Simon Rae's award-winning *W. G. Grace: A Life* received widespread acclaim on its publication in 1998. He has also edited a number of anthologies, and for five years presented Radio 4's *Poetry Please!* For nearly ten years he wrote regular topical poems for the *Guardian* and published two collections of them, *Soft Targets* and *Rapid Response*. More recently he collaborated with Ronald Searle on a book of cartoons and poems, *The Face of War*, and in 1999 he won the National Poetry Prize. His first stage play, *A Quiet Night In*, was produced in Bristol and London the same year. In 1999/2000 he was poet in residence with Warwickshire County Cricket Club and MAC at Edgbaston, and he was Royal Literary Fund Fellow at Warwick University for 2000/2001.

IT'S NOT CRICKET

A History of Skulduggery,
Sharp Practice and Downright Cheating
in the Noble Game

SIMON RAE

ff

faber and faber

First published in 2001
by Faber and Faber Limited
3 Queen Square London WC1N 3AU
This paperback edition published in 2002

Photoset by Faber and Faber Ltd
Printed in England by Mackays of Chatham plc, Chatham, Kent

A CIP record for this book
is available from the British Library
ISBN 0-571-21582-3

2 4 6 8 10 9 7 5 3 1

Here are the playing-fields where he may forget his ignorance
To operate within a gentleman's agreement: twenty-two sins
have here a certain licence

W. H. AUDEN, *The Dog Beneath the Skin*

Contents

___

List of Illustrations

———

The author and publishers would like to thank the following people and institutions for kindly granting permission to reproduce the pictures in this book: The Roger Mann Collection (2, 3, 6); The David Frith Collection (7–11); *The Southland Times*, New Zealand (12); Allsport (13, 15); Graham Morris (14); Popperfoto, Northampton (16).

Author's Note

The idea for this book came from my editor Julian Loose, and my first thanks are to him, along with his assistant Angus Cargill, who read the manuscript so attentively. Also at Faber, Brian Simmons gave me encouraging feedback, while David Kynaston, my mentor through the writing of *W. G. Grace: A Life*, gave a critical appraisal of an early draft. But I am particularly indebted to Ian Smith, who subjected each chapter to a close reading and returned the typescript bristling with instructive marginalia. Needless to say, the faults that remain are my sole responsibility.

There are a number of other people to whom I owe thanks: Bernard Wimpress gave great succour at a difficult time in the rewriting process when he invited me to send an article for his cricket periodical *Baggy Green*, and Edward Pearce provided similar stimulus by commissioning a piece for *Punch*. During the course of a convivial evening after I had handed in the manuscript, Gideon Haigh indicated several windows of missed opportunity, but did alert me to a Warwick Armstrong story that made it into the Introduction. In the wake of my Grace biography, Gerald Brodribb kindly shared with me the story of W. G. and E. M. driving Tim O'Brien to the brink of violence with their incessant chatter around the wicket while he was batting. David Frith and Roger Mann showed a generous interest in the project and raided their respective collections to provide many of the plates. My thanks to all of them.

The scope of *It's Not Cricket* has meant that it has had to be compiled almost exclusively from secondary sources, and I gladly record my appreciation of the labours, research and insight of innumerable writers on the game whose works I have pillaged. In several cases, my dependence on a particular title or author has been noted in the text; for the rest, I can only hope that inclusion in the Bibliography will suffice as acknowledgement.

I would like to thank the staff of the following libraries for their assistance: the British Library, the London Library, the Bodleian Library, Warwick University Library, and the MCC Library at Lord's, where Stephen Green and his assistant Michael Wolton have been unfailingly helpful.

I am grateful to Kit Wright for permission to quote from his poem 'I Found South African Breweries Most Hospitable' (*Hoping It Might Be So,* Leviathan, 2000).

I would also like to acknowledge the invaluable support offered by the Royal Literary Fund. Not only did they help me over a very sticky patch with a grant, but eased the final lap with an RLF Fellowship at Warwick University.

Finally, a word of thanks to my immediate family for their tolerance and support. My mother Jill Rae once again generously helped to allay financial anxieties; Siân Hughes was a mainstay against writer's block, dips in confidence, burn-out and other occupational demons, while also being a meticulous and constructive reader of the manuscript; Albertine Rae took time off from GCSE revision to offer tea and sympathy; and, last but not least, Michael arrived in the closing stages to provide a host of joyous displacement activities.

Simon Rae
Stanton Harcourt
Oxfordshire

1st April 2001

Introduction

———

This has been a difficult book to finish. It was commissioned before the Hansie Cronje revelations opened the seething vat of worms that is the match-fixing scandal, and I had only just forced a lid down on that last chapter of infamy when the England tour to Sri Lanka exploded in an exhibition of bad behaviour, bad umpiring and bad feeling.

These, as the main text shows, are in fact perennials of the so-called noble game, though judging from some of the coverage you could be forgiven for thinking that the Sri Lankan series plumbed new depths. In fact, it wasn't so very bad. What did we have? Some finger-wagging, some name-calling, some boorish behaviour from the English supporters, and a petulantly flung helmet that bounced off an advertising hoarding. And yet, under the headline 'One Step from Anarchy', Mike Gatting predicted the end of civilisation as we know it.

He was particularly exercised by Aravinda de Silva's refusal to walk in the third Test: 'De Silva nicks one to slip but stands his ground. Just what was he thinking?' Almost certainly he was thinking of the several occasions when English batsmen had stood their ground, in particular the two bat–pad catches Nasser Hussain offered during his match-winning century in the previous Test, or the even more outrageous refusal of Graeme Hick to walk having hit a straightforward return catch to Muttiah Muralitharan in the same game.

For many, of course, Gatting's position as a cricket moralist would seem compromised by his part in the famous stand-off with Shakoor Rana at Faisalabad in 1987. And that, it might be remembered, though it was the worst, was not an isolated incident. Under his captaincy the England team were renowned for their grudging, not to say surly response to decisions that went against them. The winter after the tour to Pakistan, Gatting's side went to Australia to play the Bicentennial match and then to New Zealand for three more Tests. Alan Lee, who covered the tour for *Wisden*, noted: 'England's players again allowed their on-field behaviour to plunge to unacceptable levels'. Chris Broad marred the Australian showpiece by smashing his wicket when given out – after batting for over seven hours and scoring 139 – while Graham Dilley was fined for swearing when an appeal for a catch was turned down during the first Test against New Zealand. But Lee reserved his strongest criticism not for the perpetrators of these 'tawdry incidents', but the captain, Mike Gatting, 'whose attitude to overseas umpires appeared not to have altered [from the previous tour to Pakistan]. Although Gatting indulged in nothing as overtly appalling as his row with Shakoor Rana in Pakistan, his expressions and gestures regularly spoke volumes. There were too many times when he appeared to be leading English dissent against decisions, rather than calming it.'

But to return to the 2000–1 Sri Lanka series, even if it broke no new ground it certainly provided a masterclass in unacceptable practices. Take persistent appealing. As far back as 1867, John Lillywhite's *Cricketers' Companion* declared: 'it is *not cricket* to keep asking the umpire'. But both sides in Sri Lanka appealed remorselessly with the clear intention of pressurising the umpires into making mistakes in their favour. The Sri Lankans indulged in this practice more than the Englishmen – to the extent that four of them were fined one quarter of their match fees after the first Test in Galle. One of the worst decisions was an lbw against Alec Stewart. The bowler was the Sri Lankan captain Sanath Jayasuriya, who was bowling left-arm orthodox spinners from over the wicket on or outside the leg stump. A ball pitching a good nine inches outside the leg stump turned and hit Stewart on the leg. Up went Jayasuriya, backed up by the irrepressible wicket-keeper Sangakkara, and to the amazement of everyone watching, up went the umpire's finger. Stewart publicly described it as the worst decision he had ever experienced in first-class cricket.

And yet, in the final Test at Colombo, with the off-spinner Robert Croft bowling over the wicket to a left-handed batsman and pitching outside the leg stump, a mirror image of exactly the same scenario was re-enacted. A ball pitched unmistakably wide of the leg stump, turned and hit the pad. Up went both wicket-keeper and bowler with every indication of sincere conviction.

It was the same with walking. Throughout the series, batsmen of both sides stood their ground, however palpably out, reducing the fielding sides to pantomimes of self-righteous apoplexy. You can't call your opponents cheats when you're doing exactly the same thing. Or can you?

The umpiring was undeniably poor. Of the 40 wickets that fell in the first two Tests, the *Independent* reckoned 22 were as a result of bad decisions. But then, who would be an umpire? Not only do the players put them under intense pressure, but their decisions are then subjected to dissection by a hundred TV replays. Sometimes umpires make life more difficult for themselves by refusing to use the technology available; sometimes, for seemingly arbitrary reasons, they are denied it. A case in point was the dismissal of Jayasuriya in the second innings of the second Test at Kandy. The Sri Lankan captain snicked Andrew Caddick's loosener to third slip, where Graham Thorpe took a brilliant one-handed catch. The batsman was convinced it was a bump ball, but the umpire had no recourse to the third official and gave what he saw. Unfortunately, what everybody else saw was the umpteenth replay showing that the ball had undoubtedly hit the ground before bouncing into the slip cordon. Equally unfortunately, they also saw Jayasuriya storm off, flinging his helmet from him as he left the field. Even more unhappily, that moment of petulance gave the England supporters the excuse to start chanting abuse at the Sri Lankan captain. Crowd behaviour generally was another disappointing aspect of the series.

If one substantially built and bearded former England captain thought the series teetered on the brink of 'total breakdown', what would the great W. G. himself have thought of it all? I suspect that the finger-wagging and sledging at Galle and Kandy would have seemed to him just another acrimonious day at the office. The most famous Test match ever played, England vs

Australia at the Oval in 1882, was marked by some of the worst behaviour. And Grace was right at the centre of it. At a crucial point in the Australian second innings, a young and inexperienced batsman, Sammy Jones, thinking the ball was dead, left his crease to tap down a divot, only to be run out by W. G. lurking at point. A letter written by the son of one of the other Australian players, Hugh Massie, indicates that W. G. was guilty of gamesmanship to the point of sharp practice: 'Jones nodded to Grace', establishing, as he supposed, that he was safe to venture from the crease. But it was a decoy. Grace conned him out.

Grace's blatant bad sportsmanship rebounded badly. The Australians were incensed, and Frederick Spofforth, the demon fast bowler, burst into the English changing-room in between innings and told W. G. to his face that 'he was a bloody cheat and abused him in the best Australian vernacular for a full five minutes'. His parting shot was 'This will lose you the match.' And it did. Although they needed only 85 to win, England were blown away for 77. Fired up with a venomous passion, Spofforth produced one of the greatest bowling feats in Test history, taking 7 for 44, and so the greatest trophy in cricket came into being as a result of an action which was clearly 'not cricket' performed by the greatest cricketer of them all.

Something else happened during the England tour of Sri Lanka which brought another of W. G.'s most reprehensible actions to mind. One day in May 1889, W. G. walked up to the county ground in Bristol, and after a brief inspection put up a notice saying that the nets were too wet for practice. When he returned later, he was infuriated to find his orders being flouted by a number of county colts, and when one of them answered him back, he set about him. A day or two later he penned an extraordinary letter to J. W. Arrowsmith, Gloucestershire CCC's chairman. The letter was written on club notepaper with Grace's address on, and it read, in part:

Dear Arrowsmith,
   Many thanks for saying you would see White's father *about the assault* if I wished it [my italics] . . . The lad I know bears me no ill will, but I fancy, he was kept in bed to make it look worse . . . I told the boy's father and mother

that I was sorry I had struck the boy, but that 9 out of every 10 persons would have done the same, under the provocation . . .

Fast-forward to March 2001 and a remarkably similar story, involving Arjuna Ranatunga. The former Sri Lankan captain and his brother Prasanna, a prominent politician, aided by a posse of security guards, were accused of beating up a group of students who had trespassed on to the grounds of their mother's house in search of a cricket ball. Several of the students were taken to hospital, and although most were discharged, one was detained with head injuries. As a result of their allegations Ranatunga was arrested.

The major difference is that the Ranatunga case was immediately news around the world, while Grace's misdemeanour remained dormant for over 100 years, until two researchers, Robert Lowe and I, independently stumbled upon it in the Bristol archive and published it in full in our respective biographies. No murmur of the assault, to which W. G. confessed so unrepentantly, got out into the press or the wider public, either at the time of the incident or during the rest of his life. It is fair to say that Grace would have found life in a media-saturated age impossible.

It is not entirely fanciful to suggest that Ranatunga occupies a similar position to Grace in Sri Lankan cricket. A veteran of the country's first Test side, he played more matches than anyone else, and once captain, took Sri Lanka to the greatest of World Cup triumphs when they beat Australia in 1996. And like Grace, while he was a hero to his own people, he proved something of an anti-hero to his opponents, as the England team could attest when they played Sri Lanka in a one-day international during the Ashes tour of 1998–9.

The match was played in the worst possible spirit, with Ranatunga in regular conflict both with the umpires and the England side, making what Christopher Martin-Jenkins described as 'a calculated public exhibition of himself' in his determined attempts to have the game run the way he wanted it. The stump microphone picked up Stewart's opinion that his behaviour was 'appalling for a country's captain'. Having shown an absolute disregard for the preamble to Law 42 that 'The captains are responsible at all times for ensuring that play is conducted within the spirit of the game as well as within the laws', Ranatunga compounded his defiance by turning up to the post-match disciplinary hearing accompanied by two lawyers. For Peter van der Merwe, the match referee, this was clearly not cricket, and finding himself in an uncomfortable position, he handed out a derisory £65 fine and a suspended six-match ban. Ranatunga appeared to have won hands down. It was the sort of victory that Grace used to bludgeon his way to, regardless of how many toes he trod on.

The *casus belli* on this occasion was the decision of one of the umpires to call Muralitharan for throwing. This was not the first time the Sri Lankan off-spinner had been called; in 1995, Australia's leading umpire Darrell Hair had called him in a Test match, and subsequently described his action as 'diabolical'. In 1996, the two officials standing in the Adelaide game, Ross Emerson and Tony McQuillan, had both called him in a one-day international. The Sri Lankan party had protested against their selection for the England match, but the objection had been ignored. It was not only from a Sri Lankan perspective that Emerson's no-ball call seemed premeditated. As Henry Blofeld put it, 'It is impossible to believe that he did not make the journey from Perth to Adelaide with his mind made up that he was going to call Muralitharan, come what may.'

Throughout the history of the game, umpires who have taken the drastic step of calling bowlers for throwing have been regarded either as men of principle, standing out from the ruck of timid placemen, or as publicity-seeking egotists eager to draw the spotlight away from the players and on to themselves. In the majority view, Emerson fell into the latter category. As the Sri Lankan manager remarked, 'Someone out there decided to play God today.'

That was Ranatunga's cue to play the devil, and he proceeded to push the umpires' authority to breaking point, first threatening to take his team off the field, then putting Muralitharan on at Emerson's end and instructing him to go round the wicket, while at the same time insisting that the umpire stand right up to the stumps where he could not possibly see the bowler's arm.

When Emerson showed reluctance, Ranatunga gave him a finger-wagging and told him, 'I'm in charge of this game. You'll stand where I want you to. If you don't stand there, there won't be a game.' The bad feeling poisoned the whole match and infected relations between the two teams, who ended up at daggers drawn.

Although that was one of the worst examples, it is fairly representative of the modern game, with its verbal and physical intimidation, confrontational attitudes towards umpires and a general no-holds-barred, win-at-all-costs approach to the game – in a nutshell, 'Not cricket'. Having said that, at what point did the malaise creep in; when did 'modern cricket' in this sense begin? If the 1990s were bad, what about the 1980s? That was the decade not only of the Shakoor Rana incident, and much more besides, but of an unabashed quote by the Pakistan manager in England in response to a dreadful attempt to claim an obvious bump ball as a catch off Ian Botham:

> This has now become a technique for all cricket teams, that they must pressurise the umpire to the extent that they get one or two wrong decisions in favour of the bowler, in the match. So if Saleem Yousuf picks up a half volley, all right, it is called cheating. But everyone is doing it. It has now become *absolutely necessary* in professional cricket today [my italics].

In the view of many, the 1970s was the decade that saw the pronounced downturn. According to Mike Brearley, even before the Packer revolution set out to sell the game as a gladiatorial contest, Test cricket had been turned into 'gang warfare' by the Australians under Ian Chappell, with intense psychological pressure brought to bear by verbal aggression ('sledging') as well as the physical dangers of extremely fast bowling produced by men who revelled in the intimidatory aspect of their trade. But Dennis Lillee and Jeff Thomson, and the endless succession of West Indians who followed them, were not the first fast bowlers to put the fear of God into batsmen. John Snow had helped Ray Illingworth secure the Ashes in 1970–1 amid Australian protests against his use of the short-pitched ball, and facing Wes Hall and Charlie Griffith in the 1960s was an ordeal for any batsman – especially given that Griffith was widely thought to throw his devastating bouncer. The 1960s in fact saw a massive battle to combat the problem of throwing, which had emerged to mar the 1950s. So bad did the problem become in Australia that Ray Lindwall jokingly described himself as the 'last of the straight-arm bowlers'. Peter May's well-fancied unofficial world champions were trounced 4–0 in 1958–9 by an Australian side whose main strike bowler, Ian Meckiff, was later forced out of the game. Three of the other Australians had doubtful actions, while the MCC tour party included two suspect bowlers, Tony Lock and Peter Loader.

People generally look back on the 1950s as a halcyon age, whose probity was somehow guaranteed by May's immaculate parting. But not everything in the garden was as rosy as might have appeared. Surrey won the championship year after year for seven years, and stoutly denied that they doctored the Oval wicket to help their ferocious spinners, Laker and Lock. The fact that the two took more wickets away from home suggests a case for the defence, but when it came to Test cricket, there can be little doubt that home advantage meant just that. In 1956, when Jim Laker took an unbelievable 19 wickets against the Old Enemy at Old Trafford, the groundsman Bert Flack remarked, 'Thank God Nasser has taken over the Suez Canal. Otherwise, I'd be plastered over every front page like Marilyn Monroe.' Mr Flack was not noted for his physical beauty.

The 1950s also saw strained relations between England and the West Indies. After the fantastic first West Indian victory at Lord's in 1950 engineered by those 'two little pals of mine, Ramadhin and Valentine', which led to a resounding series win, Len Hutton's touring side of 1953–4 set off for the Caribbean rather like one of the pacifying missions sent out to put down trouble in some far-flung corner of the empire. It was an approach that resulted in defensive tactics, slow over-rates, leg-stump attacks and excessive short-pitched bowling. In addition, the series was plagued by bad umpiring, a bottle-throwing riot, a 'misunderstanding' between the captain and the Prime Minister of Jamaica which necessitated a public apology, and the no-balling of Lock for throwing. But the most disastrous aspect of all was the attitude of the England squad, who had been expressly warned off the usual Caribbean convivialities. The policy of stand-offishness came from Hutton. Godfrey Evans recalled his attitude: 'We've got to do 'em. You mustn't speak to 'em on or off the field.' Writing nearly half a century after the events, in 1999, Clyde Walcott still remembered Hutton's team as 'the most unpopular ever to tour the Caribbean', adding that by the end of the tour, 'the reputation for sportsmanship of previous English touring sides lay in tatters'. The series was billed as the unofficial championship of world cricket, but was 'ruined for many because Hutton allowed some of the fieriest characters in his side to offend against both the Laws and the spirit of the Laws. Some of the language directed against our players was appalling and *would not be tolerated today* [my italics]'. It was such a public-relations disaster that there were serious moves to drag the Revd David Shepherd out of the pulpit to lead the next side to Australia. Things were not much better when the West Indies next toured England. As Frank Worrell's account of a deeply unhappy day at the Oval indicates, hardened professionals behaved no differently under the leadership of the immaculate amateur Peter May.

Nor was the domestic game in the 1950s quite as untroubled as imagined. It was, in fact, marked by disciplinary disputes which sprang from, and fuelled, the players' smouldering resentment of those who administered the game, often breaking out into headline-grabbing outbursts. As John Down wrote, 'Cricket's dirty linen was being washed in the full gaze of an eager public, and while the popular press revelled in the disease the long term effects on the game's image were extremely detrimental . . . Dating from those few years in the late fifties, the phrase "it isn't cricket" would begin to have a slightly hollow ring.'

As for the 1940s, the war left barely half a decade for the game, but there was still room for one or two unsavoury incidents. At Brisbane in November 1946, the first morning of the resumption of Test cricket between England and Australia produced one of the greatest controversies, when Don Bradman stood his ground after seemingly giving a catch to Jack Ikin at second slip. His opposite number, Wally Hammond, was incensed. 'A fine bloody way to start a series,' he spat as they passed at the end of the over. The following year, when India were the visitors, all-rounder V. M. H. Mankad made history by being the first man to run out a batsman while backing up in a Test match. The Australians were so stunned that they were all out for 107. A year later, Denis Compton was so stunned by a bouncer from Ray Lindwall that he had to be led off the field bleeding copiously. This was by no means a rare event as both Lindwall and his irrepressible companion in destruction Keith Miller employed the bouncer as a conscious strategy. It was not popular, either with the batsmen (*Wisden* went so far as to give a list of casualties) or with the British public. With a fine sense of history, Miller chose Trent Bridge for his most excessive demonstration of the fast bowler's hostility, bowling five bouncers out of eight balls at Hutton.

Trent Bridge was, of course, the home ground of arguably the most awesome fast-bowling duo, certainly of the first half of the century. Harold Larwood and Bill Voce were formidable enough under the hard-nosed captaincy of Arthur Carr, but harnessed to Douglas Jardine's unwavering will-power they turned the theory of bodyline into the terrifying reality. Both remained loyal to their skipper and the plan of action which they spear-headed, and when challenged, pointed back a generation to the terror generated by Ted McDonald and Jack Gregory on the Australians' 1921 tour to England.

The cricket played between the wars was no less keenly fought than today. Indeed, it can be argued that with far greater attendances at county matches, the championship was taken more seriously. Crunch matches, like the Roses match, always produced huge crowds and unblinking competitiveness. One veteran recalled that both teams greeted each other with surly monosyllables on the first morning and then got down to 'three days' good honest cheating'. And although in those far-off hierarchical days everyone wore caps, they were not always dutifully doffed. In a county match in 1922, Hampshire professional John Newman reacted to barracking with some 'offensive language' of his own, and then, when sent off the field by his captain, the Hon. Lionel Tennyson, kicked down the stumps on his way to the pavilion. As for the notion that the war to end wars produced a universal panacea for the combative spirit, at the beginning of the first season after the Armistice, the last man batting for Sussex was timed out on appeal at Taunton. The man in question was crippled with rheumatism – a legacy of the trenches.

Back before the Great War, the Golden Age stretches like a spotless paradise, but even there vipers lurked in the undergrowth. In 1909, Frank Woolley made his England début in the fifth Test at the Oval. Facing the first ball in Test cricket is an ordeal for any batsman, however gifted, and no bowling side is going to try to make it easy for the débutant. However, not many teams would prolong the agony for *eighteen minutes* – but that is the time Warwick Armstrong took bowling 'trial balls' before he felt ready to bowl to Woolley. Several times the ball was allowed to run to the sightscreen, and as none of the fielders seemed prepared to go and fetch it, it had to be returned by a policeman or spectator. In a characteristic understatement, Woolley described the interminable delay as 'rather a trying time for me'; in fact, it was quite clearly a cynical bit of gamesmanship on Armstrong's part. It was not for nothing that he was regularly described as 'the Australian W.G.' (As with many breaches of the spirit of the game, this one led to a revision of the Laws; trial balls were made illegal the following year.)

Another star player of the period, and a Kentish *confrère* of Woolley, developed a provoking ploy which was beyond any legislative influence. Colin Blythe, the great left-hander, liked to bowl out of the setting sun at the St Lawrence Ground. On one occasion, this particularly upset C. B. Fry, the imperious captain of Sussex. He appealed against the light, and in so doing roused the placid folk of Canterbury to barrack him so fiercely that the Kent captain had to appease them personally.

There is little evidence that the wider commonwealth of those who cared about the game appreciated that they were living through a golden age. In 1908, E. V. Lucas writing in *The Times* deplored the 'hard utilitarianism and commercialism' that in his view had dominated the county game for 'far too long': 'The forces of industrialisation have mechanised and commercialised a sporting pastime, removing its appeal to sentiment and imagination, and these forces are embodied by the professional who pursues cricket as a trade and plays with a mechanical efficiency.' Others agreed that these tradesmen cricketers, making their entries and exits through the tradesmen's entrance, were, in fact, diminishing the attraction of the game as a spectator sport. The editor of *Wisden* noted 'diminished receipts and deplorable balance sheets . . . [such that] a good many people have come to the conclusion that first-class cricket is losing its hold on the public'. In 1913, E. H. D. Sewell fulminated against efforts 'to encourage the football element among spectators' at cricket matches. In *Nothing Sacred*, Ian McLellan reminds those – and there are many – who find the modern cricket crowd intolerably raucous that if they 'want to imagine what it must have been like watching a match from the cheap seats' in the pre-Great War period (and before), they should 'go and stand next to the Barmy Army and sing along'.

As we pursue the game back into the nineteenth century we find it plagued by controversy over throwing. We also enter the great age of Grace, with the Champion's robust dedication to gaining any and every advantage over an opponent. (On one occasion it took a novice county captain until well into the first over of the match to realise that he had not in fact tossed up. W. G. and his equally formidable brother E. M. had simply emerged from the pavilion padded up, expecting their opponents to come out and bowl at them.) Grace was by no means the only one for whom gamesmanship was second nature, and the period is regularly punctuated by stand-offs and *contretemps*, both verbal and physical. Crowds were also volatile. The first game W. G. attended on his first day in Australia ended in a riot over an umpiring decision; E. M. provoked a pitch invasion at the Oval; and at the same ground a few years later, the lugubrious Yorkshire spinner Ted Peate, when appealed to for help with placating another enraged crowd, replied, 'Ah coom 'ere t'play cricket, not t'quell a riot.'

Before the age of Grace, crowds were even more dangerous. The evolution of over-arm bowling excited murderous partisanship, with games abandoned at the whim of the spectators. The Regency period was notoriously corrupt, with blatant match-rigging the order of the day, and back in the eighteenth century the game resembled the Wild West, with the umpire, assuming he hadn't been bought, taking the role of the lone lawman exposed in the crossfire. The non-striker was allowed to prevent catches by getting in the bowler's way 'anywhere within the bat's reach'; fielders regularly baulked the batsman trying to make his ground; and catches were made in items of clothing like shirts and jackets as a matter of course. It is not surprising that things regularly got completely out of hand. In 1775, William Waterfall was charged at Derby Assizes with killing George Twigg during a cricket match on Bakewell Common; a match at Brentwood in 1737 was curtailed when the players were 'met with ill-usage' by a mob of bargemen; the Dartford vs Surrey match of 1765 had to be postponed after 'several people were dangerously wounded and bruised' by the mob. The Artillery Ground at Finsbury was such a regular trouble spot that the proprietor took to patrolling the perimeter of the playing area with a 'smacking whip'. These draconian measures could not stop 'a battle royal' breaking out at a match in 1775, when 'many persons got on the wall of Bunhill Fields burying ground to see the cricket match [and started] pelting the crowd with brick bats etc. . . . several persons were terribly wounded'.

Cricket, along with all the other rural English folk games, fell into bad odour in the sixteenth century, especially when it was played in churchyards. But even before the tide of puritanism started to erode the liberty of the citizen to enjoy himself, those in authority looked jealously upon any activity that brought crowds together. The official Tudor line was that if people wanted recreation, they would be much better off practising their archery than indulging in 'idle games'. And as far back as 1369, Edward III banned something called 'club-ball' for interfering with the war effort, though as Derek Birley notes, we cannot be sure whether club-ball was 'a specific game, or whether, as seems more likely, it was a catch-all term to cover any form of ball-bashing the citizenry were apt to waste their time on'.

One thing we can be sure of is that whatever form the 'ball-bashing' took, all participants would have been bent on finding a means of getting the better of the other side – by fair means or foul. For as Stephen Potter says, the object of all games is to 'rub your opponent's face in the dirt'. This forthright statement lies at the heart of his classic, *Gamesmanship* (1947), which he defined as 'The Art of Winning Games Without Actually Cheating'. Although this penetrating and hilarious satire on human motivation was conceived on a tennis court, Potter finds room for the Noble Game. One of his chapter headings reads simply 'Dawn of Cricket – Dawn of Not Cricket – W. G.', and elsewhere he allows himself a fantasia on the modern game (while getting in a dig on the nascent Welfare State's obsession with surveys and statistics).

[A]fter five researchers had found 8,400 instances of gamesmanship in a match at Hove, reduced by rain to a bare one and a half days' play, between Sussex and Derbyshire, the investigation was completely reorganised . . . This meant, virtually, the scrapping of two years' work, when the researchers were given their new briefing, and sent out all over again in an effort to discover some game, or some act in some game, of cricket, in which gamesmanship was *not* involved.

Potter would have found much to relish in the game's more recent past. 1981 was a particularly vintage year, starting in February when Australia's Greg Chappell instructed his brother Trevor to bowl the last ball of a one-day international along the ground to deny New Zealand any chance of scoring the six they needed to win the game. Earlier in the day, Chappell had refused to walk when seemingly caught at mid-wicket. Neither umpire felt able to adjudicate as they were both watching the crease at their respective ends to guard against short runs. Ten days later, during the third Test between Australia and India at Melbourne, Sunil Gavaskar objected so strongly to an lbw decision that he ordered his fellow batsman to leave the field with him in protest. Still in February, the England tour to the West Indies was blown off course when Robin Jackman, a late addition to the party, had his visitor's permit withdrawn by Guyana because of his South African connections, even though at least three other members of the team had played or coached in South Africa. The Georgetown Test was abandoned, and the tour itself only just went ahead. A month or two later, David Frith alerted *Wisden* readers to the sale of a splendid sporting memento – the Benson and Hedges Gold Award medallion which had been withheld when Brian Rose declared the Somerset innings closed at 0 for 0 against Worcestershire, guaranteeing, mathematically at any rate, passage through to the next round, albeit at the cost of an abortive day for the crowd. And the year was rounded off by the rousing headline 'Lillee Kicks Pakistan Captain and Is Fined £120'.

The great Australian fast bowler was much given to what Potter called 'dialogue attacks', and on one famous occasion arrived at the crease in a Test match with a metal bat – surely in accordance with Potter's maxim that the point of gamesmanship is 'the creation of doubt in the opponent's mind'. There was no doubt in Mike Brearley's mind that the bat was against the Laws, and he insisted on its replacement by one made out of traditional materials. But it should not be forgotten that it was Brearley himself who had the idea of placing a close fielder's helmet at mid-wicket to tempt the batsman to play across the line in the hope of claiming 5 runs – a practice soon outlawed by the legislators.

Most of the game's Laws have originated from cricketers' attempts to steal a march on their opponents. Perhaps the patron saint of such bare-faced march-stealers should be 'Shock' White of Surrey, who turned up one day at Hambledon with a bat the width of the stumps, and pointed out, quite rightly, that no one had ever imposed a limit on the width of the blade.

As for the spirit in which the game is played, in the revised code published in 2000, Law 42, Fair and Unfair Play, now has eighteen heads – up from thirteen in the 1980 code – and runs to a dozen pages – more than double the five in the previous code. The additional stipulations cover: The match ball – changing its condition, Deliberate attempt to distract the striker, Deliberate distraction or obstruction of batsman, Time wasting by fielding side, Batsmen wasting time, Bowler running on the protected area after delivering the ball, Fielder damaging the pitch, Batsman damaging the pitch. Section 17 covers the new system of Penalty runs, and section 18 addresses Players' conduct and defines a 'breach of the Spirit of the Game' as 'a player failing to comply with the instructions of an umpire, or criticising his decisions by word or action, or showing dissent, or generally behaving in a manner which might bring the game into disrepute'. But of course, legislation on its own will never suffice to ensure the game is played in a proper spirit. After a day of persistent on-field abuse and sporadic dissent in the second Test at Kandy in

March 2001, the ICC match referee Hanument Singh recalled the words of the recently deceased Don Bradman: 'Sir Donald famously said that players are the true custodians of the game. They have fallen short of their responsibility.'

What follows is a (selective) survey of how players from all periods have fallen short of that responsibility. If it has been a difficult book to finish because of the new material thrown up virtually every month, it has also been a difficult book to set bounds to. Each chapter has produced enough material for a separate book, and I am well aware of the topics, including race and gender discrimination, clamouring for inclusion or wider coverage. I can only beg readers' indulgence and invite them to supply the deficiencies themselves.

CHAPTER I

Walk; Don't Walk

———

Sunday 26 July 1998. Trent Bridge. The fourth afternoon of the fourth Test between England and South Africa. England chasing 247 to win, and after the early loss of Mark Butcher, desperate for Michael Atherton and Nasser Hussain to stay together till stumps.

This was not only the crucial moment of the match; it was a potential turning point in the whole series. After the first Test was abandoned with honours even, the tourists had taken the second Test at England's temple of underachievement, Lord's. However, Alec Stewart's team of moderately talented but committed players confounded expectations by fighting back at Old Trafford.

After being outplayed for three and a half days by a clearly superior side, England rallied. Led by the captain, who produced a massive innings of 170, the lower order for once found enough self-belief to offer resistance, producing an unlikely hero in the Glamorgan off-spinner Robert Croft. Croft withstood the South African assault for over three hours, supported by Darren Gough and then Angus Fraser, who stayed with him to the end.

This involved surviving the final onslaught from Allan Donald. In 1998, Donald stood at the top of the Cooper and Lybrand ratings with 890 points, but no one who saw him bowl – let alone had to face him – needed statistical proof of his pre-eminence. With his direct and pacey approach to the crease, athletic delivery and lavish follow-through, he was the classic fast bowler. The use of sunblock on his boyish features – nose, cheekbones and lower lip – contributed to his appearance of lethal hostility, and equipped with a spear instead of a cricket ball, he would not have looked out of place in Peter Brook's film *Lord of the Flies*. As it was, he more than justified his nickname 'White Lightning'.

It was this predator that bounded in for the kill that afternoon in Manchester, and few watching could have given much for the chances of 'Gus', the gentle herbivore of the England tail. After some excruciating near-misses, Donald's last ball thumped into his pads, which were rooted to the crease, and the bowler unleashed a great wail of vindication and relief. In vain: the umpire's hand remained down. On to Trent Bridge, with the series still alive – just.

After their customary failure to take a first-innings lead, England did well to dismiss South Africa second time round for 208, leaving an improbable victory target of 247 to win. The last time they had made such a score to win a home Test was at the Oval in 1902. For both teams the final session of the fourth day was crucial. With the fall of more wickets, England's chronically brittle middle order would be exposed. Should Atherton and Hussain see them through to the close, there would be a very fair hope, on a pitch that remained good, of England making the runs.

This was an occasion when the South African captain Hansie Cronje demanded – and got – the most from his greatest asset. Donald revved up, and Atherton and Hussain dug in. As sometimes happens, the batsmen got stuck at their respective ends, and it was Atherton who bore the brunt of Donald's spell. The former England captain, back in the side after injury, had the chance to show home supporters the application and skill that had brought him his match-saving 185 not out at Johannesburg in 1995–6. Donald had another opportunity to duel with an accomplished opponent. It was a play within a play, gripping theatre – Test cricket at its best.

Atherton won the early rounds. Ducking and weaving away from the short deliveries, he left anything outside the off stump with an almost perfect eye. Donald had to think again, and signalled his intention to bowl round the wicket. While drastically reducing his chances of an lbw decision, coming round would give Atherton another set of angles to think about, and would also significantly increase the physical threat.

And it worked. At last Atherton's judgement proved faulty. He sparred at a ball going past his nose and wicket-keeper Mark Boucher held the ball aloft in triumph. As *Wisden* reports, 'The celebrations were loud, but short-lived. The batsman stood his ground; umpire Dunne was similarly unmoved. Donald was first incredulous, then livid.' According to his own account (in *White Lightning*), he was also vociferous: 'I was absolutely seething and I said to Atherton "You better be f****** ready for what's coming, because there will be nothing in your half . . ." Next ball, he edged me for four, when he could easily have played on. I gave him a long look and called him a "f****** cheat" – in English, and Afrikaans.'

What followed hardly required English subtitles. Donald bowled with unrelenting hostility, and Atherton hung on for dear life as ball after ball jagged venomously past his throat. Aided by a spilled catch, England finished a dramatic day on 82 for 1, with Atherton not out 27. As the non-loser, he was the winner. The next day he guided England to a deceptively comfortable win by 8 wickets, squaring the series and setting up the final Test at Headingley as the decider, which England, to the surprise of many, won.

Atherton's decision to stand his ground was crucial, not just to the outcome of the match, but to the whole series. But despite the words uttered in the heat of the moment, did the South Africans really regard the ex-England captain as 'a cheat'? At the moment of truth, when it was clear that the umpire was not going to give the decision and that Atherton was not going to make it for him, Cronje is described by Donald as 'smiling sarcastically', surely in tacit acknowledgement that things would have been no different had the roles been reversed.

And seventeen months later, at St George's Park in the second Test, they were. With South Africa on 49 for 2, Jacques Kallis edged a ball off Phil Tufnell to Chris Adams at gully. The ball went fast and low, but Adams was in no doubt the catch was good. Kallis, however, stayed put, and neither Rudi Koertzen at the bowler's end nor Steve Bucknor at square leg had a sufficiently good view to uphold the appeal. Nor could the third umpire make a decision on the evidence presented to him. This did not include Sky's multi-camera coverage, and a dozen replays later it was revealed that the catch had indeed been cleanly taken.

The England players were up in arms. A brilliant photograph shows Kallis facing up to an aggrieved triumvirate of Adams (catcher), Hussain (captain) and Tufnell (bowler). The incident proved a subject for lively debate in the press box. Mike Selvey, the *Guardian*'s correspondent and an experienced ex-player (Middlesex and England), thought that Kallis's stand represented a new low on an ever-downward graph:

> [I]t is a sad fact that cricket teams cheat, England by no means least. Nobody walks for edges to the wicketkeeper – leaving those decisions to the umpire is accepted practice now – and many try to wangle bat–pad catches where none exists and some claim catches in the knowledge that they have bounced first. But this went beyond that, if the batsman saw the catch cleanly taken; and it is hard to credit that he did not.
>
> If that was the case, with the view of both umpires obscured . . . Kallis would emerge as morally bankrupt in cricket terms, firstly in not departing instinctively for what he has seen is a fair catch and secondly for the grossly unjust implication that the fielder is the one doing the cheating.
>
> There are plenty of tales from the old days to the contrary but, essentially, if the fielder said he had caught a clean catch, his word was good enough. Those times are long gone.

To this it might be countered that perhaps Kallis hadn't in fact seen that the catch was fair, and that if this were the case, he was on sounder ground morally than Atherton at Trent Bridge (assuming that Atherton knew he'd touched the ball). Kallis might also have pointed out to his accusers that in the first innings he had walked for a catch made – and doubtless claimed in good faith – by a tumbling Caddick, only to have the television replays cast doubt on whether it indeed was a fair catch. In any case, he could certainly have taken the view that, as there was a third umpire, he would wait for – and abide by – his adjudication; after all, no one questions the sportsmanship of the batsman who waits for what is often quite clearly an inevitable red light in the case of a run-out. It wasn't Kallis's fault that the third umpire did not have access to Sky.[*]

Things were very different thirty-five years earlier. During the 1964–5 MCC tour of South Africa, a controversy arose in which one English batsman was actually accused of bad sportsmanship *for* walking.

The visitors had taken a surprise lead by winning the first Test at Durban, and under the canny leadership of M. J. K. Smith, spent the rest of the tour defending that advantage against a powerful South African side. The pitches tended to produce vast scores accumulated steadily and requiring huge mental application in the unrelenting heat. Geoffrey Boycott, Ken Barrington and Smith himself were among the leading compilers of England's bastion totals, and the South Africans became increasingly frustrated at their inability to make their perceived superiority count.

The third Test was played at Cape Town. Batting first for the first time in the series, South Africa at last had the opportunity to build their own massive first innings. The South African captain Trevor Goddard opened with the pugnacious, bespectacled Eddie Barlow. England's 'pace' attack of Price and Thomson was one of the least worrying new-ball combinations ever seen in modern Test cricket, and their job was to take the shine off the ball for the real wicket-takers, off-spinners Fred Titmus and Allen.

After a few overs, the bowling was changed, the short fielders brought in round the bat, and the battle of attrition began. Against two top-class practitioners of the same high art, and with five days stretching endlessly ahead, patience was the key for the batsmen. The English, too, had to play a waiting game, maintaining the pressure with nagging – or rather, numbing – accuracy and probing variation. There certainly wasn't going to

[*]Kallis might also have reminded Tufnell of the second Test against New Zealand at Lord's the previous July when the England tail-ender's decision to walk – for a catch at second slip – was overruled by Mervyn Kitchen on the strength of a word with the third umpire. Tufnell was half-way back to the pavilion and had to return to the square along with the far from amused New Zealand team.

be much turn. To beat the bat, the bowlers were going to have to deceive the batsman in the air.

And this is what happened. Titmus lured Barlow down the wicket, where he failed to convert a length ball into a half-volley. In what might be termed a prequel to the Adams catch at St George's Park, Peter Parfitt pouched the ball comfortably at slip. However, before the English celebrations had gone very far, it became apparent that Barlow was not making his expected way back to the pavilion. The umpire, Jack Warner, found himself unable to determine whether the ball had carried and said, 'Not out.'

At this point, Titmus said 'something uncomplimentary' to Barlow, and the atmosphere in the middle cooled noticeably. Although Titmus had the satisfaction of bowling Goddard on 80, Barlow remained immovable, adding 172 for the second wicket with A. J. Pithey. The England players made their continuing resentment apparent by omitting to applaud Barlow's century, while, by contrast, making a huge fuss of his partner when he reached three figures.

This was not how Mike Smith wanted the England team to conduct themselves, and at the end of the day's play he mounted a diplomatic offensive to retrieve the situation. According to the *Rand Daily Mail*, he himself apologised to Barlow and announced that Titmus would too. Despite oil being poured on troubled water, things were about to get much worse.

South Africa declared at 501, late on the second day, leaving England no option but to bat for a draw. Boycott and Barber got them off to a reasonable start but then departed, leaving Ted Dexter and Barrington to begin again at 80 for 2. This was England's form pair. The win at Durban had been built on Barrington's monumental 148 not out, and the draw in the second Test had been secured by their stand of 191 (Dexter 172, Barrington 121). Both batsmen settled in and looked as though they might reproduce their earlier success.

Peter Pollock, the South African strike bowler, had been brought back into the attack to try and dislodge at least one of them before they became too rooted. Barrington, on 49, played at a ball outside his off stump. It passed through to wicket-keeper Lindsay, and almost the entire team went up in an appeal which, if not based on conviction, was certainly convincing. The hapless Jack Warner, however, summoned up enough doubt to turn it down. And then, after two of the longest seconds in cricket history, Barrington left the crease and walked back to the pavilion.

And straight on to the following morning's front pages. Beneath the banner headline NEW THIRD TEST UPROAR, the *Daily Rand* questioned Barrington's motives in giving up his wicket, demanding, 'Was it a gesture of rare sportsmanship, or was it an ostentatious act which bordered on gamesmanship?' For one commentator there was no doubt at all. Under the heading 'Ugly new low in sportsmanship', Paul Irwin wrote, 'The Newlands Test has become a travesty. And the blame lies squarely on the shoulders of Mike Smith's English cricketers.'

After a reference to the tourists' refusal to applaud Barlow's century, Irwin launched into the walker. 'Perhaps Barrington imagines he was making a magnificent gesture by signifying that he got a touch to the ball when the catch at the wicket was made. If so, his ideas of cricket don't coincide with mine.'

As far as Irwin was concerned, 'All Barrington succeeded in doing was to hold the umpire up to ridicule and contempt . . . [he] appears to have passed a public vote of no confidence in Mr Warner.' The umpire, he continued, would be perfectly justified in refusing to stand for the remaining two days unless offered a public apology, before signing off: 'it seems that the England players are quite capable of umpiring the match themselves'.

These accusations rankled, and in his cricketing autobiography *Playing It Straight*, Barrington replied to them:

First, I had no intention of ridiculing umpire Warner, and in fact I felt so upset about the incident that I later offered him my apologies for unwittingly leading him into more controversy. Second, I can blame my hesitation only on my own indecision. That indecision was caused by my own thoughts and ponderings on the Barlow business . . . I got terribly involved in the rights and wrongs of walking and the moment I saw Warner wasn't going to give me out the 'dos and don'ts' seemed to flood into my mind. In the end I made my own decision with the best of intentions, and if it happened again, I'd do exactly the same.

No doubt Barrington did act with the best of intentions, but it was the highly public mental juggling act that undid him with the South Africans, most of whom emphatically endorsed the line taken by their former captain, Jack McGlew: 'You must never take control of the game out of the umpire's hands.'

'Leave it to the umpire' has generally been the Australian way, and Don Bradman was no exception. However, on one occasion, his failure to walk blew up into perhaps the most notorious of all such episodes. The 'Ikin Incident', as it came to be known, was far-reaching in its consequences. It occurred in the first Test of the MCC tour to Australia in 1946–7, and its importance was due mainly to its timing: the first Australian innings in the first Ashes Test after the six-year break for the Second World War. It affected not only the fortunes of both teams, but also those of the two captains, Wally Hammond and Bradman.

From his amazingly assured début in the 1928–9 series, Bradman had risen rapidly to a solitary pinnacle of batting supremacy. Even the Bodyline series, aimed specifically to cut him down to size, had only succeeded in reducing his average to 56. He was the most dominant of modern batsmen and the most consistent, with a century coming on average every third innings in first-class cricket. Disparaging him as a 'run machine' was neither fair nor much consolation as series after series was won on the back of his magisterial batsmanship. Had the war not intervened there is no guessing how much more impressive his record would have been, but the odds are that Australia would have won three more Ashes series.

Now that the hostilities were over, the question was would the Don's runs continue to flow as freely? Indeed, would the Don continue in cricket at all? In the build-up to the first Test there were doubts on both counts. Bradman's form was poor, and he was suffering from various ailments (for such a peerless sportsman he had surprisingly indifferent health – grounds for exclusion from active military service during the war). However, to national relief, he eventually signalled that he would resume as Australia's captain.

The England captain Hammond had said all along that he hoped Bradman would play, but there was no personal warmth between the two men. Hammond had seen his 1928–9 record series aggregate of 905 runs eclipsed by Bradman's total of 974 in 1930, and although the Englishman had topped the Don's Test record for an individual innings of 334 by 2 runs against New Zealand in 1932–3, he had had to spend the 1930s as the world's second-best batsman.

For Bradman, too, there was unfinished business. At the Oval in 1938, he and his team had faced the largest total ever compiled in a Test match. Hammond had no hesitation in telling his batsmen to occupy the crease for as long as they liked, and they batted well into the third day. The young Len Hutton, accumulating at his own pace on the perfect surface, worked steadily towards Bradman's Ashes record of 334, and passed it after 12 hours 19 minutes (as against the Don's 6 hours 23 minutes) before going on to post the new Test record of 364.

It was a terrible match for Bradman. When, in desperation, he finally brought himself on to bowl, he turned an ankle. Unable to bat, he had to spend the rest of the match an impotent spectator as his demoralised side were bowled out for 201 and 123 to lose by the scarcely conceivable margin of an innings and 579 runs. There then followed eight years during which no retaliatory action had been possible. But Bradman was a man with a long memory, and there was no doubting his motivation when he declared himself fit to lead the defence of the Ashes.

Things got off to a good start when he won the toss and batted. However, English morale soared when Hammond took a catch at first slip to dismiss Arthur Morris off Alec Bedser, and it improved further when Bradman, who had always been known as a brilliant starter, began scratchily. His old Bodyline adversary, Bill Voce, was giving him particular trouble, and when Sidney Barnes hit Doug Wright straight to Bedser at square leg, Australia were 46 for 2 with Bradman an unconvincing 7 not out.

He was joined by Lindsey Hassett, and both men set their sights simply on survival to lunch. Voce was brought back on, and just before the interval, seemed to have won the great prize when the ball sped off Bradman's bat to J. T. Ikin at second slip, who caught it above his shoulder. The ball was travelling at such velocity that he span round, but there was no doubt that the catch was clean. Nor, in English minds, was there any doubt it was fair.

The shot was played with a near-horizontal bat as Bradman attempted a dab behind cover point. The only question was whether the ball hit the top or bottom edge of the bat, and those closest to the action were sure it took the top. The entire team expected Bradman to go without prompting.

When he didn't move, an appeal was eventually mustered, but to their incredulity the umpire, George Borwick, refused to uphold it. From disbelief the mood rapidly turned to fury. According to one of his team, Hammond was 'blazingly angry', and at the end of the over, he made the famous remark, 'A fine bloody way to start a series,' as he passed his opposite number.

For his authoritative biography of Bradman, Irving Rosenwater interviewed many of the on-lookers. Norman Yardley was at gully: 'I was in the best position on the field, even better than the umpire himself to see exactly what happened.' According to Yardley, 'the ball flew from the *top edge* of [Bradman's] bat and straight towards second slip, where Jack Ikin caught it beautifully'. Ikin was 'as adamantly certain [in 1978] as he was at Brisbane in 1946 that he took the catch fairly and properly', as were Doug Wright and Alec Bedser.

And it wasn't only Englishmen who thought the Don should have been on his way. On the Australian balcony, Keith Miller, the next man in, waiting for his first Test innings, had no doubt: 'As Ikin held the ball, I instinctively got out of my seat, picked up my gloves and grabbed my bat, my heart pumping like a runaway motor out of control.' Clif Cary was broadcasting at the time 'from a position directly behind the umpire at the bowler's end', and his testimony is very interesting:

I was looking at the play through powerful 10 x 50 Zeiss glasses. The whole scene was brought to within a few yards of me, and my exact words were: 'The next ball from Voce rises as it goes away and Bradman is out . . . Bradman out, caught Ikin at second slip, bowled Voce, for 28.' To me there was no doubt about the legality of the catch and when Bradman just stood there looking down at the ground, I was astounded, and at first thought it must have been a no-ball, and I had missed the signal. I quickly realised this could not have been the case and was at a complete loss for words. Seconds went by. Then came the belated appeal and the umpire's 'no'. Why Bradman stood there as if he had never hit the ball, as though there was nothing to worry about, is a question impossible to answer . . .

In fact, Bradman never claimed he hadn't hit the ball. He clearly had – how else could it have got to second slip? In a rare statement to the press, he insisted that had he been sure it was a catch he would have walked; as it was, he had not been sure if it was a bump ball or not, and so he stood his ground and let the umpire decide. It was not only to English ears that this sounded a lame excuse. Bill O'Reilly, a life-long scourge of Bradman, dismissed it brusquely: 'To get a bump ball to go shoulder high at speed sufficient to spin Ikin side-on as he effected the catch needs some uncanny propulsion seldom seen in cricket.' Seldom, but not never. There was an example of the uncanny things a cricket ball can get up to as recently as the second Test at Kandy in March 2001. Sanath Jayasuriya was caught by Graham Thorpe diving horizontally at *third* slip. The England fielders appealed to a man, and the umpire's finger shot up, but the slow-motion television replays showed that the ball had been snicked into the ground before ricocheting away at shoulder height. Jayasuriya was clearly the victim of a miscarriage of justice.

As Rosenwater concludes, there is no way of determining the truth about what did happen that first morning at Brisbane in 1946, but the England side were left with a strong sense of injustice. Ikin himself felt that the Australian captain's 'hesitancy combined with the fact that he actually stayed at the crease, provided sufficient time to allow the mind of the umpire to be influenced in Bradman's favour, consciously or unconsciously . . .'

Hammond, who clearly had no doubt the catch was fair, was understandably bitter about the incident. Bradman scraped through to lunch, but came out after the interval a different batsman – confident, dominant, the old Don. He went from strength to strength through the afternoon, finishing undefeated on 162, having established Australia in a virtually impregnable position at 292 for 2. He went on to 187 the following day, and declared on 645. Spectacular thunderstorms then condemned

England to batting – twice – on an uncovered wicket. As *The Times* mused, 'to be caught once on a sticky wicket when facing a total of 600 runs is bad enough; to be caught twice in the same match is wicked'. They lost by an innings and 332 runs. Hammond must have reflected that had Bradman gone on 28 the likelihood was that England would have had at least some use of the perfect wicket before the weekend, and that the Don was notoriously unhappy when batting on a rain-affected surface. How different it all might have been.

Bradman had not only laid the ghost of the Oval Test of 1938, but had revived his own career, scotching any thought of retirement. But the fall-out went further. At forty-three, Hammond lacked the elasticity to bounce back and lead his team to recovery. Cocooned in the private limousine some admirer had furnished him with, he became increasingly isolated from his players and correspondingly less effectual as a captain. His own form with the bat deserted him, and his situation was made more miserable when the Australian press seized on details of his divorce as it went through the courts back in England. In Keith Miller's view, 'Cricket and the whole tour appeared to get on his nerves and become evils from which he must escape as much as possible.'

Bradman continued to rub salt into Hammond's wound. In the second Test, Australia posted an even bigger total – 659, in which Bradman and Barnes both scored 234 – and England again lost by an innings. The third and fourth Tests were drawn, and Hammond withdrew from the side at the last minute before the fifth and final Test at Sydney. He had made a mere 168 runs in eight innings at an average of 21, while from his brooding fastness at first slip he had watched Bradman accumulate 605 runs at an average of 121.

As Miller acknowledged, 'Not only the result of the match, but the result of the whole series of Tests, may have depended on that one decision.' In typically provocative vein, he found himself pondering the influence of personality on events, and, casting his mind back to W. G. Grace, wondered 'just what he would have done had he been fielding at first slip instead of Walter Hammond'. Would he, Miller mused, have 'created a rumpus'? The answer is an undoubted 'Yes'. There would indeed have been a rumpus had Grace been standing at first slip. On the other hand, had he been the batsman, he would certainly have stood his ground, possibly going through the pantomime of looking pointedly at the ground to suggest a bump ball.

Grace never walked, but he was not alone in this. If the behaviour of W. G.'s lifelong cricketing friend Lord Harris is anything to go by, the amateur tradition of walking does not go back as far as the Victorian period. Lord Harris took a touring side out to Australia, captained England in the first home Test in 1880, and as Chairman of the MCC Cricket Committee and MCC Treasurer (from 1916 to 1932) personified the cricketing establishment. He, if anyone, should provide a representative position on those vexatious 'dos and don'ts'. And, in his cricketing autobiography *A Few Short Runs*, published in 1921, he does:

> I was caught in Kent v Derbyshire twice in one season by the same wicket-keeper off the same bowler off exactly the same spot – viz. the extreme point of the thumb rubber – and given on each occasion 'Not Out' by the same umpire: no doubt he could not see the very slight impact, and would not trust to the sound . . .

Surely if ever there were a case for an honest departure, this was it. But Harris continues:

> Now, this is a case where the umpire on appeal has decided the batsman is not out, and therefore the batsman, though he knows he was out, has no business to retire from the wicket.

Why? So as not to embarrass the umpire as in the case of Barrington and Warner? Absolutely not. The umpire's feelings do not enter into it. 'For all [the batsman] knows, one of his opponents may have infringed some law which may have affected the decision.' Quite what these putative infringements might be the reader can only guess. Lord Harris offers no further elucidation, beyond summing up the case thus: 'An umpire has to be alive and on the lookout for every ball during six hours' cricket.' This, he concedes, is a very difficult task: the eye gets tired, and, well, mistakes are made, and there's an end of it.

But this has nothing to do with fair play. Harris simply advocates a shameless exploitation of the fallible old pros with their fallen arches, dropped aitches and general predisposition to give Gentlemen (let alone Lords) the benefit of the doubt, however dubious the circumstances. But if the doyen of cricket in the Golden Age not only didn't walk, but constructed a philosophy (albeit a rickety one) to suggest that it was positively *wrong* to walk, what of a later age, and a later figure of irreproachable standing?

Having played his first first-class innings under the watchful eye of W. G., Jack Hobbs succeeded the Champion as England's premier batsman, winning universal recognition as 'The Master' and raising the stature of the professionals to unprecedented heights. When the young Gubby Allen played in his first Gentlemen vs Players match in 1925, Hobbs was in his prime and probably the most respected man in the English game.

Allen opened the bowling for the amateurs, and Hobbs got an edge to the keeper. Allen appealed, but Hobbs was given not out. When he got down to Allen's end, the frustrated bowler insisted that he had touched the ball, only for the imperturbable Hobbs to deny it. Allen was aghast. 'I admired Jack Hobbs, he had helped me a lot and I thought he could do no wrong and certainly would never tell a lie.'

The breach in Allen's good opinion of his hero was soon repaired. The two men played together in a match at Scarborough and found themselves in the covers. At the fall of a wicket, Allen went up to Hobbs and said, 'Jack, you know you hit that ball in the Gents v Players match.' Hobbs replied, 'Of course I did, G.O. But you mustn't say that in front of the umpire. It's unfair on him and, furthermore, if I had, he would almost certainly have given me out at the next possible opportunity.' Allen took the lesson to heart.

Forty years later, Allen was Treasurer of the MCC, and happened to be in Cape Town for the controversial third Test. Some enterprising journalist caught him at an unguarded moment and asked for a view of the walking controversy. He was quoted in *The Times* as saying 'that in his day the custom was not to "walk" until you were given out, even if you knew that you were out'. The correspondent continued: 'Nowadays the treasurer would be regarded as an outlaw, at any rate in England.'

In an interview for the *Cricketer* (1971), Gubby Allen's exact contemporary Bob Wyatt endorsed the same policy. In the third game of the Bodyline tour of 1932–3, Wyatt pulled Grimmett for four. In doing so, he stepped back on to his stumps and dislodged a bail. 'About five Australians immediately appealed but George Hele, one of their leading umpires, had been watching the ball after I struck it and did not see the completion of the stroke. If there had been no appeal I would have walked out, but as I had been given not out I stayed and got some runs.' Allen and Wyatt were amateurs and played the game in the best spirit of the amateur tradition (Allen, for example, flatly refused to bowl bodyline in 1932–3). Both captained England, and later served the game in various capacities, including stints as Test selectors.

If Lord Harris didn't walk, and Hobbs didn't walk, and the leading amateurs of the inter-war years didn't walk, where did the practice come from? According to Mike Brearley, it came into the English game after the Second World War and, in his phrase, 'gradually grew', until 'by the early '60s anyone who did *not* walk was considered a cheat'. Even within England it was not universal. Teresa McLean, in her study of umpires, *The Men in White Coats*, gives what she calls 'this habit of "walking"' a regional bias. It used, she says,

to be considered the height of good sportsmanship, admired by players and welcomed by umpires, but only in the south of England. It has never been admired in the north, where it is scorned as a weak southern habit, giving unnecessary help to the opposition. Decisions are the umpires' job, not the players' and nothing should be done to help umpires towards any decision which might be against the team interests.

In contrast to the north, the south came late to league cricket. While it is a mistake to write off 'friendly' cricket as tame and uncompetitive, the result is clearly less important when there are no points and no position in a league table at stake. But there is a great deal at stake in a Test match, especially in an Ashes series, so the question remains: Why for some twenty years did the national team adopt a moral standard that had not been seen as necessary or desirable before?

One possibility is that it represented a final fling, the romantic swan-song of amateurism. From the moment Attlee emerged as winner of the 1945 election, the writing was on the wall for the class-based division between amateurs and professionals, but well before the distinction was finally abolished in 1963, the unthinkable had occurred: a professional had been made captain of England.

In 1925, Lord Hawke, the benevolent despot of Yorkshire cricket, made his famous remark: 'Pray God, may no professional ever captain England!' Ironically, when the citadel finally fell, it was to the Yorkshireman Len Hutton. And Hutton is rightly remembered for winning back the Ashes for the first time in nineteen years in 1953, and then retaining them in the following series (1954–5).

However, in between these two triumphs there was Hutton's tour to the West Indies, which, as indicated in the Introduction, proved a public relations disaster. Not only were cricketing relations soured; there were political repercussions as well. At the time, the Caribbean was experiencing severe instability, with the arguments for independence gathering strength. The tour was supposed to calm things down, but Frank Worrell claims 'it did just the opposite. The MCC team of 1954 pushed British prestige in the West Indies to an all-time low. The men who could have been such great ambassadors turned out to be providers of ammunition for the "enemy".'

The damage was so bad that E. W. Swanton was given official encouragement to take a strong team out two years later to mend some of the broken fences. Significantly, the captain was the young Kent amateur Colin Cowdrey. It is also noteworthy that the next two captains of official MCC tours to the West Indies were Peter May, the leading post-war amateur batsman, and Cowdrey again. On May's tour of 1959–60, the manager R. W. V. Robins was insistent that batsmen should walk. One of the most conspicuous walkers in 1959–60 was M. J. K. Smith, who played as an amateur and went on to captain England on the 1964–5 tour of South Africa.

Walking did not die out immediately amateur status was abolished in 1963, but the walking 'code' has gradually been watered down. Teresa McLean quotes the umpire David Constant as saying that, when he started umpiring, 90 per cent of batsmen walked, and when he quit, 90 per cent didn't. More recently, Mark Nicholas told Channel 4 viewers that when he started in first-class cricket in 1978 he did walk, but that he had abandoned the practice by the time he left the game in 1992. The county circuit was a fraternity built on trust, and umpires used to wait for batsmen to go and obviously 'preferred' that they should walk rather than be given out. Nicholas also recalled Alan Knott making the distinction: 'In county cricket I walk; in Test cricket I don't.' Nicholas's fellow-commentator, Dermot Reeve, cheerfully admitted that he never walked 'unless it was really obvious'.

That's a point that Mike Brearley makes in *The Art of Captaincy*. Although he recognises the virtue of 'this admirable approach', he decides against walking on the grounds that it 'lends itself to abuse':

> Many batsmen will walk when their score is, say, 53, or 77, or 143, but not on 0 or 99. Some walk for the obvious 'nicks' but not for the faint ones. There is a temptation to walk when the match is not too important, and your place in the team is safe; but not at a crucial stage of a game, or if your last five innings have yielded 10 runs and your entire career is in the balance.

Even Colin Cowdrey, according to Mike Selvey's obituary of him in the *Guardian*, was given to walking 'for obvious decisions, and then not doing so for the less obvious, in the hope that his reputation would fool the umpire'.

The selective walker is more open to charges of gamesmanship than the unwavering non-walker, though consistent adherence to the umpire's decision is not always well received by the fielding side. On the way to his hundredth first-class century in the fourth Test at Headingley in 1977, Geoffrey Boycott tried to turn the slow left-armer Ray Bright to leg and got a nick. Bright was so incensed when the appeal was turned down that he had to be physically restrained by his captain Greg Chappell. Tony Greig, batting at the other end, declared simply, 'Boycott was out, without any shadow of a doubt.' But he went on to say, 'But why should he walk? None of the Aussies did.'

Indeed they did not. In the 1975–6 series between Australia and West Indies Greg Chappell's brother Ian had a reprieve after giving an obvious catch to the wicket-keeper off Michael Holding. The West Indian captain Alvin Kallicharran lost his temper, the bowler burst into tears, and the rest of the team collectively lost the plot. Shortly afterwards, they dropped Greg Chappell on 12. He went on to score 182 not out. As untold numbers of batsmen have had occasion to remind outraged opponents, 'Australians only walk when the car breaks down.'

As captain, Brearley always regarded walking 'as a matter for the individual to decide. But I admit that, particularly in Test cricket, I did sometimes point out that our opponents were unlikely ever to walk.' But in 1982–3, some of Bob Willis's tourists felt that it was wrong to allow the individual's conscience to jeopardise the team's chances of winning, and forced a collective decision that each player would stand his ground. This suited Allan Lamb, who, having learnt his cricket in South Africa, had never been a walker – though even he was surprised by the vehemence of the reaction when he stayed put after getting a thick edge off Dennis Lillee in his first Test in Australia:

It was such an obvious one that Lillee did not stop to give me a coaching lesson as he whooped his way down towards the slips. Their greatest danger was being injured by one of the splinters, but I stood there and hoped for the best. I wandered down the pitch and tapped the divot, not looking at the umpire. Finally I had to look up and there it was. No finger. The Australians went 'ape', and I then got the most abuse I've ever heard, before or since.

When he was eventually dismissed, Rodney Marsh escorted him off the pitch, explaining that he was 'Making sure you go this time and don't change your mind, you South African bastard.' Not that the Australians held it against him. Lamb and Lillee became as firm friends off the field as they were committed antagonists on it.

When both sides abide by the same code, the potential for friction is reduced. As the Barrington episode shows, bad feeling is generated when the two sides take a different view of what is, and is not, cricket.

CHAPTER 2

The Moral High Ground

The proponents of walking regarded it as integral to the whole ethos of sportsmanship, yet it enjoyed its brief heyday long after cricket had become established as a metaphor for fair play applicable to all walks of life far beyond the boundary.

The emergence of cricket – or the term 'cricket' – as a moral yardstick by which anything underhand, sneaky or unfair could be judged and found wanting, was a Victorian development; but it did not happen overnight, and its evolution is interesting. It starts within the game itself. As cricket moved away from its informal folk origins and a set of rules began to be established for all players, there came the recognition that there were some things which, though allowed by the laws of the game, were palpably against its spirit. Sometimes this arose through an oversight. The most obvious example is the size of the bat. As bowlers developed a new style of bowling that made the ball bounce, the old, hockey-stick style of bat became redundant and gave way to something more modern. It simply never occurred to anyone that a batsman would come to the crease with a bat as big as the wicket. But it happened.

In 1771, the Surrey cricketer Thomas 'Shock' White caused shockwaves at Hambledon when, in the words of John Nyren, he 'brought a bat to a match, which being the width of the stumps, effectively defended his wicket from the bowler'. There was, as he pointed out to his appalled opponents, nothing in the laws limiting the width of the bat, but there soon was. The Hambledon committee immediately passed a resolution limiting the width of the bat to $4\frac{1}{4}$ inches, and this was subsequently adopted by the rest of the cricketing world.

'Shock' White can't have been surprised at the reaction to his innovation – indeed, the whole performance was probably something of a practical joke. More often than not, however, examples of 'not cricket' arose from new thinking and new techniques. According to Derek Birley, 'the first recorded complaint of "not cricket" about something that was within the laws' occurred in the 1790s when the young Buckinghamshire all-rounder William Fennex was batting against one of the new-fangled 'length' bowlers (i.e. someone who lobbed the ball in the air in order to pitch it 'on a length'). Fennex, instead of remaining rooted to his crease or leaping out to meet the ball, developed what we would recognise as the forward defensive shot, with the front leg advanced and the bat angled down over the ball. This new method caused a stir among the onlookers, including Fennex's father, who called out, 'Hey, hey, boy! What is this? Do you call that play?'

Some forty years later, a strong Oxford side played the outlying village of Cowley. In their first innings they scored over 200 and were clear favourites to win. But, as the Revd James Pycroft related in his classic text *The Cricket Field*, 'Cowley grew wiser; and even now [1851], a Cowley man will tell the tale how they put on Tailor Humphreys to bowl twisting underhand sneaks, at which the Oxonians laughed and called it "no cricket".' All the same, it was effective and succeeded in nullifying the superior skills of the Oxford team.

But it is another quotation from *The Cricket Field* that is generally cited as the first formulation of the 'not cricket' idea. Pycroft was writing of Harvey Fellows, a notoriously quick bowler, who could when the mood took him be positively dangerous. 'We will not say that anything that [Fellowes] does is not cricket, but certainly it's anything but *play*.' It wasn't long before 'cricket' took over the moral burden from 'play' in one of the most widely used coinages of the last 150 years.

The Oxford English Dictionary quotes the *Cricketers' Companion* of 1867 as the first instance: the editor wrote, 'Do not ask the umpire [i.e. appeal] unless you think the batsman is out; it is *not cricket* to keep asking the umpire questions.' There is no limitation in the laws to the number of appeals any member of the fielding side can make, but constant appealing makes the game fractious and even farcical. It is simply 'not cricket', not the done thing.

There are several other things which, by general consensus, are 'not done'. One is the running out of a batsman backing up at the bowler's end without a warning. This is perfectly within the laws of the game, but always generates fury on the part of the batsman and his side and draws down universal condemnation on the head of the offending bowler. From time to time someone tries it on, whether through malice, frustration or a sudden clouding of judgement. That cricketing paragon, the future Lord Harris, did it in the Eton–Harrow match at Lord's in 1870 and was roundly hooted by the Harrovian half of the crowd. He justified his action on the grounds that his victim, C. A. Wallroth, had been stealing runs by backing up before the ball was bowled, but well into the twentieth century, one of Wallroth's sisters was still indignant about it: 'That George Harris! I shall never forgive him!'

In the first innings of the 'Ashes' Test at the Oval in 1882, Hornby, the England captain, was similarly backing up out of his ground when Frederick Spofforth pulled up in his delivery stride with the words, 'I could stump you now – you're out of your ground.' Hornby replied, 'Yes . . . but surely that's not your game, is it?' Spofforth agreed that it wasn't and returned to his mark – a piece of sportsmanship which contrasted starkly with W. G.'s underhand running out of Sammy Jones later in the same match, which goaded the Demon into match-winning vengeance.

Just under a hundred years later, on England's 1977–8 tour to New Zealand, Ewen Chatfield whipped the bails off when Derek Randall was backing up at the striker's end in the second Test at Christchurch. An enraged Ian Botham told him, 'Just remember one thing, son, you've already been killed once on a cricket field' – a tasteless reference to his near-fatal injury during the previous MCC tour, but expressive of the general disgust felt by the English team.

'Not cricket' had made the transition into the wider world by the end of Victoria's reign and could now be applied across the board. The OED quotes the *Westmorland Gazette* of 1900 using the the expression in regard to a threatened General Election:

'We believe that the feeling is very widespread that it would not be "cricket" to get back to power again as the result of an appeal to the country.' By 1922, when the *Daily Mail* employed it in similar circumstances – 'I appeal to the Conservatives to do what is patriotic and honourable and to play "cricket"' – it was simply a cliché.

But it was a cliché of which those involved with the game were immensely proud. Lord Harris, writing in 1921, exulted in the fact that 'those few words, "That is not cricket"' had become the unquestioned shorthand for a complete value system. It was, he said, 'the brightest gem ever won by any pursuit: in constant use on the platform, in the pulpit, Parliament, and the Press, to dub something as being not fair, not honourable, not noble. What a tribute for a game to have won . . .!'

But it was not achieved without a considerable propaganda effort. One of the foundation stones was laid by Thomas Hughes with his enormously popular novel *Tom Brown's School Days*. This is arguably the most successful fiction produced to promote the new cult of muscular Christianity, whose first figurehead was Dr Arnold of Rugby.* The novel follows an almost identical course to *Pilgrim's Progress*, with Tom undergoing a similar programme of character (re-)forming adventures to those of Bunyan's allegorical hero. After a few terms of slacking, skiving, breaking bounds and generally leading the life of a heedless schoolboy, Tom is given the job of looking after the frail and saintly Arthur, soon falls under his influence, and within no time at all has developed into the Arnoldian ideal of the young Christian gentleman. By the end of the book, Tom has also become the school captain of cricket, and his last match is the occasion for Hughes to deliver his homily.

Tom is watching with Arthur and one of the masters. 'It's more than a game. It's an institution,' says Tom, to which Arthur replies, 'Yes . . . the birthright of British boys, old and young, as habeas corpus and trial by jury are of British men.' The master continues, 'the discipline and reliance on one

---

*Although, as J. A. Mangan points out in *Athleticism in the Victorian and Edwardian Public School*, Arnold personally had no interest in sport and 'was blind to the moral possibilities of cricket and football that later public school masters saw with such clarity and preached with such certainty'.

another which it teaches is so valuable I think . . . it ought to be such an unselfish game. It merges the individual in the eleven; he doesn't play that he may win, but that his side may.'

The importance of sport in the upbringing of the nation's youth – or at least, the tiny proportion that went to public school – became universally accepted. Indeed, in 1864, the Royal Commission on Public Schools stated: 'the cricket and football fields . . . are not merely places of exercise and amusement: they help form some of the most valuable social qualities and manly virtues'.

In his *The Return to Camelot: Chivalry and the English Gentleman*, Mark Girouard underlines the coming together of sport and an attempt to revive a high-minded ideal of behaviour seemingly lost in the pre-Victorian era:

> Chivalry helped to create the Victorian gentleman; and the Victorian gentleman created, or rather re-created, cricket. Indeed, the whole vast fabric of contemporary sport derives not just from Victorian England, but from the small percentage of Victorian Englishmen who went to the public schools. The games which the public-school men took up or invented, the rules which they laid down for them, the clothes which they wore, the settings and equipment which they devised, the language which they used and the seriousness with which they took the whole business gradually spread down the social scale and out to the rest of the world.

J. E. C. Welldon, the headmaster of Harrow, is a perfect example of a reforming educationalist who saw sport as a path to a higher spiritual plane. He told his boys from the pulpit: 'It is a good thing to resolve upon winning something, even if it be but a short-lived success in athletic games. The scrupulous honour, the self-sacrifice, the obedience without which no game can be played efficiently, are disciplines of high value for your souls.'

There has been a tendency amongst later writers to take the likes of Hughes and Welldon at face value, and to imagine that muscular Christianity swept all before it. Of course, there was a perceptible shift in moral tone from 1850s. The public schools were reformed, and a new educational and moral agenda was set in place. But it is going too far to imagine that all those exposed to this new agenda subscribed to it. There is a weight of evidence to suggest the contrary.

The 1860s saw a new generation of moneyed young men enjoying the wealth their parents had striven so hard to accumulate. For many, fresh out of public school or university, the role model they tended to follow was not so much honest, pious and ever-so-slightly dull Tom Brown, but the selfish, hedonistic and fashion-conscious Flashman. Lord Harris reminisced with obvious nostalgia about the time 'coloured club caps . . . became common about 1860'. 'The players', he recalled,

> were very proud of them, and however glaring the colours, were not afraid to display them. Perhaps the most startling illustration of this devotion was when the Oxford Harlequins played the Cambridge Quidnuncs at Lord's just before the University match . . . when you might see eleven young gentlemen in caps and shirts, quartered brown, blue, and red, with a broad stripe of the same colours down their trousers.

The rage for sartorial display was widespread. 'The "Knickerbockers" was a military club, and their costume was noticeable for white knickerbockers, and red-and-black stockings.'

R. A. Fitzgerald, who as Secretary of the MCC did so much to lift the club out of the doldrums, made an acute and satirical study of the new breed of young cricketers on whom the amateur game depended so heavily. Writing as 'Quid', he created Splasher, 'a decided dandy', who leaves one club and forms another simply to effect 'the pet object of his ambition by investing his new club in a fiery shirt and sanguineous hose'. Splasher then lures other members from his old club, especially those 'with good calves, [who] were tickled by the notion of knickerbockers' and the prospect of showing off their legs to members of the opposite sex among the spectators.

Fitzgerald went on:

> You will find at both Oxbridge and Camford, a swarm of 'butterflies,' 'grasshoppers,' 'chrysalis,' 'wasps,' 'drones,' and other ephemeral bodies, that quicken in the summer-time, under the genial influence of 'cricket'. You will have some difficulty in selecting amongst them any one in particular, for you

will probably find friends in them *all*; it will not give you much trouble to become a member of *all*; and your wardrobe, in less than a year, might be filled with the various 'insignia' of each.

In 1871, Frederick Gale, who significantly adopted the pen name 'Old Buffer', included a stinging reproach to the young in his *Echoes from Old Cricket Fields*. Addressing an imaginary offender with all the passion of the Ancient Mariner, he listed the various temptations to which he had succumbed:

1. Love of notoriety . . . 'exhibiting yourself as much as possible to the crowd'.
2. Intense selfishness . . . 'running your own runs and not your partner's . . . and sulking about the ground if you are put in last'.
3. Intense conceit . . . 'bragging of your average . . . under-rating every one in the eleven except yourself, and over-rating yourself, and generally proving your want of breeding'.

Far from the proposed exercise in manly Christianity, the game as played by those with the most privileged backgrounds was in danger of becoming positively decadent.

Lord Harris was rather more concerned with the secular, and confined himself to what might be termed the gung-ho ideology of sport in general and cricket in particular. 'Games were encouraged at Eton and the other English public schools far more than in Europe, because we believe that they are capable of producing certain qualities which improve a man, and make him better fitted for society.' Among the qualities sought were 'patience', 'self-denial' ('golf is a very selfish game'), 'courage in yourself and confidence in your comrades', and, of extreme importance, 'patriotism'. In an article he wrote in 1900, 'Recreation and "Cricket"', he told his young readers that the object of playing cricket 'should be to make you healthier and stronger and better able to do the work that is before you in life'.

Increasingly through the last third of the century, the work that called to the young men emerging from the public schools and universities involved extending, maintaining and protecting Britain's vast empire. Welldon again used the Harrow pulpit to inspire his pupils with the prevailing vision:

There is a duty, then, which lies upon England. It is a high, a terrible duty. It is to set forth, before the eyes of the men and nations, an example of elevated morality in life, in commerce, and in politics. It is to shed the rays of a pure and enlightened religion upon all dark regions of the earth . . . It is to prove that above all qualities of art and learning, above the gifts and graces of life, stands the inalienable quality of character . . . This is the mission, if I mistake it not, of England.

Lord Harris was a firm believer in England's mission, and took office as Governor of Bombay for a brief period. There were critical murmurings at his insistence on cricket, but it was a gospel he was intent on spreading with missionary zeal.

But the most famous exponent of the creed of cricket as the basis of true patriotism is Henry Newbolt. For Newbolt, as for Welldon, the pulpit could be seen as merely an extension of the pavilion. In his poem 'Clifton Chapel', he hymned the values of valour as exemplified in both sport and war:

> To set the Cause above renown,
>   To love the game beyond the prize,
> To honour, while you strike him down,
>   The foe that comes with fearless eyes:
> To count the life of battle good,
>   And dear the land that gave you birth,
> And dearer yet the brotherhood
>   That binds the brave of all the earth.

The same volume, *The Island Race*, published in 1899, contained a host of patriotic classics like 'Drake's Drum' and the famous 'Vitaï Lampada' – 'There's a breathless hush in the Close tonight,/Ten to make and the match to win,/A bumping pitch and a blinding light,/An hour to play, and the last man in' – with its sudden transformation in the second stanza to the battlefield where

> The Gatling's jammed and the Colonel dead,
>   And the regiment blind with dust and smoke.
> The river of death has brimmed his banks,
>   And England's far, and Honour a name,

But the voice of a schoolboy rallies the ranks:
'Play up! Play up! And play the game!'

A note at the back of the volume emphasises Clifton's pre-eminence in supplying army trainees. 'Thirty-five Old Cliftonian officers served in the late campaign on the Indian Frontier, of whom twenty-two were mentioned in despatches and six recommended for the Distinguished Service Order. The connection of the school with Egypt and the Sudan is hardly less memorable.'

Of course, the ideology of cricket was not exclusively bellicose. Grace himself liked to think that cricket between the different countries engendered good fellowship and secured the bonds of empire. He wrote in 'W. G.' *Cricketing Reminiscences and Personal Recollections* (1899),

> I have often thought that the power of cricket to bring peoples of different countries into friendly relationships has never been properly recognised. I believe that the interchanging of visits by cricketing teams has helped to deepen British interest in our colonies and to bind us in closer harmony with other nations. English cricketers have met and fought in friendly rivalry Australian aborigines, Canadians, Americans, Australians, South Africans, and Parsees, and I am disposed to think that the good fellowship born on the cricket-field has done more than is recognised to knit together the various sections of the British Empire and to advance the cause of civilisation.

It may seem extraordinary that when the old world shattered itself to pieces in the mud of Flanders, so many of the certainties driving it to destruction remained intact. The war seems to have made remarkably little impact on the way the world was seen and the way Britain's role in that world was perceived. The bugle call of 'cricket' was still to be heard on the world stage, enthusiastically peddled by Lord Harris's spiritual heir, Sir Pelham Warner:

> The very word 'cricket' has become synonymous for all that is true and honest. To say 'that is not cricket' implies something underhand, something not in keeping with the best ideals. There is no game which calls forth so many fine attributes, which makes so many demands on its votaries, and, that

being so, all who love it as players, as officials or spectators must be careful lest anything they do should do it harm . . . [The] aim of the Marylebone Cricket Club, of which I am a humble if devoted servant, in sending teams to all parts of the world [is] to spread the gospel of British fair play as developed in its national sport.

These words were spoken at a press conference by Warner in his role as MCC tour manager to Australia. The tour was Douglas Jardine's of 1932–3, and never was the gap between fine sentiments and the competitive realities more graphically illustrated.

CHAPTER 3

Riotous Assemblies

———

The Victorian notion that cricket could provide a model of superior conduct would have struck earlier generations as bizarre. Until the eighteenth century, cricket had been regarded as just another aimless pastime. One of the effects of Henry VIII's assault on the Old Religion was increasing intolerance of the activities associated with Holy Days. Any recreational gathering was looked on as a potential breeding ground for sedition, and in 1536, a limitation on such public holidays was justified because they were 'the occasion of much sloth and idleness, riot and superfluity'. The Crown would much prefer its younger male citizens to be practising their archery than wasting their time in such frivolous pursuits as 'cricket-a-wicket'.

Worse, in the eyes of the Church, was the tendency of cricketers to play their games in the churchyard itself, sometimes when they should have been inside attending public worship. In 1611, two young men were fined for playing cricket on a Sunday in West Sussex, and eleven years later, a larger group of malefactors was arraigned in the diocese of Chichester

> for playing at Cricket in the Churchyard on Sunday, the fifthe of May, after sufficient warning had been given to the contraries, for three special reasons: first, for it is contrarie to the 7th Article; second, for that they are used to break the Church windows with the balls; and thirdly, for that little children had like to have their braynes beaten out with the cricket batt.

It was further alleged that the players were aided and abetted

45

by 'Richard Martin Senior, and Thomas Ward, the old Church-wardens'.

In the same period, Henry Cuffin, a curate of Ruckinge, Kent, was brought before the Archdeacon's Court for 'playing at Cricketts' immediately after divine service. Cuffin defended himself on the grounds that the game was played by men of quality. Elsewhere in Kent, Thomas Wilson, a Puritan minister, identified Maidstone as another hotbed of profanity, as evidenced by the prevalence of 'Morrice-dancing, Cudgels, Stoolball, Crickets', played 'openly and publickly on the Lord's Day'. Such killjoy mentality reached its zenith under the Puritans during the Interregnum, achieving an absurd peak when cricket was banned in Ireland in 1656, even though the Irish didn't play it. (According to Peter Wynne Thomas, 'Cromwell's Commissioners clearly mistook hurling for cricket'.) But you didn't have to be a Roundhead to disapprove of cricket. The antiquarian John Stow placed it firmly at the lower end of the recreational scale: 'The more common sort divert themselves at Football, Wrestling, Cudgels, Ninepins, Shovelboard, Cricket, Stowball, Ringing of Bells, Quoits, pitching the bar, Bull and Bear Baiting, throwing at Cocks, and lying at Alehouses.'

Something very strange happened over the next hundred years, for this idle pursuit was taken up by the highest in the land. Suddenly aristocrats and even royalty were throwing themselves passionately into a game previously regarded as fit only for hired hands and servants. Historians offer various theories to explain this transformation. H. S. Altham suggests that in the 1650s the defeated royalists thrown back on their estates started watching the game 'as played by their gardeners, huntsmen, foresters and farm hands, and from sheer *ennui* would try their own hand at it and find that it was good'. Christopher Brookes argues that in post-civil war England, cricket offered an aristocracy largely shorn of its more feudal roles an opportunity of escaping 'temporarily at least from the claustrophobic predictability of court life', and also 'an opportunity to act out their personal rivalries without resorting to duelling swords . . .'

Certainly there seems to be a royalist connection. The restoration of the monarchy in 1660 brought about a complete reversal in tone and culture. With Oliver Cromwell dug up and the heads of the other regicides prominently displayed around the capital, pleasure could supplant prayer once more. Charles II adopted the new sport of horse-racing, spending much of his time at Newmarket, and although not a cricketer, his devotion to recreational procreation injected a strain of royal blood into the game. In 1677, the Earl of Sussex (married to one of the Merry Monarch's many love-children) drew £3 from his treasurer to attend 'the cricket match at Dicker' near his estate. In 1725, the second Duke of Richmond, the son of another of Charles II's illegitimate children, was recorded playing in a single-wicket challenge match. Another, rather more notable, cricketer who could claim (through Nell Gwyn) Charles as his great grandfather was Lord Frederick Beauclerk.

One of cricket's attractions for the aristocracy must have been the fact that it is a non-contact sport. Those playing it remain physically aloof from those they play against, and, of course, the batsman rules supreme. In most sports, the exertions of those taking part are more or less equal, but in cricket, the batsman can send the fielders to and fro, running his errands for him, for as long as he stays in. He is lord of all he surveys and the focus of all eyes, while a rotating labour force toils at his pleasure. The game seems naturally to embody the idea of hierarchy.

But for all its adoption by high society, cricket did not easily shrug off its earlier associations. In 1726, Mr Edwin Stead, one of the leading lights of the game, had a match in Essex rudely disrupted by a local magistrate. The officious official decided the occasion was merely a pretence 'to collect a crowd of disaffected people in order to raise a rebellion'. A constable was sent to read a proclamation and 'to disperse the few well-meaning neighbours who were innocently at that play'.

Stead wisely turned his back on Essex, and continued to get up games in Kent, Surrey and Sussex. Although hardly an incitement to rebellion, such matches could prove the spark for disorder. In 1731, a match between the Duke of Richmond's side and a team got up by a Mr Chambers was abandoned at the appointed hour as a draw. This incensed the locals, who assaulted the Duke and his men, 'some of them having their shirts torn off their backs'. Not that the game needed spectators to generate violence. In the same year a match between '11 of London' and '11 of Brompton' degenerated into a running battle when a quarrel between two members of the opposing teams developed. '[S]everal engaged on both sides for nearly half an hour, and most of the Brompton Gents were forced to fly for quarter, and some retired home with broken heads and black-eyes, much to the satisfaction of the other side.'

The presence of royalty was always likely to stir up excitement to a potentially dangerous pitch. In the 1730s, the Prince of Wales (Frederick Louis) threw himself into the game, first as a generous patron – his team, 'the Prince's men', contending with Stead's Kent side, for instance – and then as a player. In 1737, he led his Surrey side out against a Kent team on Kennington Common. A pavilion was erected for him, around which the crush was so great that 'a poor woman by the crowd bearing upon her unfortunately had her leg broke, which being related to His Royal Highness, he was pleased to order her ten guineas'.

In the days before boundaries, the game was always played at risk of encroachment by the spectators. In 1742, it was announced that the cricketers of Slinden in Sussex (in many ways the forerunner of Hambledon) would play an important match against 'eleven picked gentlemen of London'. The notice went on, 'as 'tis expected that there will be the greatest crowd that was known on the like occasion 'tis to be hoped, nay desired, that gentlemen will not crowd in . . .' In 1744, a match was played at the Artillery Ground between 'the county of Kent', led by Lord Sackville, and 'All England'. Its position in the annals of the game owes everything to the mock-heroic poem written about it by James Love. It proved a cliff-hanger, with the outcome depending on a last towering catch, which an England fielder dropped to give Kent the victory, and it attracted a large and excitable crowd. So great were the numbers that the proprietor of the ground, George Smith, paraded up and down in front of the popular seating exhibiting 'with strenuous arms the cracking whip'.

Spectators were normally expected to form a 'ring' without such harsh supervision, and in the best-conducted matches, they would part to allow the fielder to retrieve a hard hit without bias to the home side. On other occasions it was different. In 1778, the *Morning Post* reported an incident involving yet another cricket-mad peer, the Duke of Dorset. The Duke was playing for England against Hampshire and was making a very decent score. The home supporters 'very impolitely swarmed round his bat so close as to impede his making a full stroke; his Grace gently expostulated with them on this unfair mode and pointed out their dangers, which having no effect, he, with proper spirit, made full play at a ball and in so doing so brought one of the Gentlemen to the Ground'.

Ten years later, a match between Leicester and Coventry (won by Leicester) produced what sounds like a virtual pitched battle: 'a scene of bloodshed . . . scarcely to be credited in a country so entirely distinguished for acts of humanity'. The following year's fixture, while not producing an affray, had to be abandoned because of disagreement over an umpiring decision.

It wasn't only in the provinces that the game was associated with disorder. The boys of Westminster school used to make their way to the playing fields as a mob, shouting and breaking windows as they went. In 1792, one incensed householder let a firearm off over their heads. So bad was cricket's reputation that in 1796 the headmaster of Eton, Dr Keate, a notorious disciplinarian, banned the annual match against Westminster. The Etonians ignored the embargo, played the game – which they lost – and returned to face the wrath of their headmaster, who flogged every one of them.

In 1805, the chastised but unchastened Etonians accepted a challenge from Harrow and gave them a thrashing. The young Byron took part and recounted that after the match 'we dined together and were extremely friendly, not a single discordant word was uttered by either party'. However, they did not get through the night without causing trouble, Byron leading a party up to the Haymarket Theatre 'where we kicked up a row'. But then, as he admitted, 'we were most of us rather drunk'.

In 1821, the headmaster of Eton tried again to ban the match with Harrow, and Dr Butler of Harrow vetoed a match between his school and Winchester in 1824. The boys took no notice; indeed the Eton–Harrow match was for several years enlivened by a spirited re-enactment of the chariot races of the Colosseum, with the boys piling into competing post-chaises. This was eventually banned after a particularly messy pile-up.

The great public schools continued on their headstrong course, and when, in 1825, a festival of the three great elevens, Eton, Harrow and Winchester, was convened at Lord's, trouble might have been expected. The boys, as usual, got riotously drunk and at some stage set fire to the pavilion. This not only destroyed the building, but also most of the MCC records and scorebooks up to that date. It was not for nothing that Matthew Arnold in *Culture and Anarchy* described the upper classes as Barbarians.

Early nineteenth-century England was rough and rowdy. The Duke of Wellington famously said of his infantry that he didn't know what effect they had on the enemy, but they certainly frightened him, and large crowds could be extremely intimidating, even if they were friendly. In 1817, a strong MCC team ventured out of London to play an odds match at Nottingham. The whole country was in ferment in the wake of the war against Napoleon, and Nottingham then, as later, was a hotbed of radicalism. A crowd of between 12,000 and 14,000 turned up for the match, and the cricketers were far from convinced the natives were friendly. E. H. Budd was one of the MCC players:

> The concourse of people was very great: these were the days of the Luddites, and the magistrates warned us that unless we would stop our game at seven o'clock, they would not answer for keeping the peace. At seven we stopped, and simultaneously the thousands who lined the ground began to close in on us. Lord Frederick [Beauclerk] lost his nerve and was very much alarmed, but I said they didn't want to hurt us. No: they simply care to have a look at the eleven men who ventured to play two against one.

Crowds were well aware of their power to influence events. A single-wicket match was played in June 1736 between two Richmond players and a pair from London. One of the Richmond men got hit in the face by a beamer, but although he was bleeding profusely, a contemporary report stated that

> some human brutes who had laid against the Richmond men insisted that he should play on (the Londoners being then

ahead) or lose the match. The unhappy sufferer was duly bandaged up and sent out to continue his innings, but his nose started bleeding again to such an extent that he had to give up. Violent arguments ensued, but in the end it was agreed that the match should be re-played a fortnight hence.

Such Hogarthian revelry eventually palled, and towards the end of the 1780s, two lords, the Earl of Winchelsea and the Hon. Charles Lennox (afterwards the fourth Duke of Richmond) approached a third, Thomas Lord, a Yorkshireman, with the suggestion that he set up a cricket ground under their patronage. This he did, opening the first of the three grounds to be known by his name in May 1787 where Dorset Square stands today. (In 1810, the expiry of the lease required a move to a second ground, but he was soon hounded from his new premises by the decision to run the Regent canal through the outfield.)

From now on, the aristocrats retreated from the public gaze, though the game still provided much to arouse the passions of the public. But cricket grounds during the nineteenth century did not become the havens of somnolent inattention that they sometimes appeared in the twentieth. Victorian Britain is often fondly regarded as orderly and well-regulated. In fact, it had much in common with the Wild West. The forces of law and order were thinly spread, and violence and rowdyism were a daily threat to the law-abiding citizen – or cricketer. One of the earliest matches W. G. Grace ever played in – ten days after his tenth birthday (in 1858) – ended in a pitched battle between the beleaguered players and a posse of local roughs who availed themselves of 'a convenient heap of stones' to break up the play. The cricketers finally drove them off, but the match was abandoned.

This was not the last time members of the Grace family found themselves under attack. E. M., W. G.'s elder brother, once incensed the Oval crowd by dismissing the great Surrey stonewaller, Harry Jupp, in a novel and highly controversial fashion. Fred Gale witnessed it, writing later, 'The only painful exhibition I ever saw in amateur cricket was when Dr Grace tried to pitch a ball right up in the air so as to drop on the bails, leaving the batsman powerless. It was within the laws of cricket, but that was all.' The Oval crowd took an equally dim view of the dismissal, and urged Jupp to return to the crease. Shortly afterwards, there was a pitch invasion, and E. M. had to be protected by his team-mates until the spectators could be persuaded to retire.

The Oval was a much more democratic ground than Lord's, and the Ovalites were seldom shy of expressing their feelings. In 1884, there was an ugly incident when the Australians met the Players south of the river. The tourists had the better of the game and needed only 11 runs to win as lunch approached on the third day. An early conclusion would have cost the caterers dear, so it was agreed to adjourn. The crowd suspected some plot to charge gate-money for the afternoon session and surged over the outfield to lay siege to the pavilion. They were not particularly hostile – at least, not to the players. The Australian all-rounder George Giffin was cheered when he stepped on to the balcony, and Ted Peate, the lugubrious Yorkshire slow bowler, was given a similarly warm reception. This gave the Surrey secretary his cue to ask Peate to pacify them, only to receive the firm reply: 'Ah coom 'ere t'play cricket, not t'quell a riot.'

And it was not only in England that passions got out of hand. On his arrival in Melbourne in 1873, W. G. Grace's first visit was, unsurprisingly, to a cricket match. He was taken to the final of the Challenge Cup, contested by Melbourne CC and South Melbourne CC. It was a close, hard-fought game, and after the interruption caused by the arrival of Grace and his entourage, it built to a fiercely competitive climax. One of Grace's guides remarked as they were taking their seats on how well behaved the crowds were, despite the strong partisan feelings. Almost as soon as they sat down, this complacency was rudely upset by the defining incident of the game.

Having had his appeal for a run-out turned down, the Melbourne captain, who was also wicket-keeper, replaced the bails, and then removed them again when the South Melbourne batsman left his ground under the impression that the ball was dead. The umpire was pressured into giving the hapless batsman out, at which the exemplary crowd stormed the pitch, forcing the match to be abandoned. Indeed, the visiting Melbourne side needed a police escort to get out of the ground in one piece, and even then were chased down the road by a mob of 'roughs and larrikins who followed them . . . hooting and pelting them'.

The most serious Australian pitch invasion, in terms of its potential consequences, took place at Sydney in February 1879. Lord Harris was touring with an amateur team (strengthened by two Yorkshire professionals, George Ulyett and Tom Emmett). They played a single Test match in Melbourne and lost it by 10 wickets – a disappointment which, it was rumoured, caused his lordship to hurl his bat about the changing-room. Their next first-class opponents were New South Wales, and Lord Harris brought George Coulthard with him from Melbourne to stand as umpire in both matches. Coulthard was well regarded, and had the odd distinction of standing in a Test match before playing in one, but he proved a poor choice. Such was the rivalry and mutual distrust between the Australian colonies (as they were then) that a Victorian was an object of suspicion in Sydney.

The tourists lost the first match by 5 wickets, but in the second they forced New South Wales to follow on. Billy Murdoch, who carried his bat for 82 in the first innings, opened once again, but had only reached 10 when Coulthard upheld an appeal for a very tight run-out. This precipitated a pitch invasion, with most of the animosity directed at the umpire. Lord Harris moved quickly to defend his man, but in doing so was struck by a whip or stick. While the team, in now time-honoured fashion, armed themselves with stumps and formed a defensive square, 'Monkey' Hornby made after the assailant and effected a citizen's arrest, having his shirt half torn from his back for his pains. From the relative safety of his square, Harris defied the mob and refused to leave the ground, claiming later that he was worried about forfeiting the match. Claiming the match by an appeal to the letter of the laws was the last thing on the home captain's mind, but he did ask Harris to change the umpire. Harris refused.

The incident caused the hosts huge embarrassment. Dignitaries from within the game and the wider political establishment queued up to offer their noble guest abject apologies and to plead with him to continue the match. Harris accepted the apologies and agreed to resume play after the break for the Sabbath. He was, after all, in a winning position. He could not, however, leave the matter there, and penned a highly inflammatory letter questioning Australian sportsmanship and concluding: 'We never expect to see such scenes of disorder again; we can never forget this one.' Unfortunately, this was published in the British press and in due course made its way back Down Under. The resulting flurry of correspondence in both English and Australian papers helped sour relations to such an extent that when the second Australian touring team arrived in London the following year they were treated as pariahs and reduced to advertising for fixtures. It took most of the season to effect their rehabilitation, and Lord Harris took much persuading to condescend to lead the England side in the first ever home Test at the Oval in early September.

Both the pitch invasions at Melbourne in 1873 and Sydney six years later had a root cause in common: there was a great deal of money resting on the outcome of each match. At Sydney, the crowd's fury was exacerbated by the rumour that Coulthard had put money on Harris's side. This was not true, but even if it didn't benefit him, his decision was clearly going to cost many of the home supporters their stakes. There was a great deal of betting on cricket in Australia, and the game's reputation was to a large extent at the mercy of the betting fraternity. In 1873, Grace found his team's matches always attracted huge betting, and it was widely suspected that his own players were not above a flutter themselves. When they shockingly lost their first game against Eighteen of Victoria, many people thought the match had been fixed. As one newspaper put it, 'the gentlemen of the grandest nation on earth have sold themselves for lucre, and given away a match they could have won as easily as it has been lost . . . Mr Grace and his coadjutors have been wilfully and dishonourably dishonest.' There were stories that Grace himself had used the newly installed telegraph at the Melbourne ground to warn friends back in London to lay off their bets as the game slipped away from him.

Betting certainly cast a shadow over the tour. There was no respite even at the up-country matches where, Grace complained, they were dogged by 'card-sharpers and professional gamblers'. And there can be little doubt that the players did place bets on their own matches. Six weeks after their disastrous first match, they showed something like their true form when they beat a strong Combined XV at Sydney. Grace was determined to win at any cost, and the game was played in a very unpleasant atmosphere. One of the touring party, F. H. Boult, umpired and made several questionable decisions. When one of his victims refused to go, Grace led his team from the field amidst jeers and abuse from the crowd. Although that particular crisis was resolved, the visitors' victory left a very sour taste. The Englishmen had backed themselves heavily, and had clearly derived an unfair advantage from a weak or biased umpire. As one Australian commentator wrote, 'there is no doubt that the fundamental cause of our defeat was that the fine old manly English game of cricket (what a mockery to be sure) has – for this once, let us hope – transmogrified itself into a *gigantic gambling transaction* . . . [my italics].'

Betting may have been the blight of mid- to late nineteenth-century cricket in Australia, but the English were in no position to adopt a 'holier than thou' attitude. No phrase could better describe pre-Victorian cricket than 'a gigantic gambling transaction'.

CHAPTER 4

Rules of Engagement

———

Although the origins of the game of cricket are obscure, the evolution of its laws is not. The first rules were formulated to regulate gambling, for as cricket shot from its lowly origins into the dazzling glare of aristocratic patronage, it became the focal point for a whole new gambling culture. From the turn of the eighteenth century, notices began to appear in the newspapers of cricket matches in Kent, Surrey, Sussex and Hampshire got up by gentlemen and played for '£10 per head each game', or 'for eleven guineas a man'.

Such matches were played for an agreed stake between the teams, but those looking on also liked to bet on the outcome. This obsession with betting seems to have been near-universal. Almost anything would do – prize-fighting, cock-fighting, even a race 'between five turkeys and five geese to run from Norwich to London'. Christopher Brookes points to the emptiness of upper-class life to explain the obsession with gambling:

> For the landowning gentleman, the result of a bet was not as significant as the excitement it engendered. By stimulating suspense and uncertainty, betting satisfied important emotional needs for people who found their lives becoming more and more predictable . . . [T]he everyday life of a typical gentleman, securely ensconced within a social circle which admitted changes only on the occasion of death or disgrace, was extremely tedious.

Gambling gave a spice to life, but it also gave rise to less desirable complications. In the summer of 1719, a match was got up between sides representing Kent and London. It was played in Lamb's Conduit Fields, and it led to a law-suit. The *Weekly Journal* of 16 May said: 'Last Week a Tryal was brought at Guildhall, before the Lord Chief Justice Pratt, between two Companies of Cricket Players, the Men of Kent, Plaintiffs, and the Men of London, Defendants, for Sixty Pounds played for at Cricket, and after a long Hearing, and near £200 expended in the Cause, my Lord, not understanding the Game, ordered them to play it over again.' A different version of the same events reported that the Kent team 'thought they should be worsted and therefore to the surprise of a numerous crowd of spectators, three of their men made an elopement and got off the ground without going in . . . , hoping thereby to save their money'. Their excuse apparently was 'the violence of the rain'. The match was duly replayed, and 'the Kentish Men were bowl'd out after they had got 9, and lost the Match'. Considering this was played for 'a Guinea a Man each Side' and ''Tis reckoned the Law Suit will amount to £200', it proved an expensive fixture for the losers.

In the 1720s, the second Duke of Richmond became a prominent figure in the game. In 1725, he challenged Sir William Gage in a two-a-side single-wicket competition, and two years later, played twice against Mr Alan Broderick in Surrey. In such high-profile matches between men of elevated social standing more was at stake than just the sums wagered. It was, therefore, 'very much in the interests of the patrons and protagonists to minimize the chances of disagreement'.

To this end, Articles of Agreement were drawn up between the Duke and Mr Broderick, which stipulated 'that twelve Gamesters shall play on each side' and 'that each match shall be for twelve Guineas of each side'. There were several rules governing eligibility to play – 'that 'tis lawful for Mr Brodrick to choose any gamesters within three miles of Pepperharowe, provided they actually lived there last Lady Day' – and more covering disputes and the selection of umpires. These Articles are the earliest written rules of cricket to have come down to us, and although they were designed to cover the two matches in question, it is generally reckoned that they give a pretty good idea of the way the game was played at the time. The Articles go through the ways in which a batsman could be dismissed and there were clauses governing the selection and powers of the umpires, though it was clear that the final arbiters were the Duke and Mr Broderick, who would settle things according to their honour.

While aristocratic egos could clash happily over the eleven-a-side game, scope for more satisfyingly gladiatorial combat was offered by the single-wicket version of the game. Single wicket was so called because only one participant batted at a time, but single-wicket matches could be played by teams of half a dozen or so a side. Perhaps the most popular form involved two pairs of players, and one of the most memorable was the challenge match between Lord Frederick Beauclerk and Squire Osbaldeston, which took place at Lord's in 1810.

Lord Frederick was the most gifted amateur all-rounder of his day and the most powerful individual in the game. He batted with aggressive vigour and bowled slow with demonic cunning. He was, in Tony Lewis's words, 'an autocrat who usually got his way, often bucolic on the field, arrogant enough to put a gold watch on his stumps in practice and, in the absence of a full-time secretary of the Marylebone Club, he pronounced to all on the Laws and their spirit'. Despite his social rank, his position in the game and his spiritual vocation – he was a Doctor of Divinity and incumbent of St Albans – he was also an irascible competitor and a gambler who reckoned to make some £600 per annum from cricket, and, on occasion, a cheat, prepared *in extremis* to bribe the MCC scorer so that he won his wager. His track record of sharp-practice and poor sportsmanship was no bar to his eventual elevation to the presidency of MCC in 1826 – nor to his hypocritical claims for the moral standing of the game he both adorned and disfigured. In a speech made in 1838, he audaciously pronounced: 'Cricket is unalloyed by love of lucre and mean jealousies . . . the approbation and applause of the spectators being the sole reward.'

Squire Osbaldeston would have chuckled at such sentiments. He lived for sport – his autobiography is a romp through a lifetime's hunting, racing and cricket – but made no claim to be a disinterested participant. To live was to bet, and the gamester's code was a serious matter. In 1800, he won 200 guineas from another MCC member, Lord Bentinck, who made the mistake of saying 'This is robbery' as he handed the money over. Osbaldeston promptly challenged him to a duel, and according to one report, put a bullet through his hat. The Squire was nearly as dangerous with a ball in his hand, boasting that 'sometimes when I bowled a man out the bails were found fifteen or sixteen yards from the stumps'.

If a contest between the two leading amateurs of the day was not enough to excite huge public interest, each man chose a top professional as his partner. Beauclerk picked C. T. Howard, a fast bowler, while the Squire went for the greatest of the professional all-rounders, William Lambert. The match was for fifty guineas, but would have generated hundreds of pounds' worth of betting among cricket followers.

But then Osbaldeston fell ill, and when the day of the match arrived, he was in no fit state to play. E. H. Budd, who acted as intermediary, takes up the story: 'I went to Lord Frederick, representing my friend was too ill to stand, and asked him to put off the match. "No; play or pay," said his Lordship, quite inexorable. "Never mind," said Osbaldeston, "I won't forfeit: Lambert may beat them both; and if he does, the fifty guineas shall be his."' Though Lambert was initially doubtful of taking on the whole burden of the match himself, the Squire talked him round and sent back a defiant message to Beauclerk: 'Yes; play or pay, my Lord, we are in earnest, and shall claim the stakes!'

However, Osbaldeston's request for a substitute fielder was refused out of hand. Lambert then suggested that if he could take part in the game, only to the extent of scoring a run, Beauclerk would have to allow the substitute. The Squire later recalled how

[at Lambert's] earnest desire I consented and went to Lord's in my carriage. Fully half the match was over and Lambert being just then out [for 56], I went in; but from the quantity of medicine I had taken, and being shockingly weak from long confinement to my room, I felt quite dizzy and faint. Lord Frederick bowled to me; luckily he was a slow bowler, and I could manage to get out of harm's way if necessary, but it did not so happen. I hit one of his balls so hard I had time to *walk* a run . . . [M]any of the spectators cheered, all the cricketers knowing the circumstances.

This may have had an adverse effect on his lordship's notoriously volatile temper. 'He then became vexed and desired Howard to bowl; but I gave up my bat and claimed a fieldsman.'

When Lambert took the field against Beauclerk and Howard, he dismissed them for 24. He used particular cunning with Beauclerk, bowling him a disguised slower ball and following through down the length of the pitch to pluck the catch from the bemused peer's blade. Silver Billy Beldham was one of those present, and by his account, Beauclerk 'lost his temper and said it was not fair play. Of course, all hearts were with Lambert.'

Batting a second time with a lead of 32, Lambert again performed well, scoring 24 runs off the 78 balls he received. This set Beauclerk and Howard 57 to win. Howard scored 24, and then Beauclerk struck about him and looked likely to take the game. However, Lambert had one last trick up his sleeve. He started bowling the ball wider and wider outside the off stump (the wide ball, like 'Shock' White's wide bat, having failed to attract the legislators' attention up to that point), until his lordship once again lost his temper, and when finally presented with a straight ball, attempted to vent all his pent-up anger on it. As for Osbaldeston, looking on from his carriage, 'I . . . was never more gratified in my life than I was when Lambert bowled his lordship out and won the match.' William Beldham witnessed a coda to the heroics. Osbaldeston's mother, who had watched the contest with keen attention, summoned the victor: 'Lambert was called to the carriage and bore away a paper parcel: some said it was a gold watch – some suspected bank notes. Trust Lambert to keep his own secrets. We were all curious, but no one ever knew.'

There is no account of a sporting handshake between Beauclerk and Osbaldeston. The chances are it never took place. His lordship was an intensely proud man, and being made to look a fool in front of a large crowd at Lord's would have rankled far more than the loss of the wager, though fifty guineas was not a sum to be sneezed at.

Beauclerk and Osbaldeston were wealthy men, but even for the rich, betting was a risky business. For the less well-off gambler, losing could be ruinous. But there was a simple way to circumvent the risk factor, and that was match-fixing. In Pycroft's memoirs of the period, several players referred to the general climate in which the big matches were played. According to Beldham, 'If gentlemen wanted to bet, just under the pavilion sat men ready, with money down, to give and take the current odds,' while another recalled that bookies would intervene personally to swing the odds in their favour, however underhand the means: 'One artifice was to keep a player out of the way by a false report that his wife was dead.' A much more straightforward way was simply to bribe the players to under-perform. The most notorious venue for this sort of match-rigging was a London public house called The Green Man and Still, where, as a matter of course by all accounts, tankards were filled, winks exchanged and palms greased.

The temptations for rural cricketers called up to town for the big occasion were simply too much:

> Hundreds of pounds were bet upon all the great matches, and other wagers laid on the scores of the finest players, and that too by men who had a book for every race and every match in the sporting world; men who lived by gambling; and, as to honesty, gambling and honesty don't often go together.
>
> What was easier, then, than for such sharp gentlemen to mix with the players, to take advantage of their difficulties, and to say, 'Your backers, my Lord this, and the Duke of that, sell matches and over-rule all your good play, so why shouldn't you have a share in the plunder?' That was their constant argument – 'Serve them as they serve you.'

All that was required was that a bowler should send down a few wayward deliveries, or a batsman scoop a catch up before he was set. Nothing could have been easier – and why not, when the game's great patrons were known to be cheating on a far grander scale. Even the scorers – or markers, as they were known – were in on it. The *Covent Garden Magazine* commented in 1774: 'If one of these gentry should be appointed a marker, he will favour the side that he wishes to win, and diminish or increase the notches as suits his advantage.'

The bookies did not restrict their activities to the metropolis, but would travel out into the country in their attempts to snare cricketers. A pair of brothers called Bland were particularly active – and not just in cricket. One of their agents had been hanged for poisoning a horse, and, Pycroft was told, 'the Blands never felt safe till the rope was round Dawson's neck'. The same interviewee recounted how

> Joe Bland traced me out in this parish, and tried his game on with me. 'You may make a fortune,' he said, 'if you will listen to me: so much for the match with Surrey, and so much more for the Kent match –' 'Stop,' I said: 'Mr Bland, you talk too fast; I am rather too old for this trick; you never buy the same man but once: if their lordships ever sold at all, you would peach upon them if ever after they dared to win. You'll try me once, and then you'll have me in a line like him of the mill last year.' No, sir, a man was a slave when once he sold to these folk.

It could be a dangerous game – even though no one was ever hanged for rigging a cricket match – especially when the beady-eyed Beauclerk was involved. His lordship took part in a farcical game in 1817 which both sides had contracted to lose. This was an England versus Nottingham fixture, got up by his old rival, Osbaldeston. The Squire did not play, but his henchman Lambert did, and Beauclerk was perfectly aware of what was going on – painfully so, as he broke a finger trying to stop a deliberate overthrow and had to bat one-handed in his second innings. Nottingham won the match; or, to put it another way, the visitors won the contest to see who could lose it. Beauclerk took his opportunity for revenge and collected enough evidence of Lambert's corruption to be able to have him banned from Lord's for life. (He finally settled his score with Osbaldeston when the Squire resigned his MCC membership in a fit of pique and then sought to change his mind, only to find the unforgiving peer standing in his way, black ball in hand.)

Lambert's was perhaps the saddest case, because he was the most gifted professional of his time, but he was by no means the only first-class player to fall. William Fennex was also playing in the Nottingham match, and as he told Pycroft, much to his shame, he was also involved in the match-fixing:

> [M]atches were bought, and matches were sold, and gentlemen who meant honestly lost large sums of money, till the rogues beat themselves at last. They overdid it; they spoilt their own trade; and, as I said to one of them, 'a knave and a fool makes a bad partnership; so, you and yourself will never prosper.' Well, surely there was robbery enough: and, not a few of the great players earned money to their own disgrace . . . I'll tell the truth: one match up the country I did sell – a match made by Mr Osbaldeston at Nottingham. I had been sold out of a match just before, and lost £10, and happening to hear it, I joined two others of our eleven to sell, and get back my money. I won £10 exactly, and of this roguery no one ever suspected me; but many was the time I have been blamed for selling when as innocent as a babe. In those days, when so much money was laid on matches, every man who lost his money would blame someone. Then, if A– missed a catch, or B– made no runs – and where's the player whose hand is always in? – that man was called a rogue directly. So, when a man was doomed to lose his character and to bear all smart, there was the more temptation to do like others, and after 'the kicks' to come in for 'the halfpence.' But I am an old man now, and heartily sorry I have been ever since; because, but for that Nottingham match, I could have said with a clear conscience to a gentleman like you, that all which was said was false, and I never sold a match in my life; but now I can't.

Such an openly corrupt state of affairs could not last for ever. Although the authorities had assiduously trained their blind eyes on the far horizons, the scandal finally came into the open at Lord's in such a way that it could no longer be ignored: 'One day a sad quarrel arose between two of them, which opened the gentlemen's eyes too wide to close again to those practices. Two very big rogues at Lord's fell a-quarrelling, and blows were given; a crowd drew round, and the gentlemen ordered them both into the pavilion.'

Vengeful choler proved more powerful than self-preservation, and the accusations and counter-accusations flew to and fro: '"You had £20 to lose the Kent match, bowling leg long hops and missing catches" said one, to which the other retorted, "And you were paid to lose at Swaffem", only to be countered, "Why did that game with Surrey turn about – three runs to get, and you didn't make them?"' As Pycroft concluded, 'Angry words come out fast; and when they are circumstantial and square with previous suspicions, they are proofs as strong as holy writ.'

This was the long-awaited cue to start cleaning up the game, but match-fixing was not expunged overnight; nor did the betting craze fade quickly either. A match between Hampshire and 'J. W. Ladbroke, Esq., and All England' was reported in the *Weekly Dispatch* of August 1823:

> This match has excited the greatest interest in Hants and the adjoining counties, the spectators very numerous, and great bets depending. There was no odds at starting, but Hants rather the favourite. At one part of the game it was twenty-to-one on Hants, and afterwards came to three to two only. Mr Ward and Mr Budd peculiarly distinguished themselves by their fine hitting; Mr Ward got 120, and Mr Budd 67 in the first innings – Beagley 18. We understand a gentleman gave 60 guineas to receive a guinea for each run got by Mr Ward, Budd, and Beagley, consequently he was a winner of 145 guineas.

The amount won by a spectator is an unusual reason for giving individual scores in a match report, and for a more detached on-looker the whole exercise is self-serving in the extreme – and tedious into the bargain. Mary Russell Mitford, who immortalised the rural game at its best in *Our Village*, gave an account of the match in a letter to B. R. Haydon:

> I anticipated great pleasure from so grand an exhibition, and thought, like a simpleton, the better the play the more enjoyment. Oh, what a mistake! There they were – a set of ugly old men, white-headed and bare-headed (for half of Lord's were engaged in the combat, players and gentlemen, Mr Ward and Lord Frederick, the veterans of the green) dressed in light white jackets (the Apollo Belvidere could not bear the disguise of a cricketing jacket), with neckclothes primly tied round

their throats, fine japanned shoes, silk stockings and gloves, instead of our fine village lads, with their unbuttoned collars, their loose waistcoats, and the large shirt-sleeves which give an air so picturesque and Italian to their glowing, bounding youthfulness: there they stood, railed in by themselves, silent, solemn, slow – playing for money, making a business of the thing, grave as judges, taciturn as chess-players, a sort of dancers without music, instead of the glee, the fun, the shouts, the laughter, the glorious confusion of the country game. And there were we, the lookers-on, in tents and marquees, fine and freezing, dull as the players, cold as this hard summer weather, shivering and yawning and trying to seem pleased, the curse of gentility on all our doings, as stupid as we could have been in a ball-room. I never was so disappointed in my life. But everything is spoilt when money puts its ugly nose in. To think of playing cricket for hard cash! Money and gentility would ruin any pastime under the sun. Much to my comfort (for the degrading my favourite sport into a 'Science', as they were pleased to call it, had made me quite spiteful), the game ended unsatisfactorily to all parties, winners and losers. Old Lord Frederick, on some real or imaginary affront, took himself off in the middle of the second innings, so that the two last men played without him, by which means his side lost, and the other could scarcely be said to win. So be it always when men make the noble game of cricket an affair of bettings and hedgings, and, maybe, of cheatings.

The old order was on the wane. The Georgian period wound down in an atmosphere of general tawdriness. As though marking the end of an era, a peer of the realm was caught cheating at whist and the case came to court in 1837, the year Victoria ascended to the throne. William Thackeray noted that in the new moral climate inspired by the young queen, 'Play [i.e. gambling] is a deposed goddess, her worshippers bankrupt and her table in rags.' And in cricket the corrupting influence of aristocratic patronage also diminished.

But even under the new dispensation, betting on cricket continued, and the money resting on matches was such that sudden reversals in fortune were looked on askance. In 1842, Kent lost to an England team by 9 wickets, despite scoring 278 in their first innings. 'A deal of money was lost on that match,' according to Fuller Pilch (who made 98 and 0). 'When we got the 278, one of the Kentish farmers offered thirty pounds to one on Kent, and an officer at Canterbury took him four times over, and old "top-boots" did sigh when he went home for his canvas bag to pay up.' Kent were skittled out for 44 in their second innings, and the only man to make double figures was Sir Emelius Bayley, who later commented: 'The Kent people thought we had sold the match which, of course, was nonsense; but Alfred Mynn was hissed in Maidstone Market.' Whatever Bayley may have thought, the people of Maidstone knew that, for all his eminence, Mynn's finances were such that he often had to have his creditors bought off so he could play in an important match. He was by no means the last cricket hero to have the finger of suspicion pointed at him.

CHAPTER 5

Money

If even a pre-eminent amateur like Alfred Mynn had money problems, those playing the game professionally had it even harder, and some of them were not too particular as to how they made ends meet. Edward Pooley, whose first-class career lasted from 1861 to 1883, was not unique in ending his life as a pauper in the workhouse. He was unquestionably the best (English) wicket-keeper of his day, and no mean batsman, but he was also regarded as a rogue who spent much of his career under one cloud or another. In 1869, he was bound over to keep the peace after threatening a journalist with violence for adverse comments in a match report, and he had the distinction of missing the first ever Test match (at Melbourne in 1877) because he was awaiting trial in New Zealand.

In 1873, Pooley was suspended by Surrey on suspicion of selling a match against Yorkshire for £50. According to Pooley's appeal to the Committee, his betting was on a rather smaller scale: 'I took one bet of five shillings to half a crown that five Yorkshire players did not get seventy runs'; but the Committee remained adamant, and he was dropped for the rest of the season (though, typically, he still continued to play in minor cricket – for a fee).

Three years later, when he went on James Lillywhite's tour to Australia and New Zealand in 1876–7, he got into much deeper trouble. The New Zealand leg of the trip involved some undemanding matches against the odds to provide an interlude in the much more serious Australian itinerary. The England team were in Christchurch playing Eighteen of Canterbury when Pooley saw his way to making a killing. He was taking his turn as umpire, and even though the laws expressly prohibited those standing from betting on any aspect of the game, Pooley offered £1 to a shilling that he could guess the individual scores of the Canterbury team. A local man, Ralph Donkin, took the wager, whereupon Pooley simply wrote down o for each batsman, knowing full well that that was the most common score for unschooled cricketers against top professional bowling.

When four of the Eighteen duly made ducks (though none through the umpire's intervention), Pooley owed 13 shillings for the 13 scores he had 'failed' to guess correctly; but was in turn due £4 for the four he had got right, a result that Mr Micawber would have found highly satisfactory.

For Mr Donkin, however, the result spelt misery, especially as he saw that he had fallen for an old trick. He refused to pay up, claiming he was the victim of what he called 'a catch bet'. Pooley, despite his diminutive stature, was a natural bar-room brawler and promptly assaulted him. Along with the team bag man, Albert Bramall, he also trashed Donkin's hotel room, and cannot have been surprised to find himself up before the local bench. Both men were committed for trial, so the England party had not only to continue the tour without their wicket-keeper, but to carry their own bags into the bargain. Under this double handicap they lost the historic first ever Test match in Melbourne by 45 runs.

Pooley, meanwhile, loafed around awaiting his day in court, where he faced charges of injuring property 'above the value of £5'. Much to the surprise of anyone conversant with the facts, the Surrey man and his sidekick were acquitted. He had obviously acquired a certain celebrity during his enforced stay, and on the court's decision, someone organised a subscription and presented him with a gold watch and £50.*

Although Pooley was untypical in his brushes with the law, he was taken by many as a representative of the new cricket professional: brash, ill-disciplined and, on occasion, bloody

---

*The next professional tour to Australia, in 1881–2, was also notable for betting scandals. In one match most of the team backed themselves at good odds to win (which they did), only for it to emerge later that two of their number had been desperately trying to lose the match for a bribe of £100.

minded. Cricketing as a profession went back to the eighteenth century, when cricket-mad aristocrats strengthened their sides by employing the best players to work on their estates. Thomas Waymark is often cited as the first cricket professional, and he was employed as a groom by the Duke of Richmond, for whose teams he performed valiantly between 1720 and 1740. Lord Tankerville had England's best bowler, 'Lumpy' Stevens, working in his garden, Sir Horatio Mann had 'the best batsman, but a poor bailiff' in Aylwood, while the third Duke of Dorset could call upon Minshull, Miller and Brown. There was keen rivalry between the great cricketing patrons, and not a little poaching was involved in their attempts to secure satisfactorily multi-skilled gamekeepers.

While such men were bound to their employers by near feudal ties, there was money to be made by playing in matches in London (five guineas for those on the winning side, three for the losers) or the great provincial centres like Nottingham. There was also a growing call for professionals to bowl at gentlemen eager to improve their skills. Thomas Lord himself started as a ground bowler for the White Conduit Club before giving his name to the world's most famous cricket ground. Even Hambledon, between 1770 and 1790 the epicentre of the game, and on the face of it a more or less self-regulating and democratic club, was steeped in the culture of patronage. Over the shoulders of men like Richard Nyren loomed the long, aristocratic faces of Dorset, Mann and Tankerville.

The challenge to accepted (and, so far as we can tell, unresented) upper-class patronage came as a side-effect of the industrial revolution. Migration into the towns, where new factories offered an alternative to rural subsistence, ruptured the established social order and created the potential for a lucrative market in leisure activities such as sport. William Clark of Nottingham was among the first to see the possibilities.

In 1837, the one-eyed under-arm bowler with a strong appreciation of economic realities married a widow, who held the licence of the Trent Bridge Inn, and enclosed the adjacent field to turn it into a cricket ground. A decade later he tried a different tack. Cricket was becoming increasingly popular, but there was, he surmised, a large audience for the game among those who could not get to the great cricket centres. Clark therefore created the All England Eleven (AEE), a squad of professionals available to play matches wherever and whenever he could arrange fixtures. Exploiting the improved communications of the industrial age – turnpike roads and the ever-expanding rail-way network (not to mention a reliable and affordable postal service) – Clark set out to take cricket to all the corners of the kingdom, and from its first match in 1846, the AEE proved a resounding success.

Up and down the country they went, playing odds matches against local teams of eighteen or twenty-two, sometimes strengthened by a professional as a 'given' man. The disparity in standards was such that the matches often became farcically one-sided, but they were popular for all that, and demand for Clark's brand of cricketing circus outstripped supply. (Even with a breakaway group led by John Wisden forming the United All England Eleven [UAEE] in 1852, there were still enough fixtures to go round.)

The rewards were considerable for all involved, but especially for the impresario. Clark had as his travelling exchequer a hat-box from which he was inseparable, and at the end of a game he would sit at a table like an army paymaster, calling out the sum owed to each player: so much for X, so much for Y; and then, at the end, he swept the residue into his hat-box with a triumphant 'And so much for me!'

Clark's power was such that by the mid-1850s he could forbid his star players, or 'cracks', to play at Lord's when he wanted them elsewhere on AEE duty. The confidence of professional cricketers rose with their financial independence, and in 1859 two leading Surrey players, H. H. Stephenson and Julius Caesar, staged the game's first strike, informing the Oval authorities that they would not play 'without a further increase in pay'.

The 1860s were to prove crucial for determining the structure of cricket for the next hundred years, and at the start of the decade, the professionals occupied the economic high ground. Alarm bells were ringing in the amateur camp, and many com-mentators lashed out at the uppity pros who were, it was claimed, effectively prostituting the game for gate-money. Anthony Trollope described the travelling elevens 'which go caravaning about the country playing against two bowlers and twenty duffers for the benefit of some enterprising publican' as 'the monster nuisance of the day', while R. A. Fitzgerald, who became secretary of a very demoralised MCC in 1863, denounced them for having 'taken all the plums and left us generally to get on as well as we can with the dough'. *The Times* thundered:

> the cause of this unfortunate position of things is to be found in the too prosperous conditions of the players. So long as they can earn more money by playing matches against twenty-twos than by appearing at Lord's – so long as they can be 'mistered' in public houses, and stared at at railway stations, they will care very little for being absent from the Metropolitan Ground.

But neither finger-wagging nor appeals to ancient loyalties worked. It was the age of self – self-help, self-improvement, self-defined aims – and the professionals saw no reason to abandon the position they had achieved. Not only had they evolved a better system for earning their living, but they had also stumbled on what would prove the lifeblood of the game in the years ahead – international cricket. The first overseas cricket tour – to the United States and Canada – had taken place in 1859. Two tours to Australia followed in 1861–2 and 1863–4, with another trip to North America in 1868. These were all-professional parties, arranged quite independently and undertaken for profit.

Even without this extra dimension, the northern heartlands had sufficiently large populations to support those making a living out of the game, and cricket might well have gone the separatist route taken by rugby league later in the century. The promised land of a self-sufficient, independent and self-regulating cricket republic beckoned, but there was no one with sufficient strength of character and vision to lead them into it. Instead, their power was dissipated in bickering and feuding. George Parr, who succeeded William Clark as manager of the AEE, was a great cricketer and a strong personality, but disputatious and vengeful. Although he had turned down the opportunity to take the first team to Australia, he never forgave

H. H. Stephenson for accepting the invitation, and the resulting friction between Nottinghamshire and Surrey affected the wider relationship between north and south.

Lord's, gradually regaining confidence under the spirited guidance of Fitzgerald, finally lost patience with the 'cracks', and in 1868, responded to their semi-permanent boycott by passing a motion 'That a fund be established called the Marylebone Cricket Club Fund; that the fund be in the first instance available for professionals on the Lord's Ground: secondly for the relief of all cricketers who, during their career shall have conducted themselves to the entire satisfaction of the Committee of the MCC.'

The professionals might have shrugged and asked why they should try to conduct themselves to the satisfaction, entire or otherwise, of a lot of self-important gentlemen in St John's Wood. What swung the balance of power was the emergence of a single cricketer, W. G. Grace, who altered the cricketing landscape like some seismic upheaval. Making his first appearance in senior cricket in 1864, at the age of sixteen, his phenomenal batting feats soon made his name synonymous with the game itself. His sporting charisma was an incomparable asset, the ultimate trump card. And in 1869, sponsored significantly by the secretary and treasurer, Grace was invited to become a member of MCC.

The professionals had trusted to market forces. They were the best players; they could, within reason, name their price. They certainly had no need to be subservient to Lord's. But now they were confronted by a cricketer whose prowess simply beggared belief. In 1871, his batting average was *twice* that of the next best man. In an age when fifty was treated as a century is now, he scored centuries – big centuries, double centuries. He revolutionised batting, he intimidated bowlers and he delighted the crowds. He was the greatest draw ever known; the man whose popularity required the introduction of turnstiles and then set them clicking so merrily that, it was said, he provided half the bricks in the cricket pavilions of England. Once he had nailed his colours to the St John's Wood mast, the game was up for the pros. They simply couldn't compete. It was as though Grace had taken out a patent on the game. In terms of the market, he was a one-man monopoly.

Grace's amateur allegiance was far from predictable given his own financial situation. His father, Dr Henry Grace, died relatively young, leaving a wife and large family. Like all his brothers, W. G. followed in his father's medical footsteps; but it took him a decade to qualify, and during that time he had no obvious means of support. Had he and his two most talented cricketing siblings, E. M. and Fred, wished, they could have gone in with the professionals and made a fortune. However, Dr Grace's climb out of genteel poverty to professional respectability had been so hard that it was inconceivable that any of his sons would have forfeited the title of gentleman. They played as amateurs, even though they could not possibly afford to devote themselves to the game without receiving payment. W. G. was happy to throw in his lot with Lord's; all he asked in return was to be allowed to flout the central tenet of the MCC faith. And throughout the forty years of his first-class career, Lord's pretended ignorance of the fact that the leading amateur of the day made more money from cricket than any of the professionals.

But Grace did not confine himself to demanding fat expenses for appearances at Lord's or the Oval. He also revived the waning tradition of the travelling Eleven. As part of the professionals' falling out among themselves, yet another travelling Eleven, the United South, started up, taking over the southern franchise. The Sussex bowler James Lillywhite ran the side, and in 1866 persuaded Grace to play a game for him. W. G. and his younger brother Fred became USEE regulars and soon took over, like cuckoos in the nest. And with Grace in charge, it soon became a very well feathered nest. Like Clark before him, W. G. negotiated a fee for the appearance of the Eleven, paid the professionals the going rate, and kept the rest for himself.

Amateurs – true amateurs – simply didn't do this sort of thing. They maintained a rigid distance from the professionals. It was precisely to keep the Pooleys of the cricketing world at arm's length that the Victorians insisted on the Gentleman–Player divide. Wearing his class assumptions on his sleeve, Lord Harris looked back on the period and reflected, 'In the great matches of the sixties one does not find many amateurs playing for either All England or the United All England, and not much wonder, perhaps; there would have been no companionship at all touring the country with either of those professional teams.' Grace, however, was perfectly happy to rub shoulders with Old Etonians one day and old sweats like Pooley the next. Pooley, in fact, was a core member of the USEE – something Surrey took into consideration when they suspended him. To bring him to heel more effectively, they also barred him 'from playing with the United South of England Eleven until he is re-instated in the Surrey Eleven'. Grace took absolutely no notice and played him in the next four USEE matches. Throughout the 1870s, Grace travelled the length and breadth of the kingdom – including trips to Scotland and Ireland – changing in draughty tents on windswept hillsides and playing on appalling pitches. He was a one-man roadshow of indefatigable energy; and it is conceivable that he travelled as many miles as he scored runs and bowled balls.

Nor did he simply exploit his marketability at home. He was prepared to travel to the ends of the earth – for a price. When the Australians invited him to bring a team down under in 1873–4, he accepted, provided they paid him £1,500. This demand apparently 'startled' the committee of Melbourne businessmen attempting to lure him to the Antipodes, and it was, indeed, a huge sum of money – especially in view of the £175 he was offering the professionals he recruited to join him. But if you wanted Grace, you had to pay for him. The Australians stumped up.

Grace's ability to startle his hosts did not end with these preliminary negotiations. Once he arrived, he showed an almost piratical interest in transferring other people's money into his own coffers, while happily availing himself of the lavish hospitality that was laid out for him. The most breathtaking example of his mercenary ways occurred at the end of the tour. There was to be one fixture in the colony of South Australia. This Grace auctioned off to the highest bidder, which turned out not to be Adelaide but the Yorke's Peninsula Association. The price was a simply staggering £800, more than twice that paid anywhere else on the tour. However, having achieved their great aim of putting their Adelaide neighbours' noses out of joint, the men of the Peninsula looked forward to sitting back and enjoying their three days of Grace-given glory. They were to be disappointed.

Behind their backs, their smiling guest had entered into a

secret deal to play a final, unscheduled match at Adelaide. This was sufficiently well known – or at least rumoured – to deter the expected crowds making their way from Adelaide to the peninsula, and as a result the Yorke's Peninsula consortium was left heavily out of pocket. Even worse was Grace's determination to screw every last penny out of his hosts. Although contracted to play an exhibition match for free if the real fixture ended within the three days – always a likelihood given the poor wicket and the huge disparity of class between the tourists and the locals – Grace demanded £10 a head for the extra match on the spurious grounds that his men had not had an opportunity to buy any souvenirs. The Peninsula reacted to Grace's act of piracy with dignity and thoroughly justified wrath. The letter pages of the *Walleroo Times* hummed with indignation, while editorial criticism was stinging:

> The signal failure of the Yorke's Peninsula Match, in a pecuniary sense, was no doubt largely due to the non-appearance of visitors from Adelaide, and we have no hesitation in attributing their non-appearance on the Peninsula to the fact that the Adelaide cricketers, the Adelaide Press, and the Adelaide people generally, were fully apprised many days ago that this break of faith on the part of Mr Grace and his team, was fully intended from the first. We scarcely know how to characterise the mean and sordid character of this business. For the sake of securing a few pounds in Adelaide, Mr Grace or his agents for him, have forfeited any claim that they had to the character of men of their word, or gentlemen; and they may be assured they will leave the colony with that stigma attached to them.

The editor of the *Walleroo Times* was by no means the only one to doubt Grace's claim to the title 'gentleman'. Season after season he turned out for the Gentlemen against the Players, whose representatives earned a tithe of what he took from the game. His supposed fellow amateurs were not particularly happy with the situation, but Grace had the hide of a rhinoceros. He had also, early in life, cemented an important friendship with the Hon. George Harris, who as Lord Harris held sway over the game for most of Grace's extended career. Lord's had no option but to maintain the fiction and brazen it out, bearing whatever embarrassment that happened to entail.

The professionals were surprisingly muted in their response to this flagrant double standard. Partly this was because they simply had to concede that Grace was in a class of his own as a cricketer; and for all the long days endured in the field while he compiled his awesome centuries, they could see that this phenomenon was good for the game, good for business. There was no doubt he was worth whatever he could get, and the spin-offs for the professionals were worth having. Even though he creamed off a huge proportion of the profits from his personal milch cow, the United South, it was still unarguable that the beast only produced the quantities of milk it did because of him. The professionals associated with the United South may have spent rather more time than they would have liked travelling the country, but much of the time they were simply making up the numbers while Grace and his brother Fred did the hard work.

In fact it was not Grace's privileged position in the game but the arrival of the first Australian tourists in 1878 that provoked rebellious stirrings in the professional ranks. With one exception, the Australians all played as amateurs, and yet each had agreed to put up a stake to fund the tour with the expectation of receiving a dividend from the profits at the end. And profits there certainly would be. The tourists may have started as something of a curiosity, but after they beat – annihilated would be more accurate – a strong MCC team at Lord's in a single day's play, they were the hot ticket. They could fill any ground they liked, and the deal was a half share in the gate. Those initial £50 stakes proved to be an exceptionally good investment. But although they were in effect playing for money, the Australians were accorded amateur privileges: each was given the honorary 'Mr' in front of his name on scorecards and in press reports; they changed in amateur changing-rooms; and they ate their luncheons in the pavilion (instead of having to go and queue at pie stalls with the general public as the pros had to).

It is probably fair to say that the English professionals didn't much mind what the Australians were called. They were inured to the injustices of a two-tier class system within the English game, but they did dig their heels in over money. When a Players XI was selected to play the visitors, the professionals were offered £10 a head – which might have been considered generous, given that the going rate for an ordinary county match was £5. But the professionals knew that the Australians would take the lion's share of the gate and didn't see why, as cricketing equals, they should be fobbed off with a relative pittance. They said they would play, but for £20 a man. The Australians rejected this out of hand. The Players promptly boycotted the fixture, leaving the Australian manager John Conway and his agent James Lillywhite precious little time to get a second eleven of mercenaries into the field. This they did, and the substitute team did exceptionally well. The tourists scraped home by only 8 runs. For the record, they paid their near-vanquishers £20 each, though that did little to smooth the ruffled feathers of the professional body as a whole.

This militancy among the professionals, along with mutterings in the press, brought the whole question of who was paid what to public attention. This at last forced MCC's hand, and in November 1878 they issued an edict to the effect 'That no gentleman ought to make a profit by his services in the cricket field, and that for the future no cricketer who takes more than his expenses in any match shall be qualified to play for the Gentlemen against the Players at Lord's'. This was really only to restate the existing position, which, the committee then had the effrontery to claim, the club had never wittingly departed from. That was simply asking for trouble.

John Lillywhite's Cricketers' Companion was unimpressed:

The Note issued by the MCC . . . should have been issued four or five seasons ago, but cricketers must be thankful that the leading club has, however late in the day, recognised an evil which has been injuring the best interests of the game for some years past. It is satisfactory to learn at last that 'no cricketer who takes more than his expenses in *any* match shall be qualified to play for the GENTLEMEN against the PLAYERS at LORD'S'; but it is somewhat surprising to read the assertion appended to the note that 'this rule has been invariably adhered to by the MARYLEBONE CLUB . . .', for ninety-nine out of every hundred cricketers know as well as we do that this statement is, to use a mild term, hardly consistent with [the] facts. One well-known cricketer in particular has not been an absentee from the GENTLEMEN'S eleven at LORD'S for many years past, and that he has made larger profits by playing cricket than any Professional ever made is an acknowledged fact. How the MARYLEBONE CLUB can reconcile their statement with this fact, even with any reasonable amount of word-twisting, we are unable to conceive.

The 'well-known cricketer' in question was, of course, Grace. Quite apart from his United South income, W. G. made a healthy profit from his expenses. Such matters were a jealously guarded secret, but just two months after the Lord's Note, the systematic chicanery involved was dramatically exposed.

As a result of a bitter power-struggle within the club, an Extraordinary General Meeting of Gloucestershire CCC was called in January 1879. What was at issue was E. M. Grace's stewardship as club secretary, and his opponents submitted damning evidence of the expenses paid to the Gloucestershire amateurs.

Figures were produced for the previous season's match with Surrey at the Oval. They were as follows: W. G. Grace, £15, Mr G. F. Grace, £11, Mr Gilbert, £8. As all were making the same journey – G. F. (Fred) and his cousin Gilbert were actually living in the same house – the discrepancies in the amounts recorded were hard to account for. It was, in fact, blatantly obvious that the expenses were graded according to an estimation of the individual's worth, with W. G. as usual taking the largest fee.

The Grace clan successfully fought off the attempt to relax their control over Gloucestershire, but it was a Pyrrhic victory. *The Times* published a full report of the proceedings, and in doing so provided a fresh arsenal of ammunition for those intent on exposing the scandal of amateur payments disguised as expenses.

John Lillywhite's Companion, which had long highlighted 'the abuse of the term "Amateur"', seized on *The Times* report. It was fair enough that amateurs should have their railway tickets bought,

But if hotel bills are to be included, and a gentleman playing for his county is to be at liberty to drink Chateau Yquem with his dinner, and to smoke shilling cigars at the expense of the Club, and if the said Club is to be debited with £10, £15 or £20 for the privilege of retaining the services of such so-called amateurs, the MARYLEBONE NOTE is worse than useless . . . That a professional's *wages* should be £5, and an Amateur's *expenses* £10, for playing the same match, is simply absurd. It is high time that this unsavoury question was fairly met and disposed of for good and all.

This was an embarrassing situation for everyone – apart from Grace, who was as impervious to embarrassment as he was to fast bowling. What could be done? In the end, the MCC came up with a solution. They effectively offered to buy Grace off by offering him a testimonial which would raise enough money to set him up in his own medical practice when he at length qualified as a doctor. Once ensconced in his surgery, it was thought, he would not need to milk the game for his subsistence. Grace gladly went along with this, somehow managing to intimate that he would play much less cricket once established in general practice; indeed, it was rumoured that he would actually retire.

The great day came at Lord's in July 1879, and W. G. was duly presented with a cheque for £1,458, with which he was indeed able to set himself up as a GP in Bristol. Although Grace did the decent thing to an extent – he ended his connection with the United South, which promptly withered on the vine – talk of his gradual retirement from the game proved somewhat exaggerated. Despite his new responsibilities, he played more – far more – cricket in the 1880s than in the 1870s, and was just as keen to be paid for appearing as ever. Instead of being tied to his surgery, he hired a locum, largely paid for out of Gloucestershire CCC funds. So much is clear from the minutes of Committee meetings. His match expenses remain shrouded in mystery, and the club were careful not to parade their dirty washing in public in the future.

The trouble in 1878 was a direct reflection of how hard done by the professionals felt, but politically they were powerless. The pendulum had swung back, leaving them under the thumb of Lord's and their county committees. County cricket had superseded the unequal odds matches played by the old travelling elevens, and the regular visits by the Australians proved the greatest box-office attraction of all.

The Australians continued to stir up resentment among the professionals. In 1881, *two* teams arrived from down under. Neither was sufficiently strong to play a Test match, but both travelled the country reaping a fine harvest of gate receipts. And wherever they went, they were classed as amateurs. This rankled to such an extent that Alfred Shaw and Arthur Shrewsbury, respectively the leading professional bowler and batsman in the country, led a revolt of the senior professionals at Nottingham. While not agreeing with all their objectives, James Lillywhite was sympathetic to their grievances. As he wrote in his *Annual* for 1882:

> The terms upon which the Colonial Players were accepted over here were utterly false to men like Shaw, who knew that the home *status* of some was certainly not above the level of professional cricket in England . . . Then again, the readiness with which, in many cases, rather exorbitant demands from the Australian managers were met by some of our chief clubs probably had some influence in encouraging Alfred Shaw, who may be considered the leader of the movement, in believing that the withdrawal of seven most capable members of the eleven might reduce the management of a county, even one so rich in cricketers as Notts, to accede to the imposition of new stipulations in the recognised contracts.

Shaw's demands went beyond an increase in appearance money. The professionals wanted some limited security of employment and also a guarantee of a benefit, the enticing carrot dangled before them through long years of service, but only granted by the committee as a favour, not as a right. Shaw also wanted the pros to revert to organising their own matches so that they could get the sort of share of gate money enjoyed by the Australians.

There was a general outcry against such insurrectionary proposals. Even the sympathetic Lillywhite could not give the rebels his full support, declaring: 'It was not merely a question of the welfare of one county, but it involved a distinct and material alteration in the relations between paid cricketers and their employers which vitally affected the interests of every club of any importance.'

The Nottinghamshire committee rejected the demands out of hand and suspended all the players involved. This cost the club the county championship as Lancashire came up on the inside rail, but had the desired effect. By the end of the season, 'after due submission had been made', five of the malcontents were readmitted. Shaw and Shrewsbury, as 'the prime movers in the conspiracy', were left out in the cold for the winter, but mutual interest saw to it that both were back in the team the following year.

Shaw and Shrewsbury's sense of injustice can only have been increased by their next experience of touring Down Under. In 1884, they sailed with another all-professional side, and soon found themselves embroiled in distasteful wrangles over money. For the first Test at Adelaide, they met the nucleus of the Australian side that had just toured England. Under their captain Billy Murdoch, they claimed – and got – an equal share from the game. The second Test was at Melbourne, and Murdoch once again demanded a 50 per cent split. This time he was turned down flat. Neither he nor any of the 1884 tourists would play, and the Englishmen cruised to an easy victory over Horan's scratch team, taking a 2–0 lead in the series. It was only the return of Frederick Spofforth, who had publicly condemned the mercenary approach of his team-mates, that restored some balance between the two sides, and the rubber stood at 2–2 when they met for the fifth time at Melbourne. However, once again the Australian cause was fatally compromised by internal divisions, and Shrewsbury, leading from the front with an excellent century, forced the deciding victory by an innings and 98 runs.

For all its problems, touring remained a profitable exercise, and Shaw and Shrewsbury took two further teams to Australia in the 1880s. They also developed their partnership in a sports goods business, and, despite the inequalities of the system, ended up making a decent living from the game. By and large, their fellow professionals were content to follow their example, accepting the status quo, doffing their caps figuratively, and indeed literally, to those in power, making what they could as they went along and looking forward to the windfall of a healthy benefit. There was, in fact, little alternative; stepping out of line was a risky business.

However, in 1896, there was another attempt to force a change by collective action. Again the Australians were the spark, although the controversy widened to take in the continuing scandal of shamateurism and put W. G. (now England captain) in the spotlight once more. George Lohmann, the ringleader of the rebels, was unquestionably a major star – a remarkable athlete, he was a belligerent but skilful batsman and a majestic bowler. Good-looking, intelligent and articulate, he was an independent spirit with the confidence to claim what he saw as his rightful rewards. By this time, Test cricket was proving a gold mine. The matches were played before capacity crowds; the Australians continued to take their traditional share of the gate; the amateurs, as ever, were put up in great luxury and sent home with their wallets appreciably fatter; and the coffers of the host club grew heavy with the residue. The only ones left out of the loop were the professionals, who were still getting a set fee of £10.

After some disappointingly one-sided rubbers, the 1896 series was proving a great one. Australia had fought back to level at one match each, with the third and final Test to decide the series. For England, Tom Richardson had bowled magnificently, Ranjitsinhji had made his incredible début at Old Trafford, and there was universal excitement leading up to the match at the Oval. Lohmann realized there was probably no better time to make a move. When the letters went out inviting players to play in the match and outlining the terms, he and four others wrote back to the Surrey committee 'taking the liberty' of asking 'for increased terms. Viz. Twenty pounds.' Adding, 'The importance of such a fixture entitles us to make this demand.'

The players had a strong case, but the tone and timing grated. The committee were further incensed that the rebels included four of their own men (Lohmann himself, Bobby Abel, Tom Hayward and Richardson). The fifth was the Nottinghamshire batsman William Gunn. They rejected the demands peremptorily, but the pros fought back, for the first time using the press in a deliberate propaganda ploy. On the Saturday before the match, the *Daily Mail* carried an interview with one of the five, almost certainly Lohmann, who was quoted as saying:

> We want £20 apiece and expenses. The Australians will prob-
> ably take away £1,700 or £1,800 and the Surrey club will
> probably benefit to the same extent or more. We professional
> cricketers in England do not get anything like adequate pay-
> ment for our services. The enormous crowds which now fol-
> low the game benefit the clubs and, in fact, everybody but
> those who have done at least their fair share towards bringing
> the game towards its present state – the professional players.

And Lohmann didn't stop there. He extended his fire to
include the amateurs, who, he said, 'will be paid more than us
professionals'. This was incendiary stuff, and the Sunday papers
took the story up with gusto. Harry Trott, the Australian captain, foolishly added his two pennies' worth, coming out with
sanctimonious regret 'that Lohmann is the leading spirit of the
movement, especially after the handsome treatment he has
received at the hands of the Surrey Club and the English public
generally'. This gave another paper the opportunity to snipe:

> the charm of this criticism would be more apparent were Trott
> to tell an excited public the exact terms upon which he, per-
> sonally, undertook the trip to this country. If I mistake not, the
> burden of the complaint made by Lohmann and his brethren is
> that the terms are not equal all round. Given fine weather, the
> Australians will benefit to an extent undreamt of by the Eng-
> lish professionals. Of course, the Australians are amateurs . . .

First and foremost among the English amateurs stood the
England captain. W. G. was rumoured to be getting £40 for the
match, and Lohmann's remarks signalled open season on this
broad and inviting target. The *Weekly Sun* weighed in with
enthusiasm: 'My sympathies are entirely with the pros., and
whether they get what they are asking for or not, they are entitled to our respect for having raised another protest against the
shoddy amateurism which waxes fat on "expenses".'

Grace was livid and threatened to go on strike himself if the
Oval authorities did not deny the claim categorically. Which,
naturally, they did, in a statement which appeared on the morning of the match:

The Committee of the Surrey County Cricket Club have observed paragraphs in the Press respecting amounts alleged to be paid, or promised to, Dr. W. G. Grace for playing in the match England v Australia. The Committee desire to give the statements contained in the paragraphs the most unqualified contradiction. During many years, on the occasions of Dr W. G. Grace playing at the Oval, at the request of the Surrey County Committee, in the matches Gentlemen v. Players and England v. Australia, Dr Grace has received the sum of £10 a match to cover his expenses in coming to and remaining in London during the three days. Beyond this amount Dr Grace has not received, directly or indirectly, one farthing for playing in a match at the Oval.

Signed on behalf of the Committee,
C. W. Alcock, August 10, 1896

This fooled no one. Sydney Pardon, in his Notes for the 1897 edition of *Wisden*, did his best to smooth over the embarrassment with a line from the Bard: 'Mr W. G. Grace's position has for years, as everyone knows, been an anomalous one, but "nice customs curtsey to great kings" and the work he has done in popularising cricket outweighs a hundredfold every other consideration.' The quotation comes from the victorious Henry V after the battle of Agincourt. Grace held a similar position of power in Victorian cricket, and was wholly unabashed about exercising it.

Even in his late forties, Grace was indispensable. Not so the rebels. Abel, Richardson and Hayward climbed down as soon as the committee got tough. Gunn stayed firm and was dropped. Lohmann prevaricated until warned that lack of compliance would mean indefinite suspension from Surrey. He was further humiliated by having to put his name to an open letter of apology circulated to the press. The establishment had closed ranks, called the professionals' bluff, and cruelly exposed their lack of bargaining power. The mutiny was over. After what must have been one of the worst build-ups to an important match, England won comfortably under Grace's imperturbable captaincy.

Grace proceeded through the 1890s (and his forties) as he had through the 1880s, the 1870s and the 1860s, a cricketing force of nature, impervious to age, critics or opponents alike. In 1895, he astonished and delighted everybody by scoring 1,000 runs in May, clocking up his hundredth first-class century in the process. The public exhibited a frenzy of enthusiasm, which the canny proprietor of the *Daily Telegraph* seized upon to launch a shilling fund to which, it seemed, everyone in the land, from the Prime Minister to the meanest schoolboy, subscribed. This second national testimonial reached the dizzy heights of £10,000, watched keenly by its beneficiary, who, it was said, knew to the last shilling where the fund stood on any given day. As a coda, Sir Home Gordon wrote after Grace's death that Lord Burnham, who owned the *Telegraph*, 'believed that a substantial portion of this ten thousand pounds went to pay [Grace's] betting debts'.

While cricket's monarch was indulging a secret passion for the sport of kings, the weary foot soldiers of the game slogged on. Their life did get better, albeit slowly. In 1898, appearance fees for Test matches went up to the £20 Lohmann and co. had asked for; conditions of employment improved; and professionals were given winter payments to see them through the close season. But the pros remained the second-class citizens of cricket, beholden to their county committees, subordinate to amateur captains (however inadequate as cricketers), and subject to the class apartheid that hived them off to dingy dressing-rooms and required them to join their social superiors on the field of play via a separate gate. This archaic system, reminiscent of the frozen world of Gormenghast, survived the upheavals of two world wars and the loss of an empire, and finally bowed off the stage only as the Swinging Sixties burst into life.

CHAPTER 6

'Flesh Will Blacken'

———

Once at the wicket, cricketers could largely forget the social and financial inequalities that reigned so rigorously off the field of play. The ball was no respecter of rank; an aristocrat's shins bruised just as readily as a ploughman's; his knuckles bled as freely. Keeping the balance in the central opposition between batsman and bowler has always been at the heart of debate and the lodestar of cricketing legislation.

'Shock' White's wicket-wide plank was blatantly iniquitous and ruled out immediately. The lbw law was brought in when someone repeatedly stopped the ball with his foot. Mr Fennex senior thought his own son's awkward-looking but effective blocking of the length ball unfair to the bowler. But the Revd Pycroft's sense of natural justice was roused on account of the batsman:

> The principle injuries sustained are in the fingers . . . The old players, in the days of under-hand [i.e. under-arm] bowling, played without gloves; and Bennett assured me he had seen Tom Walker, before advancing civilisation made man tender, rub his bleeding fingers in the dust. The old players could show finger-joints of most ungenteel dimensions; and no wonder, for a finger has been broken even through tubular india rubber. Still, with a good pair of cricket gloves no man need think much about his fingers; albeit flesh will blacken, joints will grow too large for the accustomed ring, and finger nails will come off.

Pycroft clearly relishes the manly fortitude exhibited by players of the previous age, and is implicitly scornful of contemporaries with their 'tubular india rubber' batting gloves. (There was a similar prejudice against pads when they were first introduced.) But his tone changes when he considers the situation in which a batsman's safety – as opposed to his comfort – is imperilled:

A spinning ball is the most mischievous; and when there is spin and pace too, as with a ball from Mr Fellows, which you can hear humming like a top, the danger is *too great for mere amusement*; for when, as in the Players' Match of 1849, Hillyer plays a bowler a foot away from his stumps, and Pilch cannot face him, which is true when Mr Fellows bowls on any but the smoothest ground, why then we will not say that anything that hardest of hitters [with the bat] and thorough cricketer does is not cricket, but certainly it's anything but *play*.

Harvey Fellows was an Etonian, and over the two-year period 1848–9 was regarded as the fastest bowler in the English game. Unusually, the Gentlemen beat the Players in those two years, Fellows taking wickets in both games. Hillyer and Pilch were leading professional batsmen, so if they did not fancy him in full cry, his effect on tail-enders can be imagined. The 1849 match saw the last appearance of the veteran professional bowler William Lillywhite, who went in number eleven for the Players. Or rather, who didn't, at least not in the second innings. As the ancient scorecard reports with illuminating candour: 'Lillywhite hurt by Fellows on wrist, and refused to go in.'

As Pycroft makes clear, Fellows, a 'thorough cricketer' (and a gentleman into the bargain), was doing nothing illegal; but in his view, the level of physical risk took such bowling out of the realm of sport – 'the danger is *too great for mere amusement*'. It is a sentiment that has echoed down the years. Fast bowling is one of the most exhilarating aspects of cricket, and part of the excitement is its naked aggression, but there is always an underlying vicarious nervousness for the poor batsman under attack.

Alfred Mynn, a giant of a man, and capable himself of ferocious pace off his few grenadier's strides to the crease, came close to having a leg amputated as a result of the battering he received from the bowlers in a North vs South match at Leicester in 1837. He made a match-winning century, but was so badly injured that he had to be strapped to the roof of the London coach to reach St Bartholomew's Hospital.

A bowler who was reputedly fast enough to break a man's leg was F. W. Marcon. Although the encounter occurred before he was born, W. G. Grace gives a spirited account of the West Gloucestershire Club's encounter with this phenomenon in 1846:

Mr Marcon was in the neighbourhood that year, and played against them. Their wickets went down like ninepins, and half of the batsmen never saw the ball when he bowled. Every fieldsman was behind the wicket, and there were two longstops: the first stood fifteen yards behind, and was supposed to be the wicket-keeper; and the second about thirty yards farther away. Mr Marcon did not trouble about the length of the ball. He aimed at the wicket, and the ball flew straight from his hand to it without touching the ground; and nearly every time it hit the bottom of the stump, the stump was smashed. Runs were scored now and then from a snick to leg or slip, but not one of them could hit him in front of the wicket. A member of the team said it could be done – ought to be done – and *he* would do it!

. . . Mr Marcon came with a rush, and our enterprising member hit. The ball hit the bat high up about the shoulder, and the bat and ball went right through the wicket.

Marcon, the last great under-arm fast bowler, was another product of the public school/university system, and like Fellows did not stay long in the game. To the relief of many, he took holy orders and retired to the care of souls in Cornwall.

There was no shortage of fast bowling in the professional ranks. Whatever the numerical odds faced by Clarke's All England Eleven, the majority of their matches were one-sided affairs, leading R. A. Fitzgerald, for one, to disparage 'the inferior grade of gladiatorial exhibition'. Sometimes indeed it was more a case of Christians to the lions. John Jackson, of Nottinghamshire, was a fifteen-stone six-footer known as 'the Demon'. On the rare occasions that a batsman stood up to him, he retaliated with a deliberate head-high full-toss. Most, though, departed without provoking him to beamers. At Uppingham he once bowled six men in seven balls.

His colleague in terror was George Tarrant, widely known as 'Tear 'em' Tarrant. In contrast to Jackson, Tarrant was quite small, but with great physical strength and an aggressive temperament to match. (When George Parr took over as manager of the AEE, Tarrant acted as his minder-cum-enforcer, prepared to use his fists to settle any disputes over the finer contractual details.) Where Jackson intimidated with the beamer, Tarrant made frequent use of the bouncer, which was all the more lethal given his preference for bowling round the wicket. Lord Harris left a vivid picture of 'Tear 'em' in action: 'He was all over the place like a flash of lightning, never sparing himself, and frightening timid batsmen. He was the terror of the twenty-twos when he played for the All England Eleven, some of his long-hops bounding over their heads, causing them to change colour and funk at the next straight one.'

Although still (notionally) bound by the law forbidding delivery above shoulder height, men like Tarrant and Jackson could work up a frightening pace, and they were given enormous help by the universally low standard of the wickets. When Grace came into senior cricket as a teenager in the mid-1860s, he entered an arena dominated by the fast men. In less than ten years, Grace had changed all that, bringing about not only a revolution in batting, but, by extension, bowling too. In the words of one veteran, 'He killed professional fast bowling; for years they were almost afraid to bowl within his reach.'

But they didn't give in easily, and W. G.'s skill and courage were frequently put to the test. He usually passed with flying colours, if at the cost of some personal discomfort. In May 1870 at Lord's, he made a fearless – and famous – 66 for MCC against Yorkshire, who had a formidable pair of fast bowlers, Tom Emmett and George Freeman. Grace recalled that

[I] stood up to Emmett and Freeman on one of the roughest, bumpiest wickets we had now and then on that ground. About every third or fourth ball kicked badly and we were hit all over the body and had to dodge an occasional one with our heads. Shooters were pretty common on the same wicket, and what with playing one ball and dodging another, we had a lively and unenviable time of it.

Even the two Yorkshiremen were awed by the punishment they dished out. According to Freeman, 'Tom Emmett and I have often said it was a marvel the doctor was not either maimed or unnerved for the rest of his days or killed outright,' while Emmett himself waxed lyrical at the damage inflicted:

Freeman and I were then at our best, and Lord's was at its worst. I verily believe there wasn't one square inch of the Doctor from his ankles up to his shoulders that wasn't black and blue after that score. We barked his shins, battered his thighs, skinned his fingers, rattled his ribs, pounded his chest, thumped his elbow, and made a mark of his back . . . We never have ceased to wonder that one of us didn't either cut him over or kill him that day; the climax was reached when one of Freeman's very fastest got up so high that the doctor had only just time to duck his head, and the ball went straight into Rowbotham's hands at long stop before it touched the ground a second time.

Grace's companion at the crease was C. E. Green, who later wrote, 'to this day I carry a mark on my chest where I was struck by a very fast rising ball from Freeman'. W. G. also had vivid memories of Freeman's powers to inflict pain: 'When he hit you on the thigh it hurt. The ball seemed to sizzle into your leg.'

The dangers of fast bowling on 'those typical Lord's fiery wickets' of the time were horrifically demonstrated within a month, when Grace – and Green – were back at Lord's to play against Nottinghamshire. This was another of the many matches which filled the first-class season in the period before the county championship really counted and before the regular visit of Australian Test teams. The atmosphere was relaxed – extremely so on the amateurs' part. When the game started, or was scheduled to start, the MCC were still four men short, and the Nottinghamshire captain Richard Daft indulgently allowed them four substitutes. In that neither side was playing for anything, it was 'friendly' cricket, but that does not mean it was not competitive. Playing at Lord's was a great honour: matches were written up in the press and everyone wanted to make a name for himself by performing well, especially those making their début at the ground.

Compared to some Lord's wickets, the pitch was not too bad. But the match took place after a dry spell, and although the strip with the most grass had been chosen, it was very hard and fast, and offered considerable variations in bounce. Nottinghamshire batted first, and with Daft leading the way with 117, knocked up 267. Daft was Grace's nearest rival at the start of the 1870s, and on several occasions a good score by the Nottinghamshire man provoked an equal or better response. This time Grace equalled his score, but was stranded as the MCC were dismissed for 183 and forced to follow on.

The stoppage proved fatal to Grace, who was dismissed for a duck, but Dale, one of the first day's late-comers, and I. D. Walker made runs, and the MCC ended up with a very creditable 240, leaving the visitors a target of 157 on the final day.

This was the day that marred the match, if not the entire season. George Summers went in first wicket down to face the bowling of Jack Platts. Platts was not only making his first appearance at Lord's; he was making his first-class début. Having failed to impress in the first innings, he was determined to make a mark in the second. The first ball he bowled to Summers reared up and hit him on the head. There was conjecture subsequently that it had hit one of the stones frequently found on the Lord's square. The immediate concern, of course, was for the health of the batsman, who went down like a felled ox. At twenty-one, W. G. was merely a medical student, but he hurried up and pronounced the prostrate batsman 'not dead'. Summers was helped from the field and went back to the team digs, but, although the blow 'shook him terribly', he later returned to the ground and sat about in the hot sun. In Grace's opinion it was this, coupled with the jolting train journey back to Nottingham, that proved his undoing.

The tragic outcome could not have been guessed at the time: Summers died a couple of days later. All that was clear was that Platts 'had his tail up'. Richard Daft, the next man in, came to the wicket with his head swathed in a towel and received another bouncer first ball, to which the Nottinghamshire captain responded 'with a few choice observations expressed in the Anglo-Saxon vernacular'.

The incident appears to have divided opinion. Grace stated that the fatal delivery 'did not bump higher than many I had to play in the same match'. But then Grace was in a class of his own against any kind of bowling, particularly fast bowling on a fiery wicket. Lord Harris, on the other hand, refers darkly to 'Black Jack Platts' as though he were a notorious pirate, and Daft's gesture made it clear that he thought Platts was deliberately bowling to intimidate. After Summers's death, this view became so widely held that he was not bowled again in first-class cricket for the rest of the season. The impact on Platts went further. Grace wrote later that the bowler suffered great 'mental distraction', and not long afterwards, he changed his bowling style from fast to slow. Still later (1885) he became a county umpire.

While it was easy to blame the bowler, the responsibility for the state of the wicket lay with the MCC, as was tacitly acknowledged when the club paid for a gravestone which carried the legend: 'This Tablet is erected to the Memory of George Summers by the Marylebone Cricket Club, to mark their sense of his qualities as a cricketer, and to testify their regret at the untimely accident on Lord's ground, which cut short a career so full of promise, June 19th, 1870, in the 26th year of his age.' It cost £30, which would have been better spent on ground preparation in the first place. Although admitting no liability, the tragedy did at last force the MCC to turn their attention to the state of the square, employing a heavy roller to dampen its demons.

Grace carried on with his mission to pacify the pacemen, employing a battery of shots to fight fire with fire. The short ball held no terrors for him. One of the things that impressed the Australians on his first tour was the way he 'frequently played balls down that rose breast high in a way that surprised [local players] who were accustomed to see their own men bob their heads and let such go by'.

On that first tour, Grace met one bowler whom he would learn to treat with the utmost respect: Frederick Spofforth, the

Australian 'Demon'. Spofforth was a young man at the time, and only played in one match against Grace's team – and that without drawing much attention to himself. However, this did not stop him inventing an encounter which was so convincing it has been handed down from generation to generation:

> In those days [1873] . . . I could bowl faster than any man in the world. W. G. was at the nets . . . and I lolled up two or three balls in a funny slow way. Two or three of those round asked: 'What's the matter with you, Spoff?' I replied: 'I am going to have a rise out of that W. G.' Suddenly I sent him down one of my very fastest. He lifted his bat half up in his characteristic way, but down went his off stump, and he called out in his quick fashion when not liking anything: 'Where did that come from? Who bowled that?' But I slipped away, having done my job.

This is splendid and makes a wonderful (if retrospective) prologue to the great battles that lay ahead. The only thing wrong with it is that, although absent from his native Sydney, Spofforth was not in fact in Melbourne at the time, but on holiday in Tasmania. The legendary thunderbolt was never delivered.

But many others were, and Spofforth was certainly the most intimidating bowler of the age. This was not simply on account of his pace, though that could be considerable. It was more to do with the bowler's intense focus and the aura of hostility that seemed to emanate from him. Few batsmen could meet his baleful glare as they passed him on the way to the crease. In Beldham's action photograph of him taken long after he had retired, there remains more than a hint of the diabolic venom of his delivery leap.

As a young man, Spofforth had modelled himself on 'Tear 'em' Tarrant (who had toured Australia in 1863–4), placing a premium on out-and-out pace. By the time he came over to England with the first Australian tourists in 1878, the Demon had tempered his youthful ambition to blast batsmen out. He had learned the importance of control and variations in pace and movement off the seam. (In later life he claimed that he could swing the ball if he wanted to, but found that it affected his accuracy and therefore abandoned it.) It comes as a shock when looking up the great matches in which he was the determining factor – the Australians' one-day trouncing of a strong MCC side in 1878 and the even greater victory in the Test at the Oval in 1882 – to see that a number of his victims were *stumped*.

The psychological pressure Spofforth could exert, especially when a game reached crisis point, as on the last afternoon of the 'Ashes' Test in 1882, was extraordinary. Whether or not he had the upper hand over W. G. is a moot point. There were certainly periods when he reckoned to have the great Englishman tamed or beaten, but it would never have occurred to him to direct his fire at the great man's spreading flesh.

Indeed, once W. G. had established himself, few bowlers would. One who did was Charles Kortright in a Homeric clash of personalities at Leyton, in 1898. This was W. G.'s Jubilee year, and when Gloucestershire travelled to Essex for the first time, the Champion was only a few days short of his fiftieth birthday (and the Gentlemen vs Players match that the MCC had decreed should coincide with the milestone). The Old Man started off in celebratory mood, bowling Essex out with his beguiling slows before lunch on the first day. He wired news of his 7 for 44 back to Bristol and received in reply a telegram which made a condescending reference to rabbits. This was unfortunately pinned up in the pavilion, possibly by W. G.'s own massive thumb.

This bit of tactless triumphalism went down badly with the home side. They had already had an experience of Grace at his most roguish, when, on scooping up a ball hit back to him – clearly on the bounce, as all but the unsighted umpire could see – he shouted out, 'Not bad for an old 'un,' in a shameless – and successful – attempt to gain the dismissal.

If there was one member of the Essex side capable of a riposte, it was Kortright. He was the fastest bowler in England, and almost certainly the fastest bowler of the century. Although a member of the small but distinguished club of amateur fast bowlers, he was never picked for his country, probably because of a question mark over his action, but he was allowed to play first-class cricket unquestioned and had, in fact, been invited to play for W. G.'s Gentlemen against the Players the following week at Lord's.

No fast bowler is unaware of his most potent weapon, but while some, for all their pace, seem almost solicitous of the batsman's welfare, others clearly delight in their potential for destruction. Kortright definitely had a vicious streak. Playing an army side once he took exception to one of the officers taking his stance with a raised left toe. Kortright explained that he allowed no one but W. G. himself to cock his toe at him, and ordered the batsman to desist. When he declined, Kortright simply blitzed the offending foot with yorkers until he caught it with a direct hit and broke it.

Grace's cocked foot might have gone unchallenged, but that was about the only concession Korty allowed, and what followed after the lunch interval at Leyton was the start of a great duel. Kortright ran like fire through the Gloucestershire upper order, but could not shift Grace, whom he hit repeatedly on the gloves. His bowling was described as 'absolutely terrific. He was banging ball after ball down with almost reckless virulence, but W. G. never seemed perturbed . . .' Grace's response to Kortright's continuous short-pitched bowling was to advance down half the length of the pitch to pat the wicket where the majority of his deliveries were aimed, a gesture which did not go unnoticed by the crowd. Grace, supported only by Townsend (51), scored 126. Kortright took 5 for 41.

The wicket was still fast and true, and Essex knocked off the arrears and ran up a total of 250. This might have been more had not A. P. Lucas been given out caught behind, despite indicating that the ball had only brushed his shirt. As he retired to the pavilion a section of the crowd shouted, 'Cheats never prosper'.

The rowdy section were to have more to shout about in Gloucestershire's second innings. Chasing only 148 to win, their task seemed a mere formality. However, they were starting their innings at 5.15 p.m. with an hour and a quarter to bat before the close, and by now Kortright was seriously angry. W. G. faced his opening over and got off the mark with a single. This exposed first Board and then Troup to the English Demon's fury, and both were clean bowled for ducks that over. But it was quite clear that the man – as opposed to the wicket – in Kortright's sights was W. G. Gone was the off-stump line of the first innings. Now he aimed straight at the inviting bulk of the Champion and got him repeatedly. On one occasion, he struck him in the stomach, and play was held up for several minutes while Grace set off on a recuperative hobble round the wicket-keeper, who was standing many yards back.

Gilbert Jessop, who was waiting with his pads on, recalled that the thud could be clearly heard in the pavilion, 'an unpleasant noise – especially for those who had to come after him'. As for the bruise, it was 'quite the most extraordinary extravasation of blood that I have ever witnessed. The seam of the ball was quite clear, and you could almost see the maker's name impinged on the flesh.'

Grace's discomfort caused a certain amount of glee amidst the crowd – a correspondent informed him that 'in the covered stand where I was, a laugh was raised when Mr Kortright struck you in the chest with a fast ball [but] a cry of Order! Order! soon silenced that', and the continuing dog-fight was watched with rapt attention. Grace rose magnificently to the challenge, drawing on his inexhaustible supplies of courage, skill and cussedness. When Kortright was rested, Mead had a spell. At one point, Grace hit what the Essex team was sure was a return catch. So certain indeed that no one appealed, until they saw Grace calmly settling himself for the next delivery. On appeal, the umpire raised his finger only to retract it when Grace roared down the pitch, 'What, George?'

If Kortright had been angry before, this drove him to the pitch of homicidal fury, and he signed off a day of blood and thunder with a final burst of aggression. His last over consisted almost exclusively of bouncers, one of which Grace tipped into the slips. The chance, such as it was, was not accepted, and when W. G. overheard the incensed bowler berating the fielder as they trooped off the field, he remarked softly but audibly, 'Cheats never prosper.' In the pavilion he was rather more voluble, expressing his view of Kortright's deliberate assault 'vigorously and adjectivally'.

Battle was resumed in the morning. Gloucestershire had scored 81 of the 148 they needed, but now the wicket was deteriorating. Kortright, refreshed from a night's rest and inspired no doubt by an evening savouring his grievances, tore into the attack. Grace kept him at bay, and had inched the score up to

96 when the fast bowler summoned everything for one last fling. He hit Grace's front pad plumb in front of the wicket and appealed with the heartfelt relief of a man who knows he has achieved his aim. From half-way down the wicket he watched mesmerized as Grace, through sheer power of personality, willed the umpire to keep his finger down. Kortright snatched up the ball and returned to his mark before launching himself like a sprinter at the wicket. This time Grace got a snick to the wicket-keeper. Another clamorous appeal, another almost tangible laser beam of authority from the Champion to the umpire. Kortright took the ball in silence and wound himself up for one final, fate-defying attempt. The result was almost certainly the fastest ball ever delivered up to that time. It knocked the middle stump out of the ground and propelled the leg stump several yards.

After a momentary pause – perhaps in the hope of a late no-ball call, but more probably out of pure shock – the great man set off for the pavilion. This gave Kortright the cue for his immortal line: 'Surely you're not going, Doctor? There's still one stump standing.' Grace said he'd never been so insulted in his life – which can't have been true. But anyway, he got the last laugh in that Gloucestershire sneaked home by one wicket, and he could boast his best all-round effort since his heyday in the 1870s – 126 and 49 (plus 7 cheap wickets) against the fastest bowler in the world – ten days before his fiftieth birthday.

Deliberately intimidatory fast bowling was not, of course, unheard of in the nineteenth century, but Kortright's assault on Grace drew forth the olympian reproof of *Wisden*, which, consciously or unconsciously, echoed Pycroft's sentiments and vocabulary with regard to Fellowes fifty years before: 'Balls dropped little more than half way down the wicket at his tremendous speed bring cricket within the category of dangerous pastimes.'

Although the quarrel at Leyton meant that the two men were not on speaking terms when they met at Lord's for W. G.'s big day, they featured in a fine last-wicket stand at the end of an epic struggle with the Players, and walked off arm in arm to rapturous applause. Grace was never one to harbour a grudge; nor was he a squealer. All bowling came alike to him, and the faster it came, the faster he would dispatch it to the boundary. He even said on one occasion that he didn't mind if the bowler threw. Which was just as well, for during the latter part of his career, throwing was rife.

CHAPTER 7

The Scourge of Throwing

It is a paradox that the first wave of 'throwers' bowled with straight arms; they were penalised simply for delivering the ball away from their bodies. The origins of the round-arm revolution are disputed. Some credit the Hambledon man, Tom Walker, with the introduction of what came to be called 'the March of Intellect' style; others give pride of place to John Willes of Kent. An apocryphal story credits Willes's sister with the invention. Bowling to her brother in a bustle, she found her arm of necessity pushed wider than the traditional under-arm delivery. However he came by it, Willes certainly found that this wider delivery produced interesting results. Instead of coming straight on to him, the batsman was now confronted by a new angle and new possibilities of movement off the wicket.

Willes was delighted, but like every innovation, the round-arm style of bowling had traditionalists and partisan spectators alike up in arms. The *Morning Herald* reported in 1821: 'Mr Willes and his bowling were frequently barred in making a match and he played sometimes amidst much uproar and confusion. Still he would persever till the ring closed on the players, the stumps were lawlessly pulled up, and all came to a stand-still.'

The under-arm versus round-arm controversy heralded one of cricket's most fractious periods and threatened the newly established position of the MCC as the game's arbiter and law-giver. Lord's was the site of an early attempt to halt the new style before it could contaminate the rest of the game. When Willes took a Kent team to play MCC in 1822, he was consistently no-balled –

on the orders, it was thought, of Lord Beauclerk. The Kent man threw the ball down in disgust, called for his horse and rode out of cricket for good.

The traditionalists may have won that battle but they had not won the war. Within five years, the spectre of the new method returned to haunt them – this time in the guise of a two-headed monster. William Lillywhite and James Broadbridge both started bowling round-arm for Sussex, with eye-catching results. Where Willes could be dismissed as an eccentric amateur, here were two professionals clearly determined to take bowling on to a new level of proficiency.

They gained some support even inside the amateur citadel itself. An MCC member, Mr G. T. Knight of Godmersham Park, Kent, not only championed their cause in print, but organised three experimental matches between Sussex and All England. The first two, played at Sheffield and at Lord's, were won comfortably by Sussex. The All England team threatened to boycott the third match – at Brighton – 'unless the Sussex players bowl fair; that is, abstain from *throwing*'. This was the central question, and the paradox was that, as Knight pointed out, the new style was less like throwing than the old. It was bowled with a straight arm – i.e. the very antithesis of the throw.

Despite the bad feeling, the match went ahead, and All England narrowly won it. If it proved anything, it was that with practice the new style could be countered. Knight thought long and hard about the innovation and its implications, consolidating his reflections in a lengthy letter in *The Sporting Magazine* of February 1828. The change, he argued, was needed because batting had become more sophisticated and there was a perceptible imbalance between bat and ball. This was generally acknowledged and had brought forth a number of proposals – for widening the wicket, for instance, or reducing the size of the bat. Such measures, Knight argued, would tend to lower 'the standard of excellence, instead, if possible, of raising it'.

With more and more bowlers imitating Lillywhite and Broadbridge, the legislators' hands were forced: the MCC passed an amendment to Law X, stating that 'The ball shall be bowled; if thrown or jerked, or if any part of the hand or arm be above the elbow at the time of delivery, the umpire shall call, "No Ball".'

This proved little more than a holding operation. As framed, it was almost impossible to apply. In 1829, Lillywhite and Broadbridge played at Lord's and were both no-balled in the first innings, but allowed to deliver round-arm undisturbed in the second. In 1835, the MCC tried again, this time stipulating that a delivery was legitimate provided the hand did not rise above the shoulder. Though there was further tinkering in 1845, ultimately the law on the height of delivery was destined for abolition.

The incident that finally forced the MCC to accept the inevitable occurred at the Oval in 1862. Playing for England against Surrey, another Kent bowler, the left-arm Edgar Willsher, was no-balled six times in succession by John Lillywhite, son of William. At this, the rest of the England team, barring a couple of bemused amateurs, marched off the field in solidarity, and the ground authorities had to find a replacement umpire. Lillywhite's motives are unclear. Did he think Willsher was taking round-arm too far? Or was he acting as *agent provocateur*, intending to force the authorities into allowing the March of Intellect style pioneered by his father to achieve its logical metamorphosis – over-arm?

Whatever his intentions, Lillywhite made throwing the issue of the day. As we have seen, the 1860s opened with the MCC in the doldrums. Lord's was run down, the professionals were in the ascendant, and amateur morale was low. The wider radicalism that would lead to the second Reform Act of 1867 even led people to question the MCC's position as the game's unelected and unrepresentative law-giving body, and prompted a popular movement for a national cricket parliament. The failure of Lord's to respond consistently to the development of over-arm was seized on by opponents. A correspondent to the *Sporting Life*, the paper orchestrating the campaign, wrote in 1863 that the MCC

> first determines that the Law X shall be strictly enforced, and then suffers its umpires openly to sanction its violation, or to put their own interpretations on it. This insubordination to authority I hold to be nothing more nor less than the inevitable and mischievous result of bungling legislation, and may be, I think, adduced as one of the strongest arguments in favour of some radical change in the mode of government.

At a meeting on 10 June 1864, a slim majority (27 votes to 20) of MCC members finally defused the grenade that had rolled around cricket's deck for forty years by revising Law X so that it read simply: 'The ball must be bowled; if thrown or jerked, the umpire must call no-ball.' All references to the height of the hand had gone. From this point on, 'throwing' meant what we understand it to mean today – the gaining of unfair advantage, either in terms of pace or movement off the wicket, by straightening a bent arm in the moment of delivery.

It is a little known – or little reflected on – near-certainty that England won their first-ever home Test match, at the Oval in September 1880, as a result of throwing. Not that any of the England bowlers – Morley, Steel, Shaw, Grace (W. G.), Barnes, Lucas or Penn – had doubtful actions; the damage had been done three weeks before, at the other end of the country, and the perpetrator was an unknown amateur called Frank.

Joseph Frank was born in Helmsley, Yorkshire, in 1857, and played less than a dozen first-class games, and only one for Yorkshire. He was acknowledged a 'very fast right-arm bowler', which makes his short-lived first-class career surprising. The reason is bluntly stated in the *Who's Who of Cricketers*: 'His bowling action was very suspect.'

'Suspect' was putting it mildly. The Australians had absolutely no doubt about it when they came up against Frank playing for XVIII Scarborough and District towards the end of August 1880. Because of the bad odour arising from the Lord Harris incident at Sydney the previous year, the Australians had found it impossible when they arrived to get any first-class fixtures. Instead they had been forced to accept a programme of regional games against the odds, most of which they won easily. The previous match, against XVIII of Sunderland, produced victory by an innings and 38 runs, with Australia's two leading bowlers, Spofforth and Boyle, returning match figures of 17 for 66 and 15 for 64, respectively.

Scarborough offered sterner competition, their XVIII boasting ten men who had played first-class cricket. The game proceeded in undramatic fashion until, late in the Australians' first innings, Frank was introduced into the attack. Immediately, the visitors sat up and took notice. He was, in their opinion, clearly throwing. Nothing was said until the end of the innings, when Billy Murdoch raised the matter with the captain of the Eighteen, Henry Charlwood. The response was unsatisfactory, so the Australians then had words with Frank himself. The outcome was no better. A report in the *Sydney Mail* by one of the tourists takes up the story:

> No notice was taken of the objection as when the second innings commenced, Frank again went on. Bannerman, after getting a severe blow on the leg objected, and drew away from the wicket. Murdoch then went out and asked Charlwood to discontinue the unfair proceedings, as it was not fair cricket, beside being very dangerous. An appeal was made to the umpire, whose reply was 'That some of the balls were unfair, but it was very difficult to catch them.' During this time frequent cries were heard from the spectators of 'another Lord Harris affair,' and 'go on,' etc. After the reply of the umpire, the game proceeded, and Frank was allowed to continue, and throw in such a way that not only did he get the batsmen out but hit them so frequently and with such force, that it caused them to limp about the ground in the most painful manner. This seemed to give the spectators no end of amusement, judging from the laughter that burst out after each knock.

It was during this Punch-and-Judy travesty that Spofforth sustained the blow on his right hand (breaking the bottom joint of the third finger) that would keep him out of the side at the Oval. At that stage of the (British) leg of the tour, Spofforth had taken, in all classes of cricket, 393 wickets. It is hard to imagine that his presence would not have made a difference in the inaugural home Test match, which England won by 5 wickets after a dreadful collapse in their second innings. Two years later when England were in a similar situation, they cracked under the psychological pressure, and Spofforth saw them home to a famous victory.

Lord Harris, England's captain at the Oval in 1880, and the unwitting beneficiary of Frank's assault on the Australians, would certainly have sympathised with Spofforth. Such incidents were not isolated aberrations, and his lordship felt more strongly than most that throwing was a danger to the game as well as to individual batsmen. Over the next twenty years he led a campaign to root it out, setting his aristocratic face rigidly against bowlers with dubious actions and captains and committees that countenanced them.

The worst offenders in the 1880s were Lancashire, whose opening bowler John Crossland was notorious. Crossland was born in Nottinghamshire, but Lancashire were quite happy to look beyond the county boundaries for talented players, and the Nottinghamshire man was soon at home at Old Trafford. His Lancashire career lasted from 1878 to 1885 even though his bowling was regarded as 'pure throw' by many. In the match between Lancashire and Gloucestershire played at Clifton College in August 1883, a spectator called out 'Why don't you *bowl*?' when Crossland was introduced into the attack. Grace, who was batting, walked over to the crowd and appealed for quiet. He was quite unperturbed by the bowling change and scored a century reminiscent of his heyday a decade before.

Grace may not have minded about Crossland, but Lord Harris did. In 1883, he brokered a gentlemen's agreement not to play bowlers with suspect actions, but Lancashire opted out. It was a frustrating situation, but Harris was not to be deflected. Things came to a head in 1885, when Harris took unilateral action, cancelling the return match between Kent and Lancashire when the Lancastrians refused to exclude Crossland and the slow left-hander Nash, who 'threw every ball'. Relations were restored the following year when neither man appeared in the fixture.

Not that Lancashire conceded that their bowlers threw, pointing out that both had been selected to play for the MCC at Lord's. Crossland's undoing, in fact, proved an injudicious return to his native county for the winter of 1884, which compromised his residential qualification for Lancashire, something else Lord Harris was exceptionally attentive to. Nash, by no means the last slow bowler to attract unwelcome scrutiny, decided it would be prudent to retire at the same time.

The problem of throwing was not confined to England. Two of the main suspects in the following decade were Australians, and like Crossland and Nash, one was a fast bowler, one a spinner. Ernest Jones ('Jonah') made his début in the extraordinary first Test at Sydney in December 1894, when Stoddart's team won by 10 runs after following on, but was dropped for the rest of the series. He only came to English notice when he came over with the tourists of 1896.

Then he did make an impression, and immediately. The first match was the traditional curtain-raiser against Lord Sheffield's XI at Sheffield Park in Sussex. Grace, as usual, captained Lord Sheffield's team and, as usual, opened the innings, after the Australians had batted first on a fast and lively wicket.

Jones's opening salvo has gone down in legend, although there is conflicting evidence as to whether this was the occasion when he bowled the ball through W. G.'s beard (there are a number of eye-witnesses who claim it was in the first Test at Lord's). There is no contesting that Jonah worked up a furious pace, fast enough, according to C. B. Fry's (not wholly accurate) account, to persuade the two senior professional batsmen, Gunn and Shrewsbury, to leave the heroics to the amateurs.

Grace was for once seriously discomforted, fending one rearing delivery out of his face, while taking a number of heavy blows to the body. Nonetheless, he batted on, undaunted, and with F. S. Jackson put 50 on the board in just over half an hour, going on to 49 before he nicked another riser from Jones to the wicket-keeper. Jones was just as quick in the second innings, and just as aggressive. According to *The Chronicle of W. G.*, 'Jones was pitching the ball little more than half way down the pitch, and it was rising shoulder high and even head high.' He had the satisfaction of claiming Grace's wicket a second time (caught at slip for 26), but not before the Old Man had launched a series of slashing cuts to show that he was not surrendering the initiative to any unknown tearaway.

Word of Jones's extreme pace soon spread, and the prospect of seeing the battle resumed added spice for the first Test at Lord's. As it happened, England got their retaliation in first, Tom Richardson taking 6 for 39 as the visitors were tumbled out for 53. But even so, there was great expectancy when Grace went out to face Jones. The opening delivery, which was variously reported in the press as 'a shie' and 'very difficult to distinguish from a throw', reared viciously, and in fending it off, Grace sent it skimming away over the slips off the top of his bat handle. According to Lord Harris, it was at this point that Grace demanded, 'Whatever are ye at?' while according to Home Gordon, another seasoned watcher in the pavilion, W. G. was 'conspicuously ruffled'. He went on, 'The veteran looked volumes, [and] was so seriously discomfited that he took some time to recover his composure and then only after having made some observations to the wicket-keeper, while the twelve thousand spectators positively hummed, so general were their audible comments.'

They saw a duel develop as Jones gave it everything he'd got. But the forty-seven-year-old proved his master on this occasion, laying the basis for England's 6-wicket win with a solid innings of 66. The second innings was, if anything, more torrid. Grace and the diminutive Bobby Abel (5 ft 4 ins) had to go in to face Jones in bad light late on the second day. The paceman bounced one so far over Abel's head it went for 4 wides, and the Surrey man departed with no special show of reluctance before the close. Grace, having battled it out to stumps, then had to face a refreshed Jonah on a wicket made spiteful by overnight rain. (He was caught at short-leg off Trumble for a very dogged 7, putting on a little pantomime of innocence that involved patting down a divot and looking amazed when the umpire gave him out.)

There was a second member of the touring party whose action was dubious, though his bowling did not pose a physical threat. T. R. McKibbin, a spinner from New South Wales, had a highly questionable off-break. According to his compatriot Frederick Spofforth, now settled in England, his action was so blatantly a throw that he 'should never be allowed to play under the existing rule'.

But it was Jones who had the unwelcome distinction of being the first bowler to be no-balled for throwing in a Test match – during the 1897–8 season. The umpire was James Phillips, who gave due notice that he was suspicious in the opening match at Adelaide in front of Jones's home crowd. He called him again in the second Test at Melbourne, but despite this very public vote of no confidence, Jonah's Test career was not over. He played in all five Tests, and his 21 wickets ensured that Stoddart's second team signally failed to repeat the triumphs of his first.

Jones returned to England with the 1899 Australians and once more confronted W. G., now in his fifty-first year and at long last contemplating the unthinkable – retirement from Test cricket. The series began at Trent Bridge, and the first the crowd saw of the England team emerging on to the field was the familiar greying beard. They had to wait till the following morning for the expected fireworks of Jonah's opening spell. The wicket was very hard and very fast. C. B. Fry, who opened with Grace, called it 'perfect' for batting, but it also had something to offer a bowler of genuine pace. Grace faced the first ball, and the crowd held their breath as Jonah sprinted up to the crease. The magazine *Cricket* described the first ball as simply 'a sensation'. Jones opened with a head-high full-toss, and as the writer commented, 'if Grace had not been to some extent prepared by previous experience . . . there might have been a bad accident; as it was he ducked in time'. The drama was heightened by the cry of 'No ball!' The crowd, naturally, assumed this was for throwing, but the umpire pointed to the crease to show it was for overstepping. An over or two later, there was another cry from the umpire, just as Fry's wicket exploded. Jones was back, with a vengeance.

He took 7 wickets in the first, drawn Test – after which W. G. did, finally, call it a day. With England's great bulwark removed, Jones simply tore through the batting at Lord's, taking 7 wickets in the first innings and 10 in the match. This was the only result of the rubber, so Australia kept the Ashes that Jones had won for them the previous winter. Although Grace failed to list him in the round-up of prominent contemporaries at the end of his *Reminiscences*, Jones undoubtedly made his mark. Grace always referred to him as 'the fellow who bowled through my beard'.

Throwing remained a problem through the last decade of the century. Writing to *Sporting Life* in 1897, Spofforth satirically enquired whether the authorities 'are going to legalise throwing?' In his view,

> There is scarcely a first class county which does not include a 'thrower' amongst its cricketers, many of them men who would scorn to cheat an opponent out, and who, if a wicketkeeper were in the habit of kicking down the stumps or

knocking off the bails with his hand and appealing for a bowl out, would not hesitate to bring him before his committee, or refuse to play with him again. Still, they will not only employ a man to throw, but will actually throw themselves, and acknowledge it, their only excuse being that 'others do it' . . .

The remedy for this unfair play is rather hard to find, especially as there is no umpire in England who dare no-ball a cricketer . . . I am of the opinion the best way to put down throwing is to form a committee of all the captains of the first class counties with Lord Harris as chairman, and on anyone being reported for throwing, a vote to be taken, and if unfavourable the cricketer be suspended for a week, if brought up a second time fined and suspended, a third time he should be disqualified for the season. Brother jockeys and footballers are suspended and fined for unfairness, and why should cricketers be exempt?

Spofforth signed off with the provocative suggestion that 'if nothing is to be done in the matter, the best way is to legalise throwing, and in one season it would bring about its own cure'.

One man who bowled as though that had already been done was C. B. Fry. Fry was the glittering amateur all-rounder: a future captain of England, arguably the greatest English batsman in Grace's immediate aftermath, and a very mediocre fast bowler who quite unarguably threw the majority of his deliveries. Despite some pointed observations by the editor of *Wisden*, Sydney Pardon, not to mention general muttering on the circuit, Fry's position in the game seemed to guarantee him immunity. That changed in 1898, when he was no-balled three times. One of the umpires who called him was James Phillips, who happily sailed from Australia to officiate in the English season. *Wisden*'s editor was thrilled:

A twelvemonth ago I ventured to say nothing but good could come from James Phillips's action in no-balling Jones, the Australian fast bowler, for throwing. I did not imagine, however, that the result would be either so speedy or so satisfactory. Throwing on English cricket grounds had for such a long time been allowed to go unchecked – the umpires taking no heed of even the most flagrant offenders – that I was not prepared to see any steps taken last season. When once a man has done a courageous thing, however, he is very apt to find imitators, and such was James Phillips's case last season. For the first time within my experience – with one trifling exception – bowlers were no-balled in first-class matches in England for throwing . . . The no-balling of Mr. Fry was only a case of long-delayed justice. As a matter of fact he ought never, after his caricature of bowling in the MCC and Oxford match at Lord's in 1892, to have been allowed to bowl at all.

Despite the pessimists, the campaign gathered momentum. There were three further cases in 1899, and Fry was called once more in a county match at Hove in 1900. But the most momentous incident took place at Trent Bridge, where the bowler who failed to satisfy Phillips was Arthur Mold of Lancashire. Mold had played for Lancashire through most of the 1890s, but though there had been mutterings about his action, he had the support of his captain and committee (as had John Crossland before him). Furthermore, he had been chosen for England, though subsequently he lost his place, outclassed by the great Surrey duo of Bill Lockwood and Tom Richardson. But now his hour had come. Phillips was merciless. In Ian Peebles' words, 'he no-balled Mold in the first over he sent down with such firm intention that Mold was retired at the end of it and bowled no more in the match'.

He did not, however, retire from cricket. Indeed, he needed one final show-down with Phillips to show him the door. It came at Old Trafford in July 1901, in the match between Lancashire and Somerset. All season, the Lancashire committee had played safe, not selecting Mold when Phillips was standing. By midseason, the captain, Archie MacLaren, had tired of this shamefaced behaviour, and with the backing of the committee, picked Mold and opened the bowling with him. Phillips had no hesitation in calling him repeatedly – eighteen times in all. As the *Telegraph* conceded, 'It was rather a daring thing to no-ball Mold at Manchester, of all places in the world, but even Phillips' bitterest opponents must admit that since he took up this question of unfair bowling he has shown no lack of courage.' As for the bowler, the *Telegraph* line was unsympathetic:

So far, indeed, from thinking Mold an ill-used man, we hold a strong opinion that he was very fortunate to be allowed to go unchecked through so many seasons. It is all very well for Mr Hornby, Mr Swire, and others interested in Lancashire cricket to say that Mold is a perfectly fair bowler, but the weight of expert opinion against them is overwhelming. At the captains' meeting at Lord's in December [1900], Mr MacLaren raised a direct issue by asking for a pronouncement on the point, and on a vote being taken eleven of the twelve cricketers present gave it as their deliberate opinion that Mold's delivery was unfair, MacLaren himself constituting the minority. Surely no condemnation could have been stronger than this.

The bowler, like his captain, protested his innocence, but nevertheless conceded that the tide had finally turned. 1901 was his final season as a first-class cricketer.

In the remaining years of peace there were isolated outbreaks of throwing, but thanks to the stand Phillips took, the epidemic was over. The inter-war period was also largely free of the problem, though there were the usual murmurs against individuals. In the acrimonious aftermath of the Bodyline series, an Australian commentator cast aspersions on the action of Bill Voce, but Douglas Jardine sprang to his defence: 'It will . . . come as a shock to everyone in England to learn that Voce's bowling action has ever been the subject of comment or criticism of any kind.' And Jardine expressed caustic surprise that the unnamed critic remained silent about Bert Ironmonger: 'for years, Ironmonger has been the outstanding left-handed bowler in Australia', yet he was never selected to tour England; the only possible reason is that 'Ironmonger's action would not be allowed to pass unchallenged for one single over in England'.

There was little serious cricket between 1939 and 1945, but the period produced one of the game's most bizarre throwing incidents, during a match between Trinidad and Barbados at Bridgetown. S. Mobarak Ali of Trinidad was renowned for his prodigious off-break, but although there had been eyebrows raised over his faster ball, he had never been called for throwing. On this occasion one of the umpires intimated that he would probably call him. As The Cricketer reported:

the aforementioned umpire started no-balling him, and it mattered little what type of ball he bowled. He bowled his leg-breaks, and the umpire 'called'; so finally he . . . started bowling underarm creepers, and for a time the match was reduced to a farce. In this riot of no balls Sealy actually lost his wicket, for expecting another no ball, he had a crack, was caught, and then found the umpire hadn't called. Ali continued to bowl, and eventually the no-balling ceased.

In all he had been called thirty times.

In the decades since the Second World War, throwing has once again become a serious problem. It started in the 1950s, when Cuan McCarthy came to England with the 1951 South Africans and played in all five Tests. In a period largely lacking in pace bowlers (apart from the Australian pair, Ray Lindwall and Keith Miller), McCarthy was genuinely quick, but his arm action disturbed many. In fact, as *Wisden* revealed a few years later, he only escaped official censure because of an intervention from on high. The editor recalled an incident from 1951 when England's leading umpire, Frank Chester, was standing at square leg and looking askance at McCarthy. Clearly unhappy at what he saw, he refrained from calling him, and after lunch, 'rarely looked that way again'. The editor went on:

Some time later I asked him the reason and he told me that he had gone without his lunch in order to find out whether he would receive official support if he no-balled McCarthy for throwing. He spoke to two leading members of the MCC Committee and could get no satisfaction. They were not prepared to say that MCC would uphold the umpires. In other words Chester was given the impression that, if he adopted the attitude which he knew was right according to the Laws, there was no guarantee that he would remain on the panel of Test match umpires. Naturally, Chester was not prepared to make a financial sacrifice in the interests of cricket and McCarthy continued unchecked in Test matches.

The following year, McCarthy returned to England to take a degree at Cambridge. He played cricket for the university, but was called for throwing in the match against Worcester in June.

Although he went on to get his blue, he never played first-class cricket again after 1952.

A far more serious case was that of the Surrey left-arm spinner, Tony Lock. Lock made his England début against the Indians at Old Trafford in 1952, where his – significantly – faster ball drew comment. Shortly afterwards, he was no-balled at the Oval when playing for Surrey against the tourists. W. F. Price called him three times during the course of the match, twice in one over.

Despite that public condemnation, Lock remained in the game and in the running for England honours. However, he was called again during the first Test of Len Hutton's unhappy tour of the West Indies in 1953–4. The veteran George Headley had returned to the Test side on a wave of popular support which had even extended to raising the money to bring him home from England to play. He made only 16 in the first innings, and when he batted a second time with his side in trouble, he faced Lock. Or rather, Lock's faster ball. The great man's bat was still mid-way through its generous flourish when the wicket exploded. Although there was nothing the umpire Perry Burke could do to recall the departing Headley, he did call Lock's next thunder-bolt. Hailed as 'Shylock' by the crowds thereafter, Lock again fell foul of the officials in Barbados, where he was called by both umpires in the match against the island.

His captain, Len Hutton, was stoutly supportive, writing later, 'I am not sure whether an umpire is really within the spirit of the game in no-balling a bowler so peremptorily; he should give him previous warning.' And he was clearly aggrieved that one of his bowlers should have been shorn of his secret weapon. The no-balling, Hutton said, 'unsettled' Lock so much 'that never again in the West Indies did he try to bowl his fast ball. Consequently batsmen were not compelled to be always on the look-out for it. This clearly minimized their difficulties against Lock and decreased his effectiveness.'

As so often in throwing controversies, one accusation engenders another, and Hutton took the opportunity to cast aspersions on some of England's opponents.

I insist that Lock is no bigger culprit in throwing than 'Sonny'

Ramadhin. If 'Sonny' does not 'throw' his off-break he certainly 'jerks' it a good deal. So does Ian Johnson, of Australia. So do nearly all bowlers of similar type. It's a very tricky point and if I were an umpire I would be very careful about taking action unless I were convinced beyond the shadow of a doubt. What may look a 'throw' from one position can appear to be a perfectly legitimate *delivery* from another.

Similar arguments surrounded Muttiah Muralitharan's action forty years later.

No one suggested that Lock could swing a series, but England were convinced that when they were trounced 4–0 in Australia in 1958–9, it was because of the array of chuckers ranged against them. The guilty men in English eyes were the two spinners, Jimmy Burke and Keith Slater, and the two fast men, Gordon Rorke and Ian Meckiff. Despite 'a beautiful leisurely run-up' mildly reminiscent of Ted McDonald, Meckiff's actual delivery and follow-through showed all the symptoms of a chucker. Ian Peebles saw him turning his arm over in the nets on the morning of the first Test at Brisbane and wrote:

> his action at that moment exactly resembled a coach throwing the ball to a young pupil in a net . . . It is fair to add that at such relaxed moments Meckiff's flex and bend was exaggerated and at normal speed these characteristics, although still distinguishable, were less pronounced. Even so, when the match started, and one saw him from directly behind, the result was disturbing.

The England captain Peter May had watched exactly the same scene earlier in the tour when the MCC first came up against Victoria. Before the game, Meckiff 'was throwing the ball at a batsman. This seemed an odd way for a bowler to limber up. A few minutes later he was out in the middle bowling to Peter Richardson with exactly the same action.'

Meckiff proved relatively ineffectual in the state match, which the tourists won at a canter, but at Brisbane he took 5 wickets in the match, which Australia won by 8 wickets. He played a far more prominent role in the second Test at Melbourne, taking 6 for 38 as England were skittled out for 87.

The question of Meckiff's action raised voices both pro and con. Jack Pollard, one of Australia's most respected cricket writers, declared that Meckiff's arm had a permanent bend and could not be straightened fully. E. M. Wellings, one of the English journalists covering the tour, retorted: 'Meckiff approaches the wicket in the deliberate manner of a bowler who delivers the ball at medium pace. He runs no faster than did Hedley Verity to bowl his slow spinners. And yet the ball leaves his hand at express pace.'

No one in the MCC camp had much doubt, but it took Trevor Bailey to bring the matter up at a team meeting, saying that 'if nothing is done, he will win at least one Test match for Australia', and insisting that 'If we are going to complain, we must do it before he becomes lethal.' But diplomacy won the day. Nothing was said, either about Meckiff or about the other suspects. Burke's bowling was memorably likened by Ian Peebles to 'the chopping bent-arm motion of a constable laying his truncheon on a very short offender's head'; the giant Gordon Rorke (6 ft 5 ins) increased his velocity not only by his action but by a huge drag over the popping crease – an increasing problem with many fast bowlers, chuckers or no; while Keith Slater was another tall man, who bowled either slow off-breaks or faster medium pace. In either mode, his throw was clear, and, in Tom Graveney's view, the ball with which he castled Peter May in the state match against Western Australia was faster than anything bowled by Lindwall.

But the England party were not entirely free of suspicion either. In addition to Lock, the only man on either side to have been called in a Test match, the selectors had chosen fast bowler Peter Loader. According to Colin Cowdrey, Loader had two doubtful deliveries: 'As well as the faster ball he had a well-concealed slow off-spinner and both were suspect.'

In the exchanges between the respective press corps there was a strong element of the pot calling the kettle black; it just happened that the English pot generated less heat for the opposing batsmen than the Australian kettle. The whole Ashes series was soured by the issue, and relations between the two senior cricketing nations were as strained as at any time since Bodyline.

Paradoxically, Peter May later claimed that 'this was one of my most successful tours', because he and the MCC manager had managed to keep the bad feelings within bounds.

> The problem was that we had our own suspect bowlers . . . and even though we thought they were minor offenders compared to people like Meckiff and Rorke, Freddie Brown and I were in a difficult position in lodging formal complaints which could have been written off as the response of the 'whinging pom' to our loss of the series. But it did lead the way to removing the chuckers from the game and that is why I regard this as a successful tour . . .

At first, the Australians were reluctant to acknowledge the problem. Don Bradman had been one of their selectors for the 1958–9 season, and when he came to England for the Imperial Cricket Conference in 1960 as chairman of the Australian Board, he was adamant that the bowlers he had picked were clean. Gubby Allen remembered locking horns with him on the subject:

> He wouldn't budge an inch and neither would I. He said the Australians had no chuckers and I said that was rubbish. We agreed not to mention names. I had film of some of the worst offenders and of course we were far from blameless ourselves but Don and the other Australians wouldn't look at them. But deep in his heart he knew they had a problem . . .

Back home, Bradman collected the evidence himself, building up an archive of film footage of the suspects, and once convinced, used his massive authority to insist on action at all levels of the game. As Allen acknowledged, 'within a year or two of his return to Australia, they'd cleared the chuckers out'.

By the time the Imperial Cricket Conference met to agonise over the issue, the 1960 season had already witnessed the opening act of a personal tragedy. Geoff Griffin was a young South African fast bowler making his first tour of England (despite having been called for throwing in a match between Natal and Transvaal the previous year). When he was no-balled, by both umpires, in the tourists' match against the MCC at Lord's in May, he gained the unenviable distinction of being the first member of an overseas team to be called for throwing. Griffin offended a further eight times in the match against Notting-hamshire later in the month, and remedial action was obviously required.

Although he attended Alf Gover's famous cricket school, and got through the first Test without censure, he was called again before the second Test. The tour selectors nevertheless picked him, and, only four days after celebrating his twenty-first birth-day, Griffin took centre stage at Lord's. It was an extraordinary performance. He took 4 wickets in England's only innings, including the first hat-trick by a South African in Test cricket. He was also called eleven times for throwing by Frank Lee.

The match ended early in an overwhelming English victory, but Griffin's trial was not over. With time to spare, an exhibition match was put on, and for the first time he bowled with the redoubtable Syd Buller standing at square leg. Buller rejected four out of the first five of Griffin's deliveries, and he was reduced to completing the over under-arm. (A final humiliation was Buller's pedantic no-balling of his first under-arm delivery on the grounds that he had not warned the batsman of his change of action.) It was clearly the end for Griffin, and he did not bowl again for the rest of the tour.

For most onlookers it was a sad moment. Griffin was a tal-ented and personable young cricketer, and there were no sugges-tions that he was cynically trying to gain an unfair advantage. He had worked hard under the best advice to correct his action, but in the end failed and retired gracefully from the first-class arena.

The case of Charlie Griffith was rather different. Graduating from spin, Griffith turned to pace and, with Wes Hall, formed one of the most feared fast-bowling combinations in the modern game. He made his début in the final Test of Peter May's tour of the West Indies in 1960, but took only one wicket. A year later, he proved a much more dangerous proposition. This time it was the Indians who faced a trial by pace, and in the island match against Barbados, the Indian captain and left-handed opener Nariman Jamshedji Contractor was felled by a ball from Griffith that fractured his skull. Later in the match, while the unfortu-nate opener was fighting for his life in hospital, the umpire C. Jordan called Griffith for throwing. The incident ended Con-tractor's Test career, but not Griffith's.

He was included in the West Indies party to tour England in 1963, and was easily their most successful bowler, taking 119 wickets during the season. Although he was never called, he raised suspicions that his arm was not straight when he delivered his yorker and his bouncer – the use of which caused Buller to intervene in the first day of the last Test match. Colin Cowdrey did not get as far as the final Test, having had his arm broken – by Wes Hall – in the great Test at Lord's. But he faced Griffith enough during the course of his career to explain what made him so particularly difficult:

> The truth about Griffith was that he could bowl with a perfect action. On the occasions when he strove for extra pace, his action altered perceptibly and he could produce a most brutal, lethal delivery, fast yorkers or short-pitched bouncers . . . [B]asically the difference between facing the legal delivery and the throw is this: against the legitimate fast bowler the batsman plays the line of the arm. In other words, as he sees the bowler's arm coming to the vertical he can anticipate the direction of the ball and begin to position himself for either an attacking or a defensive shot as soon as the ball is released. With the bent arm and snapping action, the batsman has trouble picking up the ball. He does not see the ball leave the hand and is therefore groping. The direction and trajectory of the delivery are unpredictable and therefore the batsman is faced with the difficult problem of trying to play the ball off the pitch. In a sentence, the legal delivery comes out of an arc whereas the throw comes out of a muzzle.

For all the doubts over Griffith, nothing was done, and there is evidence that this was as the authorities decreed. Fred Trueman told the *Observer* (June 2000) that in 1963 he had been relaxing in the bath at Lord's 'when he heard Dick Robins, the chairman of selectors, addressing the match umpires, Syd Buller and Eddie Phillipson. "He was telling the umpires not – repeat not – to no-ball Charlie Griffith. I could not believe what I was hearing . . . Some can call it diplomacy and not wishing to offend; I call it a cover-up."'

Further evidence of special treatment for Griffith comes from 1964, when the fast bowler played in a friendly match between a West Indies XI and an England XI captained by Trevor Bailey. One of the umpires, Cecil Pepper, an expatriate Australian with many years' experience, was specifically asked by Bailey not to call Griffith. He complied, but felt obliged to submit a confidential report to Lord's, which read, in part:

> I feel . . . that having stood at square leg for the first time with Charles Griffith of the West Indies bowling, I should draw your attention to the fact that had it been other than an exhibition match I would have had no hesitation in calling him for throwing . . . It is my considered opinion after watching Griffith that he throws the great majority of his deliveries.

This report was left to gather dust, while Griffith's career continued. In 1965, Australia toured the West Indies, and, having thoroughly cleansed their own stable of chuckers, were aggressively sensitive on the subject. Although Griffith was not no-balled, and no official complaint was made about his action, the press corps, led by the recently retired Australian captain Richie Benaud, observed no such self-denying ordinance. Benaud even backed up his plain speaking with a host of photographs showing Griffith's painfully bent arm just prior to delivery.

When Benaud came to publish his book on the series (*The New Champions; Australia in the West Indies 1965*), he laid much of the blame at the MCC's door. Griffith and his supporters could point to the fact that he had passed the most rigorous examination – the scrutiny of English umpires. However, Benaud had seen Pepper's 1964 report:

> Surely, the thing for MCC to do was to pass Pepper's report on to the West Indies and Australian Boards of Control so that the series in which they were about to take part would be played in the full knowledge that Griffith's action had been queried, not only by Cortez Jordan, who once called him for throwing in Barbados, but by the people used as an excuse in the West Indies – the English umpires . . . Firm and thoughtful action in September 1964 might well have been distasteful to MCC . . . but it would have been appreciated by all who are working to eradicate bent arm bowlers from cricket.

Griffith apparently had a similar let-off during a series of unofficial 'Tests' between Pakistan and a Commonwealth side. Alf Gover managed this side, and writing in *The Cricketer* in April 1965 revealed that 'The umpires in Pakistan were most sceptical when he delivered either his bouncer or his yorker. It was only the fact that the "Test" matches we played were unofficial that stopped the umpires from calling him.'

The attention focused on Griffith when he returned to England with the West Indies in 1966 was intense, but he got through the first three Tests unchallenged. (Strangely, when he *was* called for throwing in the game against Lancashire at Old Trafford, the press failed to notice as it came during a sequence of no-balls for over-stepping.) This changed at Headingley when, in possible reaction to Wes Hall's magnificent form, Griffith reverted to tried and tested methods. With the score at 18 for 2, he bowled a bouncer at Tom Graveney, the ferocity of which made everyone sit up. The two umpires, Elliott and Buller, conferred immediately, after which Elliott spoke to Griffith: 'You can bowl, Charlie. But any more like that and I will have to call you. That delivery to Graveney was illegal.' This had the desired effect. Griffith toned it down and took only one more wicket in the match.

Griffith and men like him will always inspire fear and a measure of loathing, but the most controversial fast bowler of the twentieth century had an unimpeachable action. He just happened to allow his devastating pace to be harnessed to a ruthless vision of total domination called 'bodyline'.

CHAPTER 8

Bodyline

———

The loss of the Ashes to the 1930 Australians gave English cricket an unpleasant shock. A hard-fought series was decided in the final Test at the Oval, the difference between the two sides being the batting of the twenty-one-year-old Don Bradman. His 232 not only ensured an innings victory for Australia, but also rounded off an astonishing run of scores, including the new Test record of 334 at Headingley (309 of which were scored on the first day), and left him with an aggregate of 974 runs in the series at an average of 139.14.

After Bradman's innings at Leeds, Percy Fender, the Surrey captain, wrote in the *Observer*:

> When an outstanding personality or genius appears in the field, and the best bowlers have tried without success to tame him, there is nothing left beyond analysis of the methods of that genius and an attempt to use something dictated by the result of reasoning. I feel convinced that something new will have to be introduced to curb Bradman, and that the best way of selecting that something new is to seek it along the lines of theory.

Pelham Warner spoke for all who had witnessed the new batting phenomenon: 'One trembles to think what lies in store for bowlers during the next fifteen or twenty years.'

Despite his youth, Bradman played with supreme confidence throughout his first tour. Neville Cardus praised shots of 'incredible cheekiness', while Jack Fingleton records that, on arriving at the crease, Bradman 'looked about him with a huge grin. That grin was the cheekiest, the most challenging, and the most confident thing I have seen in sport.' It was clearly the first duty of the next England captain to wipe that grin off Bradman's face.

The man chosen was D. R. Jardine. Although he had an impeccable amateur pedigree – Winchester, Oxford and Surrey – Jardine adopted an utterly professional approach to the game. In this he was similar to Arthur Carr, the thick-skinned amateur captain of that most professional of counties, Nottinghamshire. As E. W. Docker noted in his *Bradman and the Bodyline Series*, 'To them it was the sheerest hypocrisy to believe that a match for the County Championship, let alone a Test match, was like some gentlemanly trial-at-arms in which certain practices were frowned upon as simply not cricket.' In 1932–3, the Carr–Jardine philosophy was taken to its logical – and disastrous – conclusion.

The England tour party gave a pretty clear indication of where Jardine's emphasis was going to lie. He and his fellow selectors had chosen four fast bowlers – Harold Larwood, Bill Voce, Gubby Allen and Bill Bowes – and although no one could have guessed exactly how he intended to deploy them, their selection caused alarm bells to ring in Australia. One writer predicted in the *Sydney Referee*, 'If the battery [of fast bowlers] achieves success it may be done by contravening the spirit of cricket.'

There would have been much more antipodean foreboding had word leaked out of a secret meeting held in the grill-room of the Piccadilly Hotel during the Surrey vs Nottinghamshire game some time after Jardine's appointment. Jardine invited Carr to bring along his two strike bowlers, Voce and Larwood, to discuss what could be done about Bradman.

The genesis of what came to be called 'bodyline' – the coinage of another Australian journalist – was as vehemently disputed as its morality. According to Larwood, who never deviated from the neutral designation 'Fast-Leg-Theory', the whole thing started 'in the Test match at Kennington Oval in August, 1930'. The pitch was slightly damp, and the ball popped. Larwood remembered that Archie Jackson 'stood up to me, getting pinked once or twice in the process, and he never flinched'. His next sentence is crucial: 'With Bradman it was different.' Not that Larwood managed to exploit this perceived chink in the Don's armour. Bradman went on to 232 (and Australia to 695), and Larwood to figures of 1 for 132.

But a seed had been sown. Larwood 'determined, then and there' that if selected to play against Australia again, 'I would not forget the difference.' Like all great fast bowlers, Larwood was not only quick; he was aggressive. Wally Hammond wrote that his 'greatest natural asset was a tremendous upsurge of real hostility, even anger against anybody who hit him hard'. And no one hit him harder than Bradman. For Larwood it was personal: 'When I bowled against Bradman, I always thought he was out to show me up as the worst fast bowler in the world. Well, I took the view that I should try and show him up as the worst batsman.'

Jardine could not have found a better motivated instrument, and Larwood accepted the master plan as soon as it was revealed to him:

> I went along with the idea. I could see it was my only chance. I knew I couldn't swing the ball after two or three overs and then I could see myself pounding down on the hard Australian wickets, panting and perspiring under a blazing sun . . . he had pasted me two years ago when I could swing the ball. What would he do to me in Australia?

It is quite clear that Jardine had come to the meeting with a strategy fully worked out. When he came to give his account of the tour, he adopted a positively academic tone, telling his readers 'leg-theory is considerably more than a quarter of a century old'. Furthermore, one of its originators was the great Australian, Warwick Armstrong. 'For years Armstrong bowled with all his men on the leg side except two. These tactics were certainly irritating, but no one suggested they were unfair.' The Yorkshire swing bowler George Hirst was also cited as bowling with 'two or three short-legs, a short fine-leg, a deep fine-leg and a deep square-leg; in fact, a field very similar to Larwood's. There is no doubt this form of bowling at that pace was something new to England, and carried with it great misgivings among the batsmen at the time,' though the great Australian Victor Trumper had not been disconcerted, dispatching Hirst first to leg then to off to elicit a disbelieving 'Well, I'm damned' from the exasperated bowler.

After referring to W. B. Burns of Worcestershire, who, under the captaincy of H. K. Foster, 'bowled at Lord's more than twenty years ago with seven men on the leg side, without earning the epithet "unsportsmanlike" for himself, his captain or his side', and a number of other leg-theorists of a previous age, Jardine concluded his potted history, 'In recent years McDonald, the Australian Lancastrian, Root, of Worcestershire, and Bowes, of Yorkshire, have followed the same tradition, and, with one exception, without protest.'

Many would dispute Jardine's 'one exception', and 'protest' hardly does justice to the furore stirred up by the match in question. This was Yorkshire vs Surrey at the Oval in the closing stages of the 1932 season, and the batsman involved was none other than Jack Hobbs. Bill Bowes was the bowler, and when he subjected the Master to a barrage of short-pitched deliveries, Hobbs, in the words of his biographer Ronald Mason, 'allowed his disapproval . . . to take the form of a public and unmistakable protest on the spot', protesting that 'if this goes on, someone will get killed'. The crowd certainly didn't like it, and Bowes was roundly booed. Jardine, who was captaining Surrey in the game, had a pretty accurate preview of the reaction bodyline would provoke down under.

The incident was widely publicised. Plum Warner wrote about it twice. He condemned it immediately in his newspaper column, saying that keenness was one thing, but this quite another, and going on, 'Moreover, these things lead to reprisals, and when they begin goodness knows where they will end.' As a result of the incident, Yorkshire's 'great reputation was tarnished'.

In *The Cricketer* he was even more critical:

Bowes should alter his tactics. He bowled with five men on the on-side, and sent down several very short-pitched balls which frequently bounced head high and more. That is not bowling. Indeed *it is not cricket* [my italics], and if all fast bowlers were to adopt his methods there would be trouble and plenty of it.

On the face of it, the patrician Jardine and the miner from the

Nottinghamshire coalfields had nothing in common, but despite appearing natural class enemies, they forged a formidable partnership, grounded in the pursuit of the same objective. Both men stuck to their guns with iron determination. Bodyline would not have happened without Jardine; it could not have been put into effect without Larwood. Both men were utterly committed to the strategy. This was no master–servant relationship, but one based on obvious mutual respect.[*]

Jardine was quite right in claiming that there had been precedents for Fast-Leg-Theory. An Australian fast bowler, Jack Scott, who transferred from New South Wales to South Australia, experimented with what one paper called 'ultra-modern leg-theory' in the latter part of the 1920s. Indeed, he even tried it against Percy Chapman's 1928–9 tourists, though with little success. And Bill Voce bowling his left-arm over in-swingers to a packed leg field was an accepted, if not much fancied, part of playing against Nottinghamshire. What was new in 1932–3 was the combination of Larwood's express speed with the remorseless leg-stump line.

Both Jardine and Larwood were adamant in denying that Fast-Leg-Theory was in any way a form of intimidation or designed to hit and hurt the batsmen. Larwood insisted that it could only be practised by bowlers with a high degree of Accuracy. The capital 'A' is his, and he says that from the moment of revelation in 1930 till he revealed his new weapon to the world stage, he strove for Accuracy above all else.

> The acquisition of this accuracy enables me to bowl at the pace I do without injury to the batsman opposed to me, since I can assure my readers that whether they believe it or not it would be possible for me, *if the intention was there*, which I can assure the world of cricket it never has been, to make it very much more uncomfortable for the majority of batsmen than I do.

Until it was put to the test, no one knew how effective it would be. Like all new weapons, it had to be treated with caution and

[*] Jardine's Foreword to Larwood's book appeared in the form of a letter which began, 'My dear Harold' and ended, 'Good luck Harold from a very grateful and admiring "Skipper".'

restraint, and Jardine played a very canny game in the weeks leading up to the Test series, underbowling Larwood, and rarely picking him and Voce in the same team. But there were ominous signs from the start. The tourists' first match was against Western Australia in Perth. Larwood's first ball hit the batsman who was facing him, and the sixth knocked his off stump back. *Off* stump, note. The only English bowler to incur serious barracking was Bowes, for bowling bumpers. But Jardine did not keep Fast-Leg-Theory completely under wraps. Against New South Wales, *The Times* reported, 'Voce opened the bowling with Tate, the Nawab of Pataudi, D. R. Jardine, Hammond and Sutcliffe in his leg trap and Brown on the boundary.' There was little response from the Australians.

The main focus of attention in the lead-up to the first Test was the form of Bradman. He failed so consistently against the English fast men that at the conclusion of a game between the MCC and an Australian XI at Melbourne, a month into the tour, *The Times*' correspondent wrote:

> Australia is now wondering whether Larwood has a 'hoodoo' over Bradman, just as he was supposed to have over Ponsford some time ago. Larwood took Bradman's wicket in each innings [for 36 and 13]. Another question that is being asked is whether both Woodfull and Bradman are susceptible to fast bowling generally on Australian wickets. They have played four innings against the MCC and each has been dismissed in three of the innings by fast bowlers . . . Woodfull has scored a total of only 48 . . . and Bradman has made but 62.

And Bradman was not simply suffering a bad run of form (he was still capable of plundering a double century off Sheffield Shield bowling); he had been getting out in bizarre ways and to rash shots. In Melbourne he was dismissed 'when in *attempting to hook* the ball he was out leg-before-wicket' [my italics], while in the second innings his shot selection was even more bizarre: 'After Bradman had made 13 he made a wild swing at the first ball of Larwood's fourth over and was bowled.' When MCC went to Sydney to meet New South Wales, Bradman played under the handicap of a severe bout of flu, but even so his second-innings departure prompted the headline, 'Bradman's Curious

Dismissal'. Voce had been making the ball get up consistently, and Bradman had been fortunate to survive his initial onslaught. After a rest, the Nottinghamshire left-hander returned. *The Times* describes the first ball of his new spell: 'Bradman had expected a short-pitched "bumper" which would go over his head. He therefore walked right away from the wicket, only to see the ball keep low and crash into the wicket.'

On the eve of the first Test, Jardine could look back on six dismissals, five of them by pace, three of which were the result of disastrous misjudgement. It looked as though he had Bradman on the run. At this stage of the tour there were no criticisms of Jardine; in fact, he was praised by Alan Kippax, the New South Wales captain, for his sportsmanship. When the virus that Bradman had caught also brought down the wicketkeeper Bert Oldfield, Jardine insisted that H. S. Love, one of the best keepers in Australia, should take over. Kippax called this 'one of the most sportsmanlike gestures ever made'.

After all the build-up, Bradman failed to shake off the virus and pulled out of the first Test. It was something of an anti-climax, but Jardine went ahead with his fast-bowling blitzkrieg anyway, setting leg-side fields for Voce and Larwood on the first morning of the match. This was the Australian public's first real introduction to what became universally known as bodyline. To a packed leg field, with three, possibly four, catchers ringing the (right-handed) batsman and two or more sweepers in the deep, Larwood (right-arm over) and Voce (left-arm over) aimed to angle the ball, short of a length, at the leg stump. With their pace and accuracy, there was little room for manoeuvre. Orthodox scoring shots into the off were out of the question – indeed, on occasion Larwood bowled with no fielders on the off side whatsoever – while self-defence was paramount.

Jack Fingleton, who scored a century against the tourists for New South Wales which earned him a place in the first Test, gives a first-hand account of what it was like to face bodyline:

> There was nothing half-hearted about Voce's bowling. He bowled with studied intent at the body, the ball pitching at the half-way mark and sometimes shorter; he had four to five short-legs with two men covering them in the deep . . . for the

main purpose the stumps were intended to serve, they could well have been left in the pavilion. Most of Voce's deliveries, if they did not meet a [batsman's] rib in transit, cleared the leg stump, or a space outside the leg stump, by feet.

This was bodyline in deadly earnest. It was apparent and intentional, its malice unaffected by the frequent contacts of body and ball, for a blow on the ribs would, of a certainty, be followed the very next ball by a delivery of a similar length, elevation and direction. For a time several members of the English leg-side trap either offered apologies when a batsman was hit or gave a rubbing palm in solace; but a continuation of such courtesies would, in the circumstances, have been hypocritical and embarrassing to the giver and the receiver alike. The batsman was later left to do his own rubbing in the privacy of his imprecations.

However, as Fingleton himself had proved, it was possible to make a total against bodyline, and Stan McCabe now played one of the most brilliant innings in the history of the Ashes. After Australia had slumped to 87 for 4, McCabe found a partner in Vic Richardson, and together they put on 129. McCabe decided that attack was the best form of defence, and, hooking and pulling with no fear for the consequences, he went on to a magnificent 187 not out, and lifted Australia to the reasonable total of 360. Larwood and Voce shared 9 wickets, with figures of 5 for 96 and 4 for 110, respectively. Larwood bowled 31 overs, despite having his side strapped for a strain. As Jardine's main strike bowler, he was simply not allowed to be injured.

England replied with 524, thanks to centuries by Herbert Sutcliffe (194), Wally Hammond (112) and the Nawab of Pataudi (102), which gave them a lead of 164. And that was precisely what Australia scored in their second innings. This time there was no containing Larwood, who took another 5 wickets, for just 28, in 18 overs. Sutcliffe and Bob Wyatt duly padded up once more, and the Yorkshireman scored the 1 run required to win the match by 10 wickets.

This overwhelming victory confirmed the dominance that Jardine's fast bowlers had established over the home batsmen. But the real test would be how Bradman handled it on his return.

The great man recognised the psychological dimension of Jardine's new cricket warfare. With his run of poor scores there was a serious danger of losing the upper hand he had held over England since the opening match of the 1930 tour. In the past, when he found himself in difficulties he had sometimes gone on the attack, using his superb eye to destroy the bowlers. A similar strategy seemed to be behind his first innings in the 1932–3 series.

When he came to the crease on the first morning of the Melbourne Test, the score was 67 for 2. Bill Bowes had taken over from the new-ball partnership, and Bradman clearly decided the Yorkshireman represented the weakest link in Jardine's attack. From the first ball, he went on to the offensive. It was the only ball he faced, as, in moving right across his stumps to hook a short delivery aimed at around the off stump, he got a bottom edge on to his leg stump. Fingleton was at the other end, watching in horror:

> Bowes, whose pace in Australia was not comparable with that of Voce, let alone Larwood, began his lumbering run, and to my surprise I saw Bradman leave his guard and move across the wicket before Bowes had bowled the ball.
>
> The first natural and obvious principle of batsmanship is not to make up one's mind before the ball is bowled. Not even Bradman could flout the canons of the game in such a manner . . .
>
> Bradman was outside his off stump when the ball reached him. He swung at it and hit it into the base of the leg stump. A hush fell on the ground, an unbelievable hush of calamity, for men refused to believe what their eyes had seen. Bradman left the wickets in silence.

Australia was stunned. Across the vast country people sat by their radio sets in disbelief. Bradman's invincibility was an article of faith, and now the nation's confidence in its talisman was shaken to its foundations. However, with Fingleton grinding out a stubborn 83, Australia still reached 228, which proved, on a slow turning wicket, a very respectable score. Thanks to Bill O'Reilly's 5 for 63, England managed only 169, falling 59 runs behind on first innings.

In Australia's second knock, Fast-Leg-Theory was at last given an extensive trial against the individual it had been designed for. It failed. Bradman scored a century. It may only have been 103, but it was surely one of his greatest. When he went in on the third morning of the match the score was 27 for 2. He had nothing but a string of failures behind him, and yet the result of the match rested almost entirely on his shoulders. He was again confronted by Bowes, who again dropped short to him. Bradman once more took up the challenge, hooking him powerfully away for four off his first ball. Thereafter he mixed watchful and gutsy defence with a series of improvised shots to exploit the wide gaps on the off side. As B. J. Wakley wrote, 'his defence was magnificent, and his courage in standing up to the "body-line" bowling was equally admirable'. Wakley also notes that Bradman's score represented 56 per cent of the runs scored from the bat and that 191 is the lowest total to contain a century in Ashes Test matches.[*] Only Woodfull (26) and Richardson (32) joined him in double figures.

England were set 251 to win. O'Reilly and Ironmonger bowled them out for 139. With one Test each, and, apart from the aberration against Bowes, Bradman back to his indomitable best, the series seemed evenly balanced, and the Australian public were gripped. Few can have predicted how abysmally things would have sunk by the end of the third Test at Adelaide.

England batted first, on the fastest wicket they had met so far – indeed, one of the fastest ever seen at Adelaide – and got off to a dreadful start. To the delight of the locals, Jardine was clean bowled by Wall, who, after giving him a few disconcerting flyers, also dismissed Hammond. The morning session also saw Sutcliffe and Ames succumbing to the aggressive spin of O'Reilly and Ironmonger. However, from 37 for 4 at lunch, the visitors rallied well to post a total of 341 – still fairly modest by Adelaide's standards. It was absolutely vital that England made early inroads.

Jardine opened not with Larwood and Voce, but with Larwood and Allen, whose categorical refusal to bowl bodyline had initially forfeited his captain's trust. However, his orthodox pace-bowling had been one of the revelations of the tour and

[*] M. C. Cowdrey made 102 out of 191 in 1954-5.

proved a hugely effective foil to the rest of the attack. It was a bonus for England when he had the obdurate Fingleton caught behind by Ames for 0 in his first over.

No Australian could have had any complaints about that. It was what happened next that took the match, and indeed the series, out of the realm of the traditional hard-fought, don't-give-an-inch Test cricket, into a new territory of hatred and contempt. Off the last delivery of Larwood's second over, Woodfull, the Australian captain, was struck on the chest by a sharply rising ball. He had been hit in the same spot earlier in the season during the Australian XI match, and this second blow sent him staggering about the crease in agony.

The crowd booed vigorously. Jardine spoke briefly to Woodfull, and then called out clearly, 'Well bowled, Harold.' This, of course, could have been praise for the over just completed, but Larwood for one took it as a psychological thrust at Bradman, newly arrived at the wicket in place of Fingleton. Jardine was, Larwood thought, 'trying to put Bradman off, trying to unsettle him by letting him think the ball was being deliberately bowled to hit the man and that he might get the same'.

Bradman was now on strike to Allen, and played two exhilarating, if risky, shots to deliveries anyone else would simply have blocked. 6 off the over. Larwood to bowl to Woodfull. But just before he ran in – some even claimed it was as he was beginning his run-up – Jardine intervened and imperiously waved his men into their familiar leg-side positions. This riled the crowd, who yelled and jeered as Larwood belatedly sprinted in to bowl, but far from being intimidated, he seemed positively inspired by the hubbub. The first ball was as fast as anything he'd bowled on tour, and it knocked Woodfull's bat out of his hands.

The tumult that followed was unprecedented. Sheer collective fury sent the decibels rising so that those out walking in the surrounding parks of Australia's most staid state capital must have wondered what enormity was taking place beneath the dreaming spire of their splendid cathedral. Many inside the ground were sure that if one spectator had crossed the boundary, a full-scale and potentially murderous riot would have been triggered. But the line just held, and, under Jardine's unbending gaze, so did English nerve. Larwood let up not one jot, and soon had the wicket he and his captain were sacrificing so much to take. Bradman attempted a leg glance and dollied a catch to Allen in the leg trap. McCabe followed suit shortly afterwards, and then, after his heroic resistance, Woodfull fell to Allen, leaving his team tottering on 51 for 4.

Soon after – almost certainly too soon after – there was a knock on the Australian dressing-room door. It was Pelham Warner, MCC manager. He had come to enquire after Woodfull's injury. The Australian captain was lying on the massage table recuperating. At first he said he didn't want to discuss the matter, but prompted, or rather goaded, by Warner's insistent show of good manners, he finally delivered his famous remark that 'There are two teams out there, but only one is playing cricket.' The rest of the speech has come down in various forms, but the essence of it was clear: cricket is too great a game to be spoilt by the tactics the visitors were adopting, and Woodfull for one would prefer to quit the game if the English persevered with them.

Fingleton was one of those present and he recalled his captain's 'simple words, simply expressed, with no flavour of heat or anger'. All the same, Fingleton continued, it was a devastating reproof for the 'representative band of English Public School and Varsity men' at the core of the MCC party. 'Their shoulders, doubtlessly, had often been smitten by the hand of their school captain as he told them to "Play up, play up and play the game". Moreover, they were of the traditional English type whose first lesson in life taught them that to do anything mean, ignoble or even doubtful was "not cricket, sir!".'

For the Australian captain to impugn the sportsmanship of an England captain and manager in private was bad enough, but his view soon became public. Woodfull's remark was leaked to the press (by Bradman, according to Fingleton – though he vigorously denied it when the allegation was made public), and the temperature was raised even further when Bertie Oldfield ducked into yet another furiously fast short delivery from Larwood. English protestations, backed up by an admission from the unfortunate batsman that he had totally misjudged the delivery, did nothing to quell the clamour for action, and so on 18 January 1933, the fifth day of the Test, the Australian Board of Control took the unprecedented step of cabling the MCC:

Body-line bowling has assumed such proportions as to menace the best interest of the game, making protection of the body by the batsmen the main consideration. This is causing intensely bitter feeling between the players as well as injury. In our opinion it is unsportsmanlike. Unless stopped at once it is likely to upset the friendly relations existing between Australia and England.

These words were painstakingly composed while plans were drawn up to draft in a huge police reserve in case the spectators did finally lose their self-control. The worst fear was that Bradman himself would be hit.

Things appeared very different on the other side of the world. The ABC's slur on English sportsmanship was an outrage. As Ronald Blythe put it, had the MCC been accused of *cannibalism*, the charge could not have been graver. Bridling with patrician *hauteur*, the MCC gave Jardine their unqualified support:

We, Marylebone Cricket Club, deplore your cable. We deprecate your opinion that there has been unsportsmanlike play. We have fullest confidence in captain, team and managers and are convinced that they would do nothing to infringe either the Laws of Cricket or the spirit of the game. We have no evidence that our confidence has been misplaced. Much as we regret accidents to Woodfull and Oldfield, we understand that in neither case was the bowler to blame.

If the Australian Board of Control wish to propose a new Law or rule, it shall receive our careful consideration in due course.

We hope the situation is not now as serious as your cable would seem to indicate, but if it is such as to jeopardise the good relations between English and Australian cricketers and you consider it desirable to cancel remainder of programme we would consent, but with great reluctance.

Whatever view they came to in the future, the MCC would not order Jardine to desist from using bodyline. Responsibility for calling off the tour would have to be Australia's. In the view of the more cynical observers, this was the trump card. After two financially disastrous visits by the West Indies and South

Africa, the last thing the Australian Board could countenance was the financial sacrifice of cancellation. However unpleasant for the batsmen, however unsporting in spirit, bodyline was provoking huge public interest and packing the crowds into the cricket grounds.

Meanwhile, the match continued. England piled on the runs thanks to Hammond, who was deprived of an almost certain century by an unlikely bowler – D. Bradman – and then, set an impossible 532 to win, Australia put up as defiant a show as they could muster. Woodfull carried his bat for a heroic 73 not out. Bradman made 66, but in a completely different mode. Fingleton, who, incidentally, got a pair, was again a critical witness: 'At Adelaide, when Larwood returned to bowl after a rest, Bradman hit a swishing six off Verity at the other end in such a manner that the veriest schoolgirl sensed suicide was in the offing.' When he did face Larwood, he abandoned a set stance, but instead 'moved feet to the off and then feet to the leg before Larwood delivered the ball . . . It was all very thrilling if one did not stop to think that this was a Test match, not village green cricket, and that Australia was staging a burdensome uphill fight.' He was out caught and bowled Verity, but, as Fingleton indicates, for all its personal defiance, his innings was not much help in saving the game. The rest – minus Oldfield – succumbed to the pace of Larwood and Allen, who took 4 wickets apiece and presented Jardine with victory by 338 runs.

The commotion did not end with the match; the whole cricket world was abuzz. For all his air of lofty detachment, Jardine was not as insensitive to the fury he was provoking as some of his detractors assumed. He claimed later that he came close to abandoning bodyline, and would certainly have done so if he felt he had lost the support of his team. Rumours were indeed flying around that there was dissension in the camp, and Jardine called a team meeting from which he scrupulously absented himself.

It turned out that a majority supported Jardine and his strategy. As Maurice Leyland put it: 'What, give up leg-theory just because it's got 'em licked?' A more diplomatically worded resolution was issued the following day, which stated that 'The members of the MCC England team . . . are, and always have been, utterly loyal to their captain, under whose leadership they hope to achieve an honourable victory.'

Jardine declared himself 'delighted', and determined to press steadfastly on. After all, he had no doubt as to the cause of the complaints, noting that after the first Test, 'which Australia lost in spite of McCabe's great innings, there had been very little talk about leg-theory, and, again, that after the Second Test match, which Australia won with Bradman giving every evidence of an impressive return to form, there had been nothing but jubilation.' He went on:

> The general impression to be formed after the Second Test match was that there was nothing wrong with leg-theory *provided it was mastered*, and that since two of Australia's champions had already mastered it, while others seemed to be well on the same road, everything in the garden was lovely. Had it been otherwise, surely that was the time for the Board of Control to approach us or the MCC with their views on leg-theory, instead of waiting until the Third Test match had turned in our favour.

As far as the rest of the tour was concerned, Jardine made it clear he would not lead England in the fourth Test unless the Board withdrew their accusation of 'unsportsmanlike' behaviour. As he wrote, '[I]t was as unthinkable as it was impossible that an English team should take the field with such an accusation hanging unretracted over them. The meanest intelligence can see how insidiously this latent form of incitement might have worked upon the feelings of a demonstrative crowd.' Jardine got his retraction in the form of 'a half-hearted apology on the morning of the match', and so, 'After all, there was to be a fourth Test Match.'

This went the way of the third and saw Jardine fulfil his ambition of reclaiming the Ashes, but not before Australia, batting first on a fairly lifeless Brisbane pitch, had got themselves into a sound position at 251 for 3. Jardine's observations that crowd reaction to bodyline was in direct proportion to its success or failure was borne out by the fact that the barracking which greeted the tactic in the morning had completely dried up by the afternoon when the home team were in the ascendant.

However, the overnight batsmen, Bradman and Ponsford, faced a different challenge on the second morning – Larwood refreshed and fired up. He got both of them out – bowled – quickly. Bradman, having 'shown repeatedly that he was not prepared to risk being hit', stepped away to leg to attempt a cut and lost his leg stump. Jack Hobbs, who witnessed the dismissal from the press box, wrote, 'I was convinced that Bradman would not have leg theory as bowled by Larwood. If a schoolboy tried to cut a ball on his leg stump you would smack his head. Yet here was Bradman doing it.' He made 76. The rest of the batting showed little resistance and Australia were all out for 340.

England just beat that thanks to Eddie Paynter, who rose from his hospital bed (tonsillitis) to score an invaluable 83, and then Larwood and Allen ran through the Australians for 175. Larwood once more claimed Bradman's wicket as the Don again stepped to leg, this time hitting the ball to deep point. England lost 4 wickets in scoring the 162 required to win the match, series and the Ashes.

Interest in the fifth Test back at Sydney largely focused on the gladiatorial contest between Larwood and Bradman. Larwood bowled his man, for 48, in the first innings, but it was quite clear that simply dismissing him was not enough. The two men were playing a different game, one that was dangerous and personally motivated.

But before they could resume their personal duel, Larwood had astonished – and, in fact, rather won over – the crowd by making 98 as nightwatchman, which helped England sneak a small first-innings lead. All through the series the sides had been neck and neck on first innings. It was in the second that the Australians fell away, and this must have been due to the cumulative strain of having to face bodyline a second time around.

Bradman continued to bat in his own inimitable way. After Richardson bagged the second Australian pair in the series, he came in and produced 'an astonishing tennis-racket slam' to dispatch Larwood's bumper. The gauntlet was thrown down once more – and for the final time. Fingleton takes up the commentary:

Bradman's stumps were left wide open not once but a dozen times. An ordinary straight ball from Larwood would have been sufficient then to end Bradman's innings, but it really seemed that the stumps were of minor concern to both Bradman and Larwood. It seemed that Larwood was anxious to claim a hit on Bradman in this final Test – a thing the Englishman had not done previously. And Bradman seemed just as determined Larwood shouldn't. Larwood got a hit, late in Bradman's innings, with a stinging blow high on Bradman's left arm.

Larwood too was in pain – his feet had taken huge punishment on the hard Australian wickets – but although he was limping badly, Jardine wouldn't let him leave the field. Not until Bradman's wicket was finally secured. When it was – bowled by Verity for 71 – Jardine nodded to his injured fast bowler, and the two great antagonists left the field together. Not a word passed between them.

Set 164 to win, England set about a straightforward task in a professional manner. There was something for the crowd to cheer about when 'Bull' Alexander, drafted into the Australian side as a partial answer to Larwood, struck Jardine a few painful blows. The crowd booed the England captain when he complained about Alexander's follow-through, but he continued to ignore them. After giving his side a solid start, Jardine returned to the pavilion to watch Hammond and Wyatt steer the side home to a comfortable win by 8 wickets.

Jardine had done what he had set out to do – tame the Bradman run machine and inflict a crushing defeat on the Australians. It would take some time for the full cost – for Jardine, for Larwood and for the game itself – to become apparent. Back home in Britain people were delighted, and attributed the furore over bodyline to the fact that the Australians had lost and didn't like it. Even the rabidly anti-establishment Hugh MacDiarmid could be found writing a disparaging squib about 'damned colonials howlin'/Against body-line bowlin''.

But though they had bitten the bullet, or at least their tongues, in order to preserve the tour, the Australians had plenty to say once it was over, and the post-mortem was protracted and passionate. Gradually the enormity of bodyline was brought home to those in the seats of power at Lord's. The victory started to appear tarnished, and those most closely associated with it an embarrassment.

Having backed Jardine so strongly, the MCC could not turn round and publicly condemn him, but as the depth of the wound inflicted on Anglo–Australian relations became apparent, many wished they had been party to the views of his old cricket coach at Winchester, who on hearing of the appointment remarked, 'Well, we shall win the Ashes – but we may lose a Dominion.'

If there was a barely perceptible withdrawal of official support, Jardine never lost the loyalty of those he had led. For his senior professional, Herbert Sutcliffe, he was 'one of the greatest men I have met':

> [he] had the courage of his convictions . . . it was unfortunate for him that they did not meet with general approval, but that did not alter his outlook. He planned for us, he cared for us, he fought for us on that tour, and he was so faithful in everything he did that we were prepared on our part to do anything we could for him. A great cricket captain.

The same could not be said for the managers. For the first time ever, England had two managers, Pelham Warner and R. C. N. Palairet. Warner was obviously the senior figure, but found it impossible to reconcile his publicly expressed dislike of leg-theory and the requirement to support his captain and his team. He gave no leadership at all, and, like a small man entrusted with a ferocious mastiff, he ended up a rather pitiful figure (though Gubby Allen denied that 'he took to the bottle over it'). Warner's embarrassing predicament was clear to his hosts, and the great Australian Test veteran Monty Noble noted, 'It is a most remarkable thing, that in all this fuss over bodyline we have not heard one single word from the MCC managers. Where does Warner, in particular, stand on these extremely doubtful bowling tactics?'

Warner was very clear what his views were after the tour. In *Cricket Between Two Wars*, he differentiated between leg-theory ('a form of bowling which has been in use in this country for

fifty years') and bodyline, which 'is absolutely and entirely different . . . One of the strongest arguments against this bowling is
that it breeds anger, hatred and malice, with consequent
reprisals. The courtesy of combat goes out of the game.'

That was all very well after the event. The question, as Fingleton later insisted, was 'what Sir Pelham thought of bodyline
in Australia' (my italics). One (Australian) insider related that

> Warner was terribly distressed about the whole business and I
> really think did all he could to stop it. He and his co-manager,
> of course, were approached on the subject by members of the
> Board in Adelaide before the cable was sent. Warner was right
> up against the tactics and sent a report to the MCC after the
> first Test in Sydney roundly condemning bodyline and urging
> prompt action to stop it.

But his attempts at curbing Jardine were pathetic. He was
once overheard pleading with his captain, 'Don't put so many
men on the leg-side, Douglas.' Jardine showed his contempt for
him by simply packing more into the leg trap. Warner was one
of life's natural appeasers, but had he really wanted to stop
bodyline, he was not without power to influence events, if only
by the threat of resignation.

Fingleton's case against the senior MCC manager is a strong
one:

> Warner idolised cricket. He was keenly and naturally parti-
> san, like many Australians, in that he wanted his own side to
> win, but all his writings suggested clearly that the game was
> his chief concern. What could it mean to him had his team
> won the whole cricketing world if he lost his cricketing soul?

In the heat of the crisis, Warner elected to sacrifice his sense of
fair play, his sense of what was 'cricket', to 'what he was pleased
to call loyalty', 'blind allegiance to the MCC'. And Fingleton
concludes: 'Silence in such a case could be construed only as
consent to the embracing of bodyline.'

Paradoxically, Jardine comes out of the 1932–3 tour better
than Warner. There was no hypocrisy in his position. By his own
blinkered lights he and his team did nothing wrong, and his
defence of his conduct of the tour, *In Quest of the Ashes*, is as

finely argued, if as selective in its detail, as any barrister's final address to the jury.

The man most obviously in the dock was, of course, Larwood, and he too remained unapologetic – rather too unapologetic for his own good. In his own book, *Bodyline?*, he time and again denies the intimidatory core of his and Jardine's strategy, but the repeated assertions of innocence rapidly lose their force. When Larwood writes, 'none of the less accomplished batsmen among the Australian players was ever hit', the reader has to ask what liberties are being taken with the language. In Adelaide, for instance, Ponsford scored a determined 85. Docker describes how, 'his body literally bulging with padding, [he] turned his back on most of the short ones and looked safer against Larwood than he had ever looked. *Eleven enormous bruises* from shoulder to hip were the price he had to pay however' [my italics]. And we have seen how, in his last encounter with Bradman, Larwood was not satisfied until he had landed a blow on the elusive body of his adversary. What Larwood in fact seems to mean by 'hit' is actually knocked down, or otherwise physically incapacitated. He writes, 'the only player who was hit on the head [was] Bill Oldfield, who said to me himself, the moment after the blow, that it was not my fault; while the only one at all severely struck on the body was that essentially firm-footed and almost immobile player WM Woodfull'.

In fact, as he develops it, Larwood's defence becomes as belligerent and reckless as the bowling he is trying to justify:

Inasmuch as throughout the last tour in Australia . . . only two batsmen were at all severely struck by the ball, one of them, by his own frank admission, owing to his own fault, I hold that it is finally proved that
(i) my Leg-Theory bowling is *not* Body-Line bowling.
(ii) my Leg-Theory bowling is not more physically dangerous to the batsman than is any very fast bowling.
(iii) actually it is *much* less physically dangerous than is very fast bowling for which the bowler has not set the legside field which warns the batsman what to expect.
I have no excuses to make for bowling which I shall always hold needs no excuse.

My conscience is absolutely clear that I have never bowled at any batsman, and I know that I never shall. I am afraid that any who do not take my word for this must make the best they can of doing the other thing.

Larwood also seemed eager to keep the battle with Bradman going, declaring in the press that the Don had been 'frightened' of him. This riled Bradman into a reply: 'I resent Larwood's accusation and deny it emphatically. According to Larwood's idea, it would seem that to adopt orthodox methods and get hit is displaying courage. Any other methods whereby his theory might be defeated evince fear.' More contentiously, Bradman went on, 'Actually, my method of playing Larwood exposed me to considerably more danger than the orthodox way. Anybody who understands cricket knows that.'

Although handicapped by Woodfull's moral scruples from retaliating themselves, the Australians were keen to see how the English would react if and when they became the victims of bodyline. Their wish was granted when the West Indians toured England in 1933. Their two fast bowlers, Learie Constantine and E. A. Martindale, gave a lively display of bodyline in the second Test at Old Trafford. Jardine took the medicine uncomplainingly and scored a courageous century, but the sight of Hammond retiring from the crease with a cut chin brought home to the English public the realities of this new cricketing warfare. As worrying was its growing prevalence in first-class cricket. Even with Larwood out for most of the season with his damaged foot, Arthur Carr remained in favour of bodyline, while Bill Bowes continued his dangerous course around the county grounds. He hit two Glamorgan batsmen at Cardiff amid scenes of crowd fury, and in June knocked out Frank Watson at Old Trafford amidst a pandemonium of disapproval. Bodyline was even used in the Varsity match.

As the Australians had rightly suspected, one season's worth of bodyline was enough. *Wisden* condemned it unequivocally: 'It is definitely dangerous, creates ill-feeling, invites reprisals and eliminates all the best strokes in batting.' Even Carr – one of the three county captains to resist pressure for a general ceasefire – acknowledged that 'Somebody is going to be killed if this sort of bowling continues . . . Sooner or later something will have to be done, so why not do it now[?]'

There was, however, the continuing problem of bodyline's main exponent. Although Jardine missed the third Test against the West Indies, he was available for the first tour to India with Test matches. Larwood, Voce and Bowes were not on the tour, but E. W. Clark of Northamptonshire and M. S. Nichols of Essex were, and Jardine had no hesitation in setting the bodyline field for them. This was almost laughable overkill, and the predictable list of casualties swelled as the series went on. Fingleton, a self-appointed connoisseur of Jardine's follies, provided a running tally: 'Merchant had his chin split; Naomal had his eye cut open; a ball at Madras narrowly missed the Maharajah of Patiala's turban and bitterly incensed the crowd. Dialwar Hussain was hit on the head in the Calcutta Test, and . . . was carried off the field.'

Things were clearly getting out of hand. It was one thing bowling bodyline at the world's best batsmen, but a very different thing bowling it at far less experienced players. One of the umpires in that Calcutta Test was the Australia and Middlesex all-rounder Frank Tarrant. When Clark hit Hussain, he intervened, telling Jardine that he would stop Clark from bowling. Jardine retorted that he would stop Tarrant umpiring, and he did.

The scheduled visit of an Australian team in 1934 remained in the balance over that winter. With second-string MCC bowlers knocking Maharajahs' turbans about on the subcontinent, it is hardly surprising that the Australians were hesitant about committing themselves. They were not encouraged when the *Sunday Times* gleefully announced that the 'Bradman–Larwood duel' would be resumed in the Test matches. 'Many think leg-theory will be abandoned, but it will be employed if it promises success and does not savour of undue intimidation.'

But that was the issue. During the exchange of telegrams the previous winter, the MCC position had been clearly stated: 'We agree, and have always agreed, that a form of bowling which is obviously a direct attack by the bowler upon the batsman would be an offence against the spirit of the game.' But having supported Jardine against the charge that that was exactly what he was encouraging his bowlers to do, they were left in a tricky position. They could hardly sack Jardine, whose record as captain was outstanding. And yet to reappoint him without some agreement on leg-theory would have resulted in the cancellation of the tour, with all the loss of face and revenue that would have entailed. The Australians had them over the same barrel the MCC had deployed to ensure the Bodyline tour continued.

All eyes in the cricketing world were on Jardine. After keeping his own counsel for several months, he finally announced that he would not be available to captain England in the coming series. The relief was palpable, but it was not universal. Larwood, for one, suffered a shattering blow with the withdrawal of his old captain. Seeing which way the wind was blowing, the great bowler showed a modicum of tact by declaring himself unfit in the run-up to the first Test match at Trent Bridge, but he was fit enough to put the wind up Lancashire, taking 6 wickets for 1 run in an awesome demonstration of raw pace. There were angry exchanges at the end of the match, and although there was great public pressure for Larwood's recall to the Test side, Tommy Higson, the President of Lancashire and an England selector for three years, was adamant that there should be no more incidents.

Instead of holding his peace, Larwood went public and had his say on the front page of the *Sunday Dispatch*. Even if picked for the second Test at Lord's, he said, 'it will not matter. I have definitely made up my mind not to play against the Australians in this or any of the Tests.' The whole furore he regarded as a clear 'conspiracy to bury leg-theory and brand me as a dangerous and unfair bowler. The MCC have given way to political or other influences determined at all costs to placate Australia.' Bill Voce was equally outspoken, asserting in the *Sunday Express* that the Australians now had the power of veto over the English Test side. Is the Australian Board, he asked, 'to be allowed to ruin English cricket? . . . Through Larwood we are only giving the Australians what Gregory and McDonald gave us in 1921.'

Larwood was not picked for the Test at Lord's, nor did he ever play for England again. Voce too was out of favour, and gave vent to his feelings with a vintage display of bodyline when the Australians played Nottinghamshire at Trent Bridge. This was vociferously approved by the crowd, intent on repaying some of the barracking the English tourists had received down under, but was unacceptable to the Australian captain. Having been assured his side would be safe from bodyline, Woodfull told the committee that if Voce took the field the following day, the Australians would not. Voce was diplomatically indisposed. Carr, who had been rested as captain, had nonetheless been at the ground. 'I saw Voce bowl,' he said; 'there was nothing unfair. If I had been captain, Voce would have bowled even if the Australians had walked off the field. When I am captain, I shall not restrain anyone from bowling as they think fit.'

But by this time, bodyline's days were numbered. The MCC report made their position (belatedly) clear: 'There was evidence that bowlers had made direct attacks upon batsmen in the season of 1934. This attack could be defined as persistent and systematic bowling of fast, short-pitched balls at the batsmen standing clear of the wicket. The MCC has always considered this type of bowling to be unfair and it must be eliminated.' From now on, umpires were instructed to caution offenders and ultimately to bar them from bowling. Bodyline as practised by Larwood and Voce in Australia was dead.

It had been a grim chapter in the game's history, but it had not been entirely an accident. In previous years, the balance between bat and ball had become heavily weighted towards the batsman, as demonstrated by the huge scores made on shirt-front wickets first by Ponsford and then, even more consistently, by the Don. For Fingleton, bodyline 'was nothing more nor less than a revolution against Bradman'. But for all its apparent success, it was a revolution that failed. Jardine's victory was a Pyrrhic one, with England ultimately the loser. The withdrawal of Larwood and Voce tilted the 1934 series Australia's way, and in 1936–7, Allen and Voce were severely constricted in their use of even the legitimate bouncer.

The tragedy of bodyline was that it was unnecessary. In 1932–3, the MCC had the chance to defeat Australia by fair and honourable means, with batting of equal or greater depth and far stronger bowling. Jardine's battery of pace, employed fairly, might well have exposed Bradman's Achilles heel; and even if not, the party included a top-class spinner in Hedley Verity, and in Maurice Tate, one of the finest medium-pace bowlers ever to play for England. Bodyline may have been a shorter route to victory, but in delivering the great prize, it devalued it. The tour is not remembered as the triumph of a great side, but only for one of the most disreputable campaigns in the game's history.

The greatest damage bodyline did was to cricket itself. Jack Fingleton started the 1932–3 season as a young cricketer full of excited expectancy. When he battled his way to the century that guaranteed his Test place, he fulfilled every Australian cricketer's highest ambition:

> I should have been deliriously happy as I returned to the pavilion, for was this not a complete realisation of a youthful dream? Could one have wished for a better answer to one's prayers, with Test selection against England also in the offing?
>
> There was, on the contrary, no wild thrill about it. I was conscious of a hurt, and it was not because of the physical pummelling I had taken from Voce. It was the consciousness of a crashed ideal. Playing against England in actuality had proved vastly different from what boyish dreams and adventure had imagined it to be. The game was not the thing, but almost seemed to be the last thing.

It was not only the young cricketers who felt that way. Fingleton wrote, 'I do not think there was one single batsman who played in most of those bodyline games who ever afterwards recaptured his love for cricket.' Relations between the two sides soured early on. 'Players snapped at each other and never gave a thought to mixing off the field in social enjoyment or in cementing those oft-quoted "bonds of Empire" which this game of cricket, allegedly more so than any other sport, had fostered over the years.' And, at the end of the tour, not a single Australian player appeared to bid farewell to the MCC team.

CHAPTER 9

Trial by Fire

━━

Although bodyline was the most devastating deployment of fast bowling seen up to that time, it was not the first demonstration of fast bowling's power to reduce batsmen to shell-shocked cannon-fodder. After the moratorium on indiscriminate pace imposed by W. G. in his prime, the fast men staged a dramatic come-back for his golden twilight, to establish themselves as the game's most ruthless cutting edge. The old orthodoxy of opening the attack with a slow bowler in tandem with a quick disappeared, and although the laws were miserly with new balls (one per innings), captains were suddenly keen to get the best out of the shine while it lasted. Pelham Warner started playing for Middlesex in 1894 and found 'the stream of fast bowlers at flood-level'. There was no escape: 'batsmen who disliked extra pace had to face it on every county ground. If you could not play fast bowling you might just as well give up any claim to batsmanship.'

Head and brawny shoulders above the rest of this muscular throng stood Tom Richardson and Bill Lockwood. They were the dominant force throughout the 1890s, and their success in tandem, either for Surrey or for England, was spectacular. As David Frith notes in *The Fast Men*, 'Here was the first great fast bowling combination, the earliest example of pace bowlers of rare hostility and endurance *hunting as a pair*.' When Surrey won the championship in 1899, it was for the ninth time in thirteen seasons, and they owed much to their great fast-bowling combination. The duo also proved highly effective at Test level, especially on Stoddart's first triumphal tour of 1894–5. Richardson was sometimes barracked for embarrassing, not to say bruising, the

Australian batsmen, especially when he made the diminutive Harry Graham curtsey repeatedly under his shorter deliveries.

But batsmen, especially short batsmen, had to get used to short-pitched bowling. Richardson's Surrey colleague Bobby Abel was a prolific accumulator, especially on the billiard table of his own Oval square. But he had a marked disinclination for true speed, and would unashamedly shuffle to leg rather than get in line. Such was his eye, though, that he could still score runs, however exasperated the bowler became in the process. Charles Kortright in particular took irate exception to Abel's evasion tactics. According to the fast bowler's Essex team-mate P. A. Perrin, 'It was bad enough when Abel ran away and chopped yorkers off the middle stump through the slips; but when he ran away so far that he cut him inside the leg stump and to the left of the wicketkeeper for four "Korty" really did say something.'

Kortright was temperamentally as hostile as fast bowlers get, and, as in the case of his duel with W. G. at Leyton, positively relished the personal duel. Gilbert Jessop, who watched that encounter with some trepidation, was, in addition to being one of the game's most destructive batsmen, a tearaway fast bowler himself. As a mature student at Cambridge he quickly gained a reputation for short-pitched bowling, and in the 1896 Varsity match he created quite a stir. As his biographer, Gerald Brodribb, records, 'he attacked so savagely with bumpers from round the wicket that he not only broke a stump, but damaged several of the batsmen, especially Leveson-Gower, and knocked out his own wicket-keeper'. Jessop's aggression even merited a mention in a *Times* leader:

> We are very far from charging the Cambridge fast bowler with a desire to destroy human life. He would not, for example, wish to harm his own excellent wicket-keeper! Yet several of his bumped down deliveries were of almost unexampled shortness . . . This may be, and doubtless is, the result of a rather demoniacal style, and the bowler may be recommended to modify his manner.

But Jessop made no attempts to amend his ways and continued on his genial course of terror. A year later, on a bad wicket at

Gloucester, a Warwickshire batsman was so intimidated that, in Brodribb's words, 'he used to yelp every time he thought the ball was going to rise and hit him'. C. L. Townsend, who played with him for many years in the Gloucestershire side, said, 'I never saw Jessop bowl at a man in his life,' adding, 'Such a thing was not done in my day, thank goodness.' But then Townsend was writing in 1934, when most members of the 'old school' were keen to dissociate themselves from bodyline.

According to David Frith, leg-theory was already embryonic on the eve of the First World War. In 1913, Warwickshire played four fast bowlers: Field, Foster, Jeeves and Howell. F. R. Foster was the pick of them: 'Six feet tall, fast left-arm, with a high, fluid action, he swung the ball prodigiously from around the wicket, was exceedingly fast off the pitch, and claimed many of his wickets in the leg-trap of close catchers.'* Combined with the surly genius of S. F. Barnes, Foster made up one of England's greatest opening attacks. On the tour to Australia in 1911–12, they took 66 wickets between them, Foster 32 at an average of 21.62, Barnes 34 at 22.88.

There were other lesser but equally dangerous bowlers in the pre-war period, including William Baumont Burns and Neville Knox. That pace represented a real threat to life and limb, whatever the bowler's intentions, was acknowledged by the Middlesex batsman Cyril Foley in an article he wrote denouncing the open, 'two-eyed' stance. He cites an innings of his own against Burns and Knox:

> The wicket was rough, and I do believe that had I adopted the two-eyed stance I should have been killed twice and permanently injured four times, if you follow me. Balls grazing my eyebrows would have hit me in the eye; balls that hit me on the shoulder would have hit me on the heart; balls that hit me on the thigh would have hit me elsewhere, and so on . . . In my humble opinion bowling at the batsman *in order to get him out* is a justifiable and unavoidable challenge to the two-eyed stance.

*Foster was happy to give Jardine advice on field placing before the 1932–3 tour, but was unhappy with the outcome, writing to Australian friends, 'I am sorry my experience and advice were put to such an unworthy use.'

This is remarkably candid coming from a batsman. But Foley hadn't finished: 'the bowler bowls at the batsman, for the very good reason that there is nothing else for him to bowl at. If the bowler happens to bowl short and fast the batsman says it is dangerous. So it is – damnably. But whose fault is that?'

After the great blood-letting of the First World War, English cricket seemed positively anaemic. Australia bounced back with far more vigour, and in Jack Gregory and Ted McDonald, produced the game's next great fast-bowling double act. They were first paired half-way through the 1920–1 series against J. W. H. T. Douglas's side, but really came into their own in the English summer of 1921. They took 16 wickets between them in the first Test at Trent Bridge, and carried on in similar vein to take 46 wickets and help Australia win the rubber 3–0 and retain the Ashes.

McDonald and Gregory were magnificent bowlers, both highly skilled and extremely fast. Under Warwick Armstrong's unsentimental captaincy, they did not take many prisoners. Notable victims included Ernest Tyldesley, hit in the face by a lifter from McDonald in the first Test; Tyldesley's fellow Lancastrian J. R. Barnes, who was also hit on the head; P. A. Perrin of Essex got one in the stomach; and during the last Test, England's Lionel Tennyson was struck over the heart, holding play up for a considerable time until he was fit, or at least able, to continue.

A professional soldier who had seen action from the earliest days in 1914, Tennyson was clearly in his element in cricket's equivalent of the front line. He had been drafted in for the Lord's Test to inject some spirit into an England team reeling after its sixth consecutive defeat by the Australians. Having failed in the first innings, Tennyson simply refused to concede an inch to the Australian fast men and scored 74 not out, at the end of which he was 'black and blue all over'. It was an innings to compare with Brian Close's act of aggressive defiance against the West Indian pacemen on the same ground in 1963.

For the third Test at Leeds, Tennyson was promoted to captain and produced more heroics. He split the webbing of his left thumb and forefinger while fielding, but nevertheless decided to bat. Playing with only one hand, he managed the second top

1 W. G. Grace: steered a piratical course through Victorian cricket

2 Lord Frederick Beauclerk: the gaming cleric who ruled Lord's with an iron fist
3 William Lambert: banned from Lord's for throwing a match
4 Lord Harris: conducted a one-man campaign against throwing
5 Charles Kortright: a natural intimidator

ONE FOR THE UMPIRE.

TOM. B.

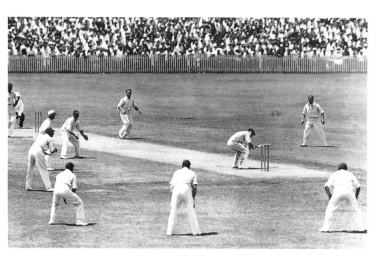

6 *One for the Umpire* by Tom Browne, the outstanding postcard painter of the
1900–1914 era
7 One for the batsman: Bradman ducks a bouncer from Larwood bowling to
the full bodyline field, Adelaide, 1932–3

8 Jack Ikin's catch that wasn't: first Test, England vs Australia, Brisbane, 1946.
'A damned fine way to start a series,' according to the England captain,
Wally Hammond
9 Ian Meckiff just before the call for throwing which was to put him out of
first-class cricket: Australia vs South Africa, Brisbane, 1963

10 N. J. Contractor, the Indian captain, felled by a Charlie Griffith special, Bridgetown, 1962

11 How low can you sink? Trevor Chappell's infamous underarm to prevent any chance of New Zealand hitting the six required to win a one-day international, MCG, 1981

12 Michael Holding shows all the grace of a supreme athlete in this act of
dissent: West Indies vs New Zealand, Dunedin, 1980
13 Merv Hughes, master of 'the art of sledging', giving Graeme Hick a few
things to think about on his way back to the pavilion:
England vs Australia, 1989

14 The classic confrontation between Mike Gatting and Shakoor Rana, Faisalabad, 1987

15 Jacques Kallis faces his accusers Hussain, Tufnell and Adams,
Port Elizabeth, 1999
16 Hansie holds his hand up: the disgraced former South African captain,
Hansie Cronje, before the King Commission, 21 June 2000

score of 63. He got through the fourth Test at Old Trafford unscathed, but was back in the firing line at the Oval. Facing Gregory and McDonald required great nerve, and though he led by example, Tennyson was not altogether successful in inspiring courage in others. As he wrote in his autobiography, 'I remember one amateur who played for England being so nervous that he could hardly hold his bat, while his knees were literally knocking together. I endeavoured to put some heart into him by a few timely words when I joined him at the wicket, but it was useless; his nerve was gone, and the first straight ball was enough for him.' The lesson that the physical threat of fast bowling produced cumulative psychological strain was not lost on the Australians' hosts – though it would be some time before they could retaliate in kind. Bill Voce was not the only one to justify bodyline by claiming he and Larwood were only imitating the concentrated hostility of McDonald and Gregory.

English batsmen may have heaved a sigh of relief when the Australians boarded the boat in 1921, but they were going to see a lot more of Ted McDonald. Taking up the lucrative offer of Nelson CC to play in the Lancashire League, the Australian settled in England, qualified for Lancashire, and played for them from 1924 and 1931, taking over 1,000 wickets. Never a comfortable proposition, when the mood took him he could be the very devil. Neville Cardus suggests something of his menace in the description of him running 'along a sinister curve, lithe as a panther, his whole body moving like visible, dangerous music'.

A terror to batsmen, he was revered by fellow fast bowlers. Bill Bowes, for instance, never forgot McDonald's words after Holmes and Sutcliffe had put on 323 for Yorkshire against Lancashire in 1931. 'You see what happens when they get things their way. They rub it in. There's no mercy. When things go your way, have no mercy. Give 'em hell and they'll think more of you for doing it.' Bowes took the advice to heart, admitting, 'I never said "sorry" to a batsman whom I had hit; never went to inquire how he was. I tried to keep my face expressionless at all times.'

Bowes was not the only one to follow the example of Gregory and McDonald. 1928 saw something of a speed war between Larwood and the West Indian Learie Constantine. According to Frank Chester, Constantine's opening salvo in the first Test at

Lord's was as quick as anything seen in England since the days of Kortright and Ernest Jones. He may have said so to Larwood, because when the visitors batted the Nottinghamshire paceman produced an even quicker spell, hitting Martin on the head, and rearranging the headgear of another West Indian batsman. Though deprecated by the doyens of English batting, Jack Hobbs and Wally Hammond, who understandably would have preferred to go about their majestic business without short-pitched deliveries flying around their ears, this duel between the fast bowlers injected a bit of interest into a somewhat one-sided series.

Constantine did not hold back in county matches. R. E. S. Wyatt going out to bat for Warwickshire against the tourists at Edgbaston passed the previous batsman coming back into the pavilion unconscious on a stretcher. Unabashed, the West Indian paceman greeted him with two ferocious bouncers which both glanced off his head to the boundary.

The West Indies had a potent weapon in Constantine but they were reluctant to use him as ruthlessly as Jardine was prepared to use Larwood. When the West Indies went to Australia in 1930–1, Constantine bowled a few short ones at Ponsford, and found himself taken off immediately. The requirements for a bumper war were not simply bowlers capable of the pace and ferocity to deliver, but captains prepared to unleash them, and G. C. Grant, the West Indies captain, would have none of it. The series in Australia passed off peaceably – the lull before the bodyline storm.

The new post-bodyline period lasted until the end of the 1930s. With Larwood in disgrace, England were deprived of the best strike bowler in the world, and so sensitive were relations on the next tour that even those fast bowlers that were sent (including Bill Voce) felt constrained to keep the ball up, depriving them of even the occasional shock tactic of a bouncer. (England, under Gubby Allen, still managed to surprise everybody by winning the first two Tests, only for Bradman to regain form and sweep his side to victory in the remaining three. It was a great series, and everything anyone could have required on the diplomatic front.)

Just as after the Armistice, Australia emerged from the Sec-

ond World War with a new and formidable fast-bowling partnership: Ray Lindwall and Keith Miller. Lindwall had been
cricket-mad as a boy, and just as Spofforth was inspired by
watching Tarrant bowl, so Lindwall wanted to emulate Larwood. Miller had been a fighter pilot based in Britain, and
never lost his cavalier approach to life. One of the game's great
natural talents, he could be an inspiration with either bat or
ball. But for all his *joie de vivre*, he played the game hard, and
both he and Lindwall attracted plenty of odium for their use of
the bouncer.

In 1948, the duo were a vital component of Bradman's all-
conquering machine (especially as a revised ruling gave the fielding captain a new ball after only 55 overs) and sent shudders of
apprehension through changing-rooms up and down the country. The Middlesex batsman Jack Robertson found himself in
hospital after being hit in the face by a ball from Lindwall, while
in the third Test at Old Trafford, Denis Compton was subjected
to a succession of bouncers from Lindwall, one of which – a no-
ball – he mis-hit on to his forehead. Miller had shown a similar
enthusiasm for short-pitched deliveries in the first Test. This was
at Trent Bridge, the home of bodyline, and in fact the last venue
where it had ever been practised against an Australian team.
Late on the Saturday, when the light was bad, Miller bowled five
bouncers in eight balls at Hutton, hitting him high up on the
arm, and getting so vigorously barracked by sections of the
crowd that, before play resumed on Monday morning, an
appeal to leave the conduct of the game to the umpires was
made over the public-address system.

Wisden took its traditional dim view of the fast bowlers' tactics. Having credited Lindwall with constituting 'the single
biggest weapon on either side', the almanack went on to say of
Miller that, although he caused 'no comparable physical damage', his bumpers provoked a more vocal response from the
crowds. 'His habit of wheeling round, flying into an abnormally
fast start and tossing back his head before releasing the ball gave
an impression that petulance more than cricket tactics dictated
his methods at such times.' And there were Australian voices
expressing doubts as well. Bill O'Reilly, Bradman's long-standing antagonist, remained critical to the end, damning the over-

use of the bouncer as identical to bodyline except for the packed leg-side field.

With the Don producing runs in volume right up to that dramatic second-ball duck in his last appearance at the Oval, Australia would have beaten England in 1948 even if their fast bowlers had kept the ball right up to the batsmen. The same cannot be said about the series between Australia and the West Indies in 1951–2. The short ball was a deliberate part of the Australian strategy as a counter to the imperial splendour of the visitors' batting. Post-Bradman, no side could match a middle order of Worrell, Weekes and Walcott, and these legendary stroke-makers were subjected to a bumper barrage.

The contrast between the two sides was heightened by the fact that the West Indies relied heavily for their wickets on the spinners, Sonny Ramadhin and Alf Valentine, and although they bowled tidily and for long spells, they were simply no answer to Lindwall and Miller. With the exception of the surprise collapse (to Frank Worrell's seamers) on a rain-affected pitch in the third Test, Australia maintained the upper hand throughout.

They did not, however, occupy the moral high ground. Even with the series decided, there was no let-up for the batsmen. The fifth Test at Sydney saw Lindwall just as aggressive as at the start, and on the last day he bowled with true venom. The West Indies began the day on 112 for 2, chasing an improbable 416 to win. Jeff Stollmeyer and Everton Weekes were the not out batsmen, and, according to Lindwall's biographer John Ringwood, faced 'perhaps the most hostile attack seen since the Bodyline days'. In one over Lindwall bounced Weekes four times, tempting him to hook, while the batsman's captain, standing at the other end, insisted that he resist the temptation. In the end, caught between instinct and caution, the great batsman succumbed, top-edging a nothing shot to give an easy catch to the keeper. That signalled the beginning of the end, and the whole team were bowled out for 213.

For those with long memories it was a throwback to 1932–3. The radio commentator Alan McGilvray expressed concern at what he was witnessing, while Bill O'Reilly in the press box was adamant in his condemnation, recalling years after the event: 'I was completely unhappy. I was unhappy with Ray Lindwall and

I let all the people know that I was unhappy. And when he spoke to me about it I told him then, too, that I was very unhappy about it. I didn't think he'd ever do it.'

At the time, O'Reilly wrote in his column that he thought the umpires should have stepped in, invoking the law against the use of 'systematic short-pitched balls'. With two short legs, and a man on the leg-side boundary, Lindwall was operating as near to Larwood's formula as possible, and to a veteran of the body-line series, it was unacceptable. O'Reilly warned that it wouldn't be long before 'the same stuff is bowled back to us. That will happen as soon as another country has bowlers fast enough to do it.'[*] This was to prove all too prescient. As David Frith notes, 'No Test series ends with the final ball: when West Indies had the fire-power in later years they used it – without hesitation. There are no treaties in international cricket.' When it finally came, the great West Indian fast-bowling juggernaut of four rotated pace-men would crush everything in its path.

But there were a lot of bruised rib-cages and cracked bones before that ultimate batsman's nightmare. England at last found reinforcements for the tireless Alec Bedser. Fred Trueman ter-rorised the Indians of 1952, reducing them to 58 all out at Man-chester in the third Test, with personal figures of 8 for 31. Always keen to live up to his nickname 'Fiery', Trueman gained a reputation for surliness and insensitivity. He made himself highly unpopular on the 1953–4 tour to the West Indies. On one occasion he struck the legendary George Headley a painful blow on the elbow, and then, as the rest of the team approached the stricken batsman, walked pointedly back to his mark. Even his hard-bitten captain Len Hutton was critical: 'In my view, any bowler who bowls a ball which hits a batsman should show con-cern about the nature and extent of any injury,' and admitted that 'frankly, to me in the West Indies, he was something of a problem child'.

With this reputation as a troublesome tourist established, Trueman was left out of the party to Australia the following

[*] Lindwall vigorously defended himself against the charge, claiming he was simply exploiting Weekes' position. The batsman himself concurred: 'He's perfectly right. Beautiful psychology – having me caught between instinct and instructions . . . I wasn't intimidated; nothing like that.'

winter (1954–5). Strangely, he wasn't missed. His replacement, a 'broad-shouldered, balding, scholarly-looking man', arrived in Australia as a virtual unknown. By the end of the series his name was on everybody's lips, often coupled with the nickname 'Typhoon'. Frank Tyson didn't have the staying power of a Trueman or Statham, but for one glorious tour he reached the heights of greatness, spreading panic through Australian dressing-rooms.

As Tyson later wrote, 'No batsman likes quick bowling, and this knowledge gives one a sense of omnipotence.' On Australian wickets Tyson was frighteningly fast, but he started the tour something of a novice. After the first Test, in which he took 1 for 160, he had a conversation with Ray Lindwall during which he admitted he didn't know how to bowl an effective bouncer. Lindwall generously offered to show him when the occasion arose. Lindwall chose the second Test at Sydney for his tutorial, but did neither himself nor his colleagues any favours when he had the Northamptonshire man carried off in the second innings. As the South Africans discovered forty years later when they disturbed the sleeping giant Devon Malcolm, if there's one way to get the best out of the opposition fast bowler, it is to hit him on the head with a bumper. Sporting a lump the size of an egg on the back of his head, Tyson steamed into the attack in Australia's second innings, and the relatively modest target of 223 for victory and a two-match lead in the series suddenly began to seem out of reach. Tyson turned the game and the series with a return of 6 for 85, and did even better at Melbourne, where he took 7 for 27 on a sporting wicket to give England the third Test and lay the foundation for a series win.

As we have seen, the later 1950s and early 1960s were dominated by the problem of throwing, but for all the attention focused on Ian Meckiff, Geoff Griffin and Charlie Griffith, there was a great deal of brutish bowling by those with straight arms. Wesley Hall, hailed for the near-perfection of his run-up and delivery, was widely regarded as relying too heavily on the short-pitched ball. Cricket writers like Ian Wooldridge made no distinctions between Hall and Griffith, whom he described at the start of the 1963 series as 'two huge hired assassins'. It was

Hall, not Griffith, who broke Colin Cowdrey's arm in the second Test at Lord's.

Cowdrey was batting on the fifth day when the light, in his words, 'had diminished to a heavy grey gloom'. He had reached 19 when

> Hall switched round to bowl from the pavilion end where, in those days, there was no sight screen. He let loose two very nasty ones and then, by chance, pitched one only just short of a length. It reared straight up and would have struck me under the chin at full speed had I not flung up my left arm in an instinctive parry.

Cowdrey's 'by chance' is typically generous.

On that extraordinary last day, Brian Close took the fight to the assassins, giving both fast bowlers the charge. They saw to it that his audacity did not go unpunished, and he returned to the dressing-room with a portfolio of bruises. The 70 that Close pillaged on his foolhardy raid kept England in with a chance, and also ensured that when the ninth wicket fell in the last over, Cowdrey made his unforgettable way through the MCC members with his hand in plaster to watch, from the safety of the bowler's end, David Allen keep out Hall's last two deliveries. No one knows what Cowdrey would have been required to deal with had he been on strike.

It probably isn't true to say that there was a changing attitude among fast bowlers in the post-war period. Fast bowlers have always known they carried a potentially lethal weapon in their hand, and few can have resisted the temptation to use their speed on occasion in a retaliatory or intimidatory way. Jim Laker records Peter Heine's snarl of frustration to England's makeshift opener on the 1956–7 tour to South Africa – 'I want to hit you, Bailey . . . I want to hit you over the heart' – but he would hardly have admitted to such sentiments in a press conference. But from the 1970s on, the fast men became less reticent about their aggressive agenda.

John Snow, who followed Frank Tyson in effectively settling an Australian Ashes series through sheer pace, declared:

> I'm not ashamed of leaving a trail of fractures among the

opposition – a finger, a thumb, a whole right hand and one foot on the latest count. After all, that's what I'm there for. Not to inflict deliberate injury, of course, but to rough up a batsman, make them apprehensive and destroy their confidence. I never let them forget the game is played with a very hard ball.

In 1970–1, Snow's use of the bouncer, especially when bowled from round the wicket, disconcerted Australian batsmen and infuriated Australian crowds. In the fourth Test, he forced his fellow fast bowler Garth McKenzie to retire hurt with a bad face wound from one that lifted from a length, and in the final Test a month later dealt another tail-ender, Terry Jenner, a sickening blow on the head with a bouncer. This brought warnings from the umpire, hotly contested by both Ray Illingworth and Snow, who claimed he was simply bowling rib-ticklers. The crowd saw it differently and the fast bowler was met by a hail of beer cans when he returned to his position near the boundary. His shirt was also grabbed by a spectator, and Illingworth took his team off the field until officials warned him he was in danger of forfeiting the match. Snow later injured his hand on the fence and so could not bowl in the second innings, but he still finished with 31 wickets in the series, and 24 of those were top-order batsmen.

At home in county cricket Snow was a far less awesome prospect, unless he was riled. There were certain batsmen who could stir him out of his lethargy, and Geoffrey Boycott was one. As England team-mates the two had nearly come to blows on the West Indies tour of 1967–8. At Hove in 1969, Boycott's goading coupled with his refusal to walk when he clearly gloved a catch to Jim Parks produced a sensational riposte. Boycott played the next ball away for runs, and when he got up to Snow's end, gave the bowler a tap on the legs with his bat. Snow swung round and kicked the bat away, causing Boycott to stumble on his way to a second run. Snow then announced that he was coming round the wicket. His intention was unmistakable, and the result, according to Jim Parks, was 'the best bouncer I have ever seen in my life. It was perfect, chest high, straight into Geoff who had to protect himself with his left hand.' The resultant fracture caused Boycott to miss the rest of the season, including a Gillette Cup Final.

Illingworth's success in 1970–1 produced such a tide of euphoria that little notice was taken of a significant début in the penultimate Test of the series, that of D. K. Lillee. He took a creditable 5 for 84, but England nevertheless made a commanding 470. When Australia came to England to try to retrieve the Ashes in 1972, Lillee announced himself by causing Boycott to retire for a while on the first morning of the first Test, and went on to establish himself as the tourists' leading bowler with a haul of 31 wickets, a record for Australia in England. However, back trouble threatened his career, and on his come-back it was assumed that his pace would be reduced. Mike Denness's team set off for the 1974–5 series confident of retaining the Ashes. None of them had heard of Jeff Thomson.

The new-boy Thommo took 9 wickets in the first Test at Brisbane, and with a revived Lillee simply blasted England out of contention. Friends rather than rivals, the two fast bowlers were great showmen, and they made no secret of the joys of being the world's top fast-bowling combination. These were no hired assassins; they did it for the sheer love of it. In his book *Back to the Mark*, published before the series began, Lillee announced: 'I bowl bouncers for one reason, and that is to hit the batsman and thus intimidate him . . . I try to hit a batsman in the rib cage when I bowl a purposeful bouncer, and I want it to hurt so much that the batsman doesn't want to face me anymore . . . not many batsmen recover from a really good bouncer.' Thomson struck a less reflective note in a magazine interview: 'The sound of the ball hitting the batsman's skull was music to my ears.'

The change that overtook cricket in the 1970s is generally associated with the Packer revolution, which deliberately played up the gladiatorial aspects of the game. While it remained a non-contact sport, Kerry Packer's circus was not for the faint-hearted as batteries of fast bowlers were incited to make batsmen hop about the crease. According to Simon Wilde, Packer 'was the godfather of fast bowlers'. But like all successful revolutions, Packer's was climbing on a bandwagon which was already in motion. In 1974–5, Lillee and Thomson were doing all the things Packer would demand. The crowds were chanting 'Lill-ee,

Lill-ee, Lill-ee' and 'Kill, kill, kill, kill' as the bowlers ran in to bowl, and the two stars of the mayhem were also talking up a storm in the media. On the eve of the first Test in Brisbane, Lillee went on television to explain clinically – or cynically – which parts of the body he targeted when bowling short to a batsman. Mike Denness, England's unfortunate captain, complained in his book *I Declare*, 'if people are allowed to perform in this frame of mind, spectators could be encouraged to come along just to see a bit of blood and thunder. I don't think cricket fans really want to see a lot of people being hit on the head or going down with broken ribs.'

The evidence pointed the other way. The Australian crowds revelled in their heroes' aggression and in the damage they inflicted. The roll-call of walking wounded was impressive. Dennis Amiss and Bill Edrich had their hands broken; David Lloyd's box was, in his own words, 'completely inverted'; Luckhurst, Fred Titmus and Derek Underwood all took crunching blows; and Thomson got a ball to cannon into the covers via Keith Fletcher's skull. Lillee bowled a beamer at Bob Willis, while the bumper he bowled at Geoff Arnold was described by Jim Laker as the most vicious ball he had ever seen. Willis, Underwood and Arnold were all established tail-enders.

But it wasn't just the Australians who tore up the unwritten treaty sparing lower-order batsmen from the short stuff. In the first Test Peter Lever had let fly three bouncers in a row at Terry Jenner, the man John Snow had felled on the previous MCC tour. On this occasion, Lever was warned by the umpire, but generally, like negligent schoolmasters ignoring fights in the playground, the officials let the players mete out their own rough justice.

After the injuries sustained by Amiss and Edrich in the first Test, Colin Cowdrey was flown out as a replacement on the eve of his forty-second birthday for his sixth tour of Australia. He found himself forced straight into the firing line, batting at number three in England's first innings in the second Test after barely half a week's acclimatisation. Intensive nets and judicious exposure to the burning sun could offer little preparation for facing the world's fastest bowling combination on Australia's fastest pitch, the WACA, Perth.

It is the stuff of cricket mythology that, in the middle of the blitzkrieg that met him on his return to the Test arena, Cowdrey took the opportunity of a drinks break to introduce himself to Thomson. Thommo, who had responded to the announcement that Cowdrey was on his way with the gangster-like one-liner 'He'll cop it as quick as anyone!', bemusedly shook the hand offered before returning to the task of roughing up England's avuncular veteran.

Though the reflexes that had allowed him to take centuries off the likes of Hall and Griffith a decade before had slowed so that he was limited to watchful, and often painful, defence, Cowdrey showed no diminution of courage. Those that saw him at Melbourne where he made his highest score, 35, in the third Test, remember him being hit time and time again as he stuck doggedly to his task.

It was Cowdrey who had pioneered some rudimentary body protection on earlier tours to the West Indies, but now he and the other English batsmen resorted to a full range of protective clothing. Denness recalls, 'never before had I seen such a variety of armour as was available at Perth . . . There were forearm shields and chest and rib protectors, made from polystyrene material which, although clinging quite tightly to the body, allowed one to move comfortably.' It is interesting that even then the idea of 'crash helmets and face masks' would, according to Denness, have indicated that the tourists were 'scared'. It is astonishing how long that attitude held sway, but its days were numbered.

The year after he got back from Australia, Cowdrey wrote about short-pitched fast bowling in his memoir M. C. C. Despite his equable tone and scrupulous even-handedness, he was unmistakably critical of the modern trend:

> Today, if there is any semblance of pace in the wicket one comes to expect a bouncer three or four balls an over – even more at times. This then becomes intimidatory bowling, contravening the law, and it has been terribly difficult for the umpire to intervene and adjudicate fairly. Where there are too many bouncers bowled, tempers fray and bad blood is spilt.

Actually, of course, it is perfectly good blood that is spilt, and *that* is what generates the bad blood.

Ironically, it was an England fast bowler's assault on a tail-ender that came closest to producing a fatality on the 1974–5 tour. After their battering at the hands of Lillee and Thomson, the MCC party flew on to New Zealand for what they trusted would be an altogether easier encounter. This it proved, with the batsmen coming out of their bunkers, blinking in the benign sunlight of Eden Park, Auckland, before running stylishly amok, with the pair who had lost form and face against the extreme speed leading the way: Denness 181, Fletcher 216. England total: 593.

New Zealand were bowled out for 326 and asked to follow on. They were failing comfortably to make England bat again when Ewen Chatfield, the number eleven, playing his first Test match, joined the middle order batsman Graham Howarth on the fourth evening of the match. They stuck it out to stumps and pushed the match into its fifth day. This was Tuesday 25 February 1975. Not one of the players or spectators scattered around the ground to witness England complete the innocuous task of taking the last wicket could have guessed they would be present at one of the most alarming incidents in just over a century of first-class cricket.

Chatfield was obviously enjoying his unexpectedly extended innings and was determined to continue in the same vein. Eventually English patience ran out, and Peter Lever let him have a short one. It was the near-perfect bouncer, exemplifying all the attributes Lillee had publicly commended – nasty, brutish and short. Chatfield coped with it to the extent of getting a glove on it, but only succeeded in deflecting it on to his temple. He collapsed near the wicket, twitching alarmingly, and for an agonising moment his heart stopped beating. His life was saved by the prompt action of the MCC physiotherapist Bernard Thomas and the local St John's Ambulance man, who gave immediate mouth-to-mouth resuscitation and heart massage.

Chatfield was taken to hospital, the end of his innings officially recorded as 'retired hurt'. It had been an extremely narrow escape – and no one felt more relief than Lever, who must have experienced many of Jack Platts' emotions when he felled

George Summers. He was reduced to tears, knowing full well that in his frustrated desire to clear the last obstacle out of England's way, he had deliberately bowled a ball beyond the competence of the batsman.

While Lever struggled with his conscience, the wider world indulged in a spate of regret, condemnation, demands for a limit on bouncers, and suggestions for sensible protective clothing. But for all the public hand-wringing, those who had pace in their armoury were not inclined towards disarmament. When the West Indies followed England to Australia in 1975–6, they received exactly the same welcome at the hands of Lillee and Thomson. Alvin Kallicharran had his nose broken by a bumper from Lillee, and then took a blow to the back of the head from Thomson which made him throw up by the side of the wicket. The hosts won by five Tests to one, and although the series had seen Lance Gibbs, the West Indian off-spinner, pass Trueman's record Test wicket haul of 307, Clive Lloyd was left in no doubt that the way to fight fire was with fire.

Fast bowling was doubly effective against opposition that didn't have any. When the Indians toured the Caribbean in the spring of 1976, their triumvirate of spinners, Bishen Bedi, B. S. Chandrasekhar and Srinivas Venkataraghavan, helped them win the third Test and square the series 1–1, but their powerful batting was no match for the naked aggression of the West Indian pace attack when they played the decider on a pitch of unpredictable bounce at Sabina Park, Jamaica. Michael Holding in particular relied heavily on short-pitched deliveries, and three batsmen were injured in India's first innings: Viswanath had a finger broken when he was caught, Gaekwad spent two days in hospital after being struck on the head, and Patel had to have stitches in his mouth. The Indian captain Bedi was so disgusted that he declared to save his tail-enders, himself included, from being exposed to what he saw was concerted intimidation, and in the second innings, India ceded the match with only 5 wickets down. It was, as Simon Wilde notes in *Letting Rip*, 'the nearest anyone has ever come to surrendering a Test match'.

The West Indies toured England later in the year, and the pattern of four fast bowlers – Andy Roberts, Holding, Wayne Daniel and Vanburn Holder – rotating, slowly, throughout the day was established. Tony Greig's pledge to make the visitors 'grovel' was hardly an incentive to tone down the aggression, but the ferocity of the all-pace attack revived the doubts expressed by the Revd Pycroft in the nineteenth century: could cricket involving such high risks of serious physical injury still be classed as a game? The England captain, with his matador psychology, was never happier than when goading opponents into trying to kill or maim him, but even he must have had moments of wondering what on earth he was doing at the crease. He recalls hitting Holding back over his head for four at Lord's and receiving a beamer in reply. This was beyond the bounds of what even Greig considered acceptable: 'I was angry enough to throw my bat down and words were passed both on the field and afterwards.'

The hostility reached a peak at Old Trafford when England's ageing openers Edrich and Close were peppered with short deliveries in an eighty-minute passage of play on the Saturday evening. Close, back in harness at the age of forty-five, was hit so many times that he needed pain-killing injections before he could even contemplate lying down that night. His colleagues, peering out into the gloom praying that a wicket didn't fall, were awestruck into silence. Bob Willis, no stranger to the power of pace, said it was 'the most sustained barrage of intimidation' he had ever seen. Holding was eventually warned by umpire Bill Alley, and the West Indies manager Clyde Walcott condemned the excessive use of short-pitched bowling. Even Clive Lloyd admitted, 'Our fellows got carried away.'

Even so, Lloyd had no intention of changing a winning formula. An anarchic spirit was at large, and, in Simon Wilde's words, 'teams roamed the cricket grounds of the world committing violent and bloody deeds'.

CHAPTER 10

Sledging: The Verbal Battle

Those who saw cricket declining into aggressive mean-spirited-ness in the 1970s could point to a new development, or at least, a new word: 'sledging'. Mike Brearley describes sledging as 'the use of language to abuse or intimidate an opponent . . . a totally unwelcome aberration in the game, inane, humourless and unacceptable'. John Eddowes is equally scathing in his *The Language of Cricket*: 'oaf's parlette: the verbal harassment and insult of a batsman by the bowler, wicket-keeper or fielders'. For its derivation, he quotes Ian Chappell, who dates it to an occasion when the fast bowler Grahame Corling swore in front of a waitress and was told he was 'as subtle as a sledgehammer'; the expression transferred easily from using bad language in front of a woman to directing it at your opponents on the cricket field.

Whatever its etymology, Chappell is widely credited with encouraging the teams he captained to use sledging systematically as a weapon of psychological warfare, and since the 1970s it has become integral to the Australian win-at-all-costs mentality. Dennis Lillee was a notable practitioner. Bob Woolmer recently recalled for radio listeners his marathon innings in the Oval Test of 1975. Intent only on saving the match, he started the final day with a trio of edges through the slips off the Australian paceman before settling in and grinding out the slowest Ashes century made by an Englishman (six hours thirty-six minutes), during the course of which, he said, he became fully acquainted with the Australian alphabet: 'It started with f and ended with f.' Viv Richards, who also played against Chappell's all-powerful team that winter, has similar memories, pointing out how difficult it is to concentrate when someone is snarling 'Fuck off, you black bastard' as the bowler approaches the crease. As Henry Blofeld noted in his tour summary for *Wisden*, the home team were 'tougher opponents when the pressure was on [and] admirably single-minded about the job of winning'.

That same single-mindedness resurfaced at the end of the following decade, which had been marked by a sharp decline in the Australians' performance. Ian Botham remembers the 1989 series, when, after a second consecutive Ashes defeat, Allan Border returned to England with only one objective: victory. Criticised for an over-friendly relationship with the England cricketers in the past, he now 'made a definite decision to become Captain Grumpy' at the head of a team 'prepared to snarl, sledge and play dirty if necessary'. While fast bowlers Merv Hughes and Geoff Lawson were the leading sledgers, Border himself developed a streak of unpleasantness that took the England players by surprise. When Robin Smith asked for a drink while batting, Border responded, 'What do you think this is, a f***ing tea party? No, you can't have a glass of water. You can f***ing wait like all the rest of us.'

Smith displayed as much resolution as any during his England career, and it's unlikely that verbal aggression or gratuitous nastiness ever did much to undermine his resolve. But not all batsmen have the psychological strength to match their technical ability, and sledging is designed to expose that fallibility. According to Hughes, abuse is a necessary component of the fast bowler's arsenal: 'If he's mentally weak and I don't try to put pressure on that side of his game, then I'm not doing my job.' And no one took the job of bowling fast for Australia more seriously than he did. A particular target was Graeme Hick, and one photograph shows Hughes screaming at Hick from very close quarters even after he'd got him out – presumably as part of the softening-up process for the next innings.

Apart from those with a perceived lack of moral fibre, it's the novice who seems to be most aggressively targeted. Just as tyro hookers in rugby are welcomed to the front row with an upper-cut, so the new boy is singled out for a verbal going over. It's a rite of passage. Allan Donald was put through his initiation cer-

emony by Rodney Hogg when he played for the President's XI
against the rebel Australians in 1985–6:

> He lined me up in the second innings when I came out to bat.
> I was last man and the Aussies were looking for an early fin-
> ish . . . [Hogg] was unimpressed when I kept playing and miss-
> ing, then fluked a leg-side three. Hogg started to bowl
> bouncers at me and when another whizzed past my nose, he
> followed through to me and shouted in my face, 'Listen you
> little . . . , I'll bounce you back to f***ing school!' I was
> shocked, I'd never been sledged before, and I was so upset I
> thought I was going to burst into tears. I had no idea how to
> handle it, and Hogg kept bouncing and cursing me. That
> made me angry and I steeled myself not to get out to this rude
> guy.

As a result of this educational foray into the big boys' game,
Donald concluded that 'you need a bit of the bully in you to
dominate as a fast bowler. A touch of the Rodney Hoggs, in
fact.' It is rare for senior players to intervene to protect their
younger team-mates from what in any other context would be
called bullying, but in 1997, the West Indies vice-captain Brian
Lara took exception to the constant stream of abuse his young
partner Robert Samuels was subjected to during their stand of
208 in the fifth Test at Perth. Not only were acrimonious words
exchanged at the wicket, but Lara made his feelings abundantly
clear at that evening's press conference. (He continued his
aggressive defiance of the Australians by coming out as a runner
for his captain Courtney Walsh the following morning, which
caused another confrontation that had to be firmly defused by
the umpires.)

Even Australians have expressed doubts about the prevalence
of sledging and other forms of aggression in their game. As *Wisden* reported in 1980, the New South Wales Cricket Association
had become so concerned with falling standards of sportsmanship that they issued a firm reminder of the standards they
required:

> The game of cricket has long been known to epitomise the
> highest levels of conduct and sportsmanship. It is a competitive

game to be played in an atmosphere of comradeship and enjoyed by players, umpires and spectators alike.

Bad behaviour by players is bringing the game into disrepute. It is alienating public support and making it almost impossible to recruit and hold umpires.

This is followed by a list of unacceptable practices, among which are:
– Fieldsmen swearing at a batsman in an attempt to break his concentration.
– Fieldsmen directing a dismissed batsman to the pavilion with a torrent of abuse.

After noting that 'captains have a special responsibility to exercise control over their players in these matters', the message ends with a warning to those who step out of line: 'Let it be clear – the Association will not hesitate to impose severe penalties on any player reported for bad behaviour in the future. If you are a player reported by an umpire, then be prepared to watch your team from the sidelines.'

Unfortunately, despite such official utterances, echoed more recently by the ICC, the temptation of gaining the least psychological advantage from verbal aggression has been hard to resist. Tourists in a hotel in New Zealand were surprised to find a note thrust under their hotel-room door on the eve of a Test match reminding them of the need to verbally harass the opposition. Whoever had been distributing the notes for the Australians had got the wrong room number.

The phenomenally successful Glenn McGrath seems to have appointed himself Australia's strike sledger as well as their leading fast bowler. On the last Ashes tour of 1998–9, he pushed official tolerance to the limit, finally driving the series referee John Reid to take action in the fourth Test.

During the tour, Charles de Lisle interviewed Bob Hawke, Australia's former prime minister and a fanatical sports fan, who confessed to being 'troubled' by one aspect of the team's dedication to winning.

Hawke said he would like to see the team cut down on the 'sledging'. 'I still think it's important to play fair,' he said. 'I don't think our blokes have played unfairly, they've not cheated, but they push things reasonably hard on the pressure and at times they've gone over the top. For example, I've got enormous admiration for Glenn McGrath. He's a marvellous young man and a great bowler. But I think at times he does himself a little bit of a disservice by excess belligerence in a personal sort of sense.

Such 'excess' has not, of course, been a purely Australian preserve. Sledging is like spying, deplored as widely as it is practised. But some teams seem to integrate it into their approach to the game more readily than others. Since their return to international cricket in 1991, the South Africans have joined in with a will. As Brian McMillan, their militant all-rounder, put it:

> If you play against the Australians you can bash one another out on the field and have a beer afterwards. The English are a little different. If you give them a go they think you're the biggest so-and-so under the sun and they won't have a beer with you. You can abuse the Indians all day long, they just nod their heads and carry on.

It's unlikely that the Indians regard this as a weakness, but there are English voices suggesting the national team should be more aggressive. When England lost their fifth consecutive Ashes series in 1997, vice-captain – now captain – Nasser Hussain declared: 'We have to get a bit of nastiness into our game . . . In Australia, even in grade cricket, they are abusing you, rucking you and making it very clear that they want you back in the pavilion pretty quick.' Two years later, when England finally secured the position at the bottom of the Test league table by losing a home series to New Zealand for the first time ever, Christopher Martin-Jenkins noted ruefully of the Lord's match that, in addition to being out-played, they had also been 'out-sledged'.

But the idea that the English game is endemically too soft is not entirely well-founded, any more than the notion that sledging only came into cricket in the 1970s. That decade may have brought more of it and given it a name; but it was not invented then. The deliberate undermining of morale, confidence and concentration by means of sustained verbal assault has a long and far from glorious history. One of the many cricketers interviewed by David Marshall for his book *Gentlemen and Players* was Don Kenyon, Worcestershire's captain in the 1950s. He recalled batting with the novice Peter Richardson in the latter's first match against Glamorgan. The Welsh team's captain was Wilf Wooler, who

> stationed himself very close in at forward short-leg and began to give [Richardson] his famous tongue-lashing. After an over or two, Peter came down the wicket to me and said, 'What do I do with this chap? He's talking non-stop and cursing me up hill and down dale and suggesting that I'm lacking in many things as well as my batting.' So I, knowing Wilf, just said, 'There's only one way and that's to give it straight back to him. If he curses you, you curse straight back at him and make it worse. On top of that, you might apologize to him in advance by saying that your hands get rather sweaty when you're batting and it's quite possible that you may lose control of the bat and if it should come flying out and hit him in a vulnerable spot you know he'll understand.'

A much more serious case from the same halcyon decade involved the West Indies when they played Surrey on their tour of 1957. In those days counties put their strongest sides out against tourists, rather than resting their stars, and Surrey had four players – Peter May, Jim Laker, Tony Lock and Peter Loader – who had helped England win the fourth Test just four days previously, along with Micky Stewart, Ken Barrington and both Bedser twins. This was the nucleus of the side that won the championship seven years in a row, and they regarded themselves as a match for any visiting side. The year before, they had humiliated the Australians as Laker took 10 wickets in an innings, and they were not prepared to lose to the West Indies – at least not graciously.

May set the visitors 270 to get in five hours twenty minutes, and as *Wisden* put it, 'their chances of success appeared slender'. However, thanks to a good second-wicket partnership between Gary Sobers and A. G. Ganteaume, they had the foundations for an assault on the target. In the end they romped home with relative ease thanks to an unbroken stand between Clyde Walcott and Frank Worrell of 137 in an hour and three-quarters.

This should have been one of the most memorably happy

passages of the tour, but in fact, as Worrell makes very clear in his memoir, it was a miserable time, made so by the increasingly heavy barrage of abuse that built up as it became apparent the visitors were going to win. According to Worrell, May had made a sporting declaration, and while doing everything in his power to win the match, was perfectly happy to take the result if the visitors were good enough to get the runs. But to the rest of the team, 'victory was everything, and they apparently were not interested in giving the public an exhibition of cricket'.

The mood, as so often, was soured by an umpiring decision. Worrell was caught at slip off his thigh, and given not out.

One of the Surrey players said to me, 'Why don't you so-and-so's go when you play the ball?' . . . Throughout the whole innings we had to put up with this barracking from the Surrey players. For the first time in my life I went through an innings without talking to any of the fielding side, and things got so bad that I did not even exchange any conversation with Clyde Walcott . . . We were abused when the players were changing ends at the finish of each over, and while few of the remarks were addressed directly to either Walcott or me, the Surrey players made certain that we heard them . . . and that we knew whom they were talking about. The incessant talking even went on among the close-in fielders while the bowler was running up to bowl! And if that didn't unsettle us, the Surrey players appealed for anything and everything.

It was a nightmare, but it probably boomeranged on the Surrey lads, for the more they barracked the more Clyde and I resolved to stick where we were. True, Peter May tried to pull his side together, and more than once he told his men to 'steady on'. But the captain who handles the England side so well did not appear to get the same response from his own county on this occasion.

When West Indian supporters in the crowd started sensing victory and cheering the runs, the Surrey players got rattled and increased the verbal contribution. Worrell describes the remarks as 'colourful . . . and much more violent than anything that we had ever heard before during a game'. It is probably not too fanciful to read 'colourful' as a euphemism for racist.

In summary, Worrell declared,

The whole day was completely ruined as far as I was concerned, and I could not help thinking that if Surrey use the same tactics against some of the young and inexperienced players they meet in County Championship matches it is little wonder that some sides collapse against their attack. For this incessant barracking and chattering is a greater weapon even than Jim Laker and Tony Lock at their best. After all, if they will behave as they did against us in an exhibition match, I shudder to think what they do when vital championship points are at stake. We all got the feeling that *Surrey want to be appellants, judges and jury* in their own cases.

The entire West Indian touring party was shattered by this experience. We never knew cricket could be played like that, and we began to wonder what sort of treatment we would have received if we had been winning in the Test series instead of being well beaten. Never in my life did I ever think I would advocate giving to cricket umpires the power of a football referee – the power to send a player off the field for the rest of the match – but my experience at the Oval has taught me that such a reform is necessary. If the umpires at the Oval had possessed such powers, some of the Surrey side would not have remained on the field!

If we had behaved half as badly as Surrey behaved on that last day we would have been dubbed as a lot of savages – and deservedly so. No wonder then I left the Oval that August as a very sad man. I could hardly believe – no, not even after what had happened in 1954 – that English cricketers could behave so badly, and the people I really felt sorry for were the well-behaved players, who must have been terribly embarrassed by this disgusting display of bad sportsmanship by a few of their colleagues.

And Worrell concludes with a gentle, but damning final judgement:

Now there is nothing wrong with wanting to win. There is nothing wrong with winning. But there is a lot wrong with getting so carried away by success that you can no longer play the game in the proper spirit, that you can no longer go through a day's cricket without swearing, abusing and bar-racking.

Surrey may go on winning championships, but after my experience at the Oval in 1957 I will never regard them as a good *cricket team*. In fact I will not even regard them as any sort of a *cricket team*.

For what happened at the Oval certainly was not cricket.[*]

But sledging – or barracking, as Worrell called it – was not an exclusively twentieth-century phenomenon. Verbal exchanges were no rarity in Victorian cricket, especially when any of the Grace clan were playing. All five Grace brothers were brought up playing with and against each other, no quarter given or asked for. And the habits formed as boys lasted them a lifetime.

The two worst offenders were W. G. and E. M., who both fielded close to the bat and whose constant commentary caused many a batsman's concentration to falter. In one match against Middlesex at Clifton, they goaded the visiting captain, Tim O'Brien, into direct action. It was in the days of 'off-theory' – over after over was bowled wide of the off stump, reducing the game to stalemate. On this occasion, the slow left-armer W. A. Woof was wheeling away outside the off stump and the Grace brothers were chatting away as usual. Gilbert Jessop takes up the story:

> Whether it was that O'Brien thought that proper concentra-tion was endangered by the persistent commentaries, or whether the wideness of the bowling produced an intense feel-ing of boredom is known to Tim alone: anyway he must have thought that the circumstances prevailing called for drastic action no matter how unorthodox, and it was pretty unortho-dox when eventually it did come, for upon the arrival of the next wide ball, Tim turned and hit it left-handed past the heads of the waiting fieldsmen in the slips.

According to C. D. Foley, who was playing in his first season for Middlesex, the man most endangered was E. M. 'W. G.,

---

[*]It is only fair to note that, in *Over to Me*, Jim Laker denies that the sledging was excessive, and claims that the disputed catch that sparked it off was defi-nitely out.

whose fraternal affection was aroused, said to O'Brien: "You mustn't do that, Tim, you'll kill my brother." O'Brien, who disliked E. M., replied: "And a good thing too," and promptly did it again, and W. G. marched off the field with his colleagues.' Foley's account ends with a stand-off between an outraged O'Brien waving a bat threateningly in the Gloucestershire changing-room, while E. M. took shelter behind his brother's massively interposed bulk.

There is no mention of this incident in J. R. Webber's magisterial *The Chronicle of W. G.*, and it looks as though the story must take its place in the Grace apocrypha. However, like most good stories about W. G., it has a kernel of truth. Few cricketers – if any – incited more fury in their opponents than the Graces, and if E. M. were the more abrasive of the two, W. G. took his shameless commitment to winning into more important arenas than county and club matches.

A case in point is the Oval Test of 1882 which, as a result of Australia's surprise win, gave birth to the Ashes. Grace's contribution, in luring the young Sammy Jones out of his ground with a nod and then running him out, was probably the most important factor in that victory – and it produced a vintage specimen of Australian sledging. Spofforth in particular was incensed, and he stormed into the English changing-room to tell Grace he was 'a bloody cheat' and abuse him vigorously 'in the best Australian vernacular for a full five minutes'.

Grace, thoroughly unperturbed, put his pads on and went out to start England's quest for the 85 runs they needed. When he arrived at the crease he was met by the one man in the game who could look down on him, the giant G. J. Bonnor, who, seconded by Tom Garrett, gave him another ear-bashing. The Champion's only recorded reply is his innings of 32, which should, under normal circumstances, have seen his side home. But these were not normal circumstances. Spofforth was inspired – 'Irresistible as an avalanche', as one team-mate put it – and swept England to defeat with figures of 7 for 44; a far more eloquent riposte to Grace's cynical gamesmanship than mere abuse.

CHAPTER 11

Umpires

———

Grace's action at the Oval in 1882 not only called down an unprecedented storm on the heads of his own team, but also put one man in a difficult position – Bob Thoms, the umpire. Thoms was one of the most respected of the Victorian umpires, and there was no suggestion of home bias in his decision. However, in the case in point – Jones's run-out – there were clearly two views; and there are two versions of Thoms's response. In the English version, Thoms had no doubts about the probity of the appeal and gave the decision without qualm, but according to Tom Horan, one of the Australians who was amazed by the decision, the umpire was at least reluctant to give Jones out, saying, 'If you claim it, sir, it is out.' Horan goes on to admit that 'In strict cricket no doubt Jones was out,' but expressed the general view of the visitors when he added, 'I do not think it redounds much to any man's credit to endeavour to win a match by resorting to what might not inaptly be termed sharp practice.'

This was by no means the only occasion in Grace's long cricketing life when umpires must have wished they were standing elsewhere. From a very early stage umpires showed a marked reluctance to give him out. As the apocryphal story has it, one of them told a disappointed bowler that the crowd had come to watch Grace bat, not him bowl. Occasionally an umpire could be found who was impervious to the great man's furrowed brow and ominous stare. Titchmarsh, the old Hertfordshire player, once gave him out lbw twice in the same match. Leaving the crease the first time, Grace shook his bat and said, 'A bad decision, Titchmarsh.' In the second innings, the finger went up even faster, followed by the audible commentary, 'I'm not so sure he *was* out that time, but I wasn't going to be told off by him.' When another old pro gave him out, W. G. squeaked in his comically high-pitched voice, 'Which leg did it hit, which leg did it hit?'

Of course, when there were other members of the family involved in a match, the umpires' predicament became even more uncomfortable. In one local match, W. G. was ranged against his brothers Henry and E. M. He hit a ball to the boundary, where it was caught. W. G. claimed the fielder carried the ball over the boundary; Henry and E.M. were vehement that the catch was fair. The umpire was caught in the force fields of three very powerful personalities, but in the end Henry pulled rank as the eldest brother with the command, 'Be a man and give him out.' Grace went, but with very poor grace. He made his views on E. M.'s judgement abundantly clear on a similar occasion when he told an umpire, 'Take no notice of *him*. It's when I appeal that it's out.'

For the most part, though, the brothers were on the same team (J. R. Webber found only *one* first-class match when they were on opposite sides), and so backed up each other's – frequent – appeals with gusto. This, like so much of their cricket, annoyed opponents greatly. The captain of Middlesex, I. D. Walker, became exasperated by Grace's persistent appeals from point, and remonstrated with him: 'You really should not appeal from point, W. G., as you can't possibly see from there.' Grace, quite unabashed, replied: 'I *shall* appeal, and so shall E. M.,' who, according to C. P. Foley, 'happened to be fielding at *square leg*!'

Grace took his uncompromising standards of sportsmanship with him wherever he went. His second tour to Australia in 1891–2, when he was forty-three and really should have known better, was a sorry catalogue of disputes with and relating to umpires. In the second Test at Sydney he used his powers of subterfuge to dismiss George Giffen's younger brother Walter, who was playing in his first Test. The young batsman hit the ball back to George Lohmann, who, in an attempt to catch it on the half-volley, scooped it to Grace at point. W. G. put on a pantomime of triumph, and the unsighted umpire was persuaded the catch was clean. As *The Australasian* commented, the England captain 'assisted in the deception by tossing up the ball'. This was particularly rich given that he had vigorously protested a perfectly fair catch to dismiss one of his own men in the first Test. As another Australian paper put it, 'he plays the game like a professional card-sharp; the veteran is master of every form of "bluff", and appeals on the slightest pretext'.

This unappealing aspect of the tourists' play not only antagonised opponents, but irritated umpires, among them E. J. Briscoe, who stood in the return match against New South Wales. Late in the home side's first innings, the Englishmen went up for a catch behind off Lohmann's bowling. Briscoe gave the batsman the benefit of the doubt. Grace left him in no doubt as to what he thought of the decision, though as so often there are different accounts as to what was said. Grace claimed he said: 'I wish you would pay attention to the game; we all heard the catch.' According to Briscoe, the words used were: 'You will give no one out. It is unpardonable. You must be blind. We might as well go home tomorrow.' Whatever was said, Briscoe went home that afternoon, refusing to continue to officiate in the remainder of the match, saying he was not going to be insulted or called a cheat by anyone.

Nor did he let the matter rest. Grace was pursued by letters from the New South Wales Cricket Association, to whom he replied with some asperity: 'I did not insult Mr Briscoe, nor did I think him a cheat.' He did, however, admit he was far from satisfied with the standards of umpiring he had found on the tour: 'The umpiring question will have to be gone into thoroughly, and some new plan adopted or cricket will not be worth playing as there is not the slightest bit of pleasure in playing under the present system of umpiring in Australia.'

This particular bee was still buzzing loudly in Grace's bonnet when he arrived in Adelaide for the final Test. He wanted Australia's best umpire, James Phillips, to stand in the match but was told he couldn't have him. In turn, he refused Flynn, an equally respected man, which not only caused great offence, but also led to the match being given over to two relatively inexperienced umpires, whose lives Grace proceeded to make hell.

England had racked up the huge total of 490 for 9 on the first two days before heavy rain delayed the start of the third day. Grace growled impatiently round the pavilion, making disagreeable insinuations as to why play was being delayed, before he finally resorted to marching the two officials out to the square every quarter of an hour until they succumbed and allowed his team to complete a massive but hollow victory by an innings and 230 runs.

It was a sad end to a tour marked by quite as much shabbiness as Grace's first nearly twenty years earlier. As Tom Horan, now a veteran of the press corps, said, more in sorrow than in anger,

> Grace is . . . a bad loser, and when he lost two of the test matches in succession he lost his temper too, and kept on losing it right to the finish . . . [He] seems to have developed a condition of captiousness, fussiness, and nastiness strongly to be deprecated. His objection to Flynn was nothing short of a gratuitous insult to a first-class umpire, and I regret to be obliged to say this . . . [but] the great cricketer has only himself to blame for any strictures passed upon his conduct by those who were inclined to view him in the best light.

Grace was neither the first nor the last to recognise the pivotal importance of the umpire. In the first set of written rules that have survived, those of 1727 governing the matches between the Duke of Richmond's team and that of Mr Broderick, it was declared that 'If any of the gamesters shall speak or give their opinion on any point of the game, they are to be turned out, and voided in the match.' So far, so good; but the umpires were the appointees of the two patrons, so naturally this rule 'is not to extend to the Duke of Richmond and Mr Broderick'. Indeed, it is made quite clear who would act as final arbiters in any dispute: 'If any doubt or dispute arises on any of the aforesaid articles, or whatever else is not settled therein, it shall be determined by the Duke of Richmond and Mr Broderick on their honours, by whom the umpires are likewise to be determined on any difference between them.'

Early eighteenth-century cricket has been called 'a full-blooded financial brawl patronised by aristocrats, bookies, publicans and the socially and locally ambitious', and in the climate that prevailed it would have been fanciful to expect umpires to be independent. Not only would the officials favour those upon whose patronage they relied, but in the heyday of match-fixing it was as profitable to nobble an umpire as a player.

The 1727 rules took the form of articles of agreement between two individuals. The first published laws of cricket date from 1744, when, under the patronage of the cricket-mad Prince of Wales, a committee of 'noblemen and gentlemen of Kent, Surrey, Sussex, Middlesex and London' drew up a schedule of regulations designed to cover the game wherever it was played. In 1755, a revised version printed under the straightforward title 'The Game of Cricket' was issued by several clubs, led by the Star and Garter in Pall Mall, which later merged with the White Conduit Club, Islington, which in turn evolved into the Marylebone Cricket Club, the guardian and copyright holder of the Laws of Cricket to this day.

The new code gave some attention to the umpire, boosting his position by stating that 'no person shall have any right to question him'. Umpires were also given total authority in the potentially tricky question of substitutes, being designated 'the sole judges of all hurts, whether real or pretend'. And hurts there were. Cricket was more of a contact sport in the eighteenth century. For one thing, to complete a run the batsman had to poke his bat into the popping hole between the two stumps, while to run him out the fielding side had to get the ball into the hole first. This was simply an invitation to physical confrontation, and the new code recognised the abuse of obstruction. The umpires could now order a run to be notched up if, in their opinion, the batsman had been deliberately baulked, but the non-striker still had the right to prevent a catch by getting in the bowler's way 'anywhere within the bat's reach' – an obvious recipe for mayhem.

As Teresa McLean observes,

> The frame of mind in which a batsman was prepared to intervene physically to obstruct a catch does not suggest the tranquillity of spirit in which the game should ideally be played. Other ploys found generally throughout the game included making catches in items of clothing like a shirt or jacket. A great deal of the eighteenth century game would strike the modern viewer as distinctly Not Cricket.

One fairly typical match that came to a bloody and inconclusive halt was a challenge between Kent and Surrey in 1762. The report quoted in *Kent Cricket Matches* says that the dispute was 'about one of the players being catched out, when Surrey was 50 a-head the first innings; from words they came to blows, which occasioned several broken heads, as likewise a challenge between two persons of distinction; the confusion was so very great, that the betts were all withdrawn'. In a climate of potential violence the umpire must have felt like a lone lawman trying to bring peace to feuding gangs in the Wild West.

There are instances of brave men preserving the rule of law against heavy odds, and one dates from 1789 and a keenly contested derby match between Coventry and Leicester. One Coventry batsman, Clarke, was declared out – by both umpires – at the end of the first day's play, and yet the following morning he shamelessly made his way back to the wicket. He was aided and abetted by a Mr Needham, a local bigwig, who was reported as saying, 'Clarke, keep to your stumps,' before turning on the visiting Leicester umpire with 'Damn ye, Brown, why do ye not call play?' Not getting any satisfaction out of Brown, Needham then swore 'that if Mr Bunbury, the Coventry umpire, would not let him go in again, the match should not be played out'. To the great credit of Messrs Brown and Bunbury, the game was not played out, and Mr Needham was left impotently fuming.

As the game evolved, different laws came and went. The 1744 code cast anathema on 'standing unfair to strike', but made no mention of Leg Before Wicket. In the age of curved bats and under-arm bowling along the ground, it wouldn't have occurred to anyone to get his legs anywhere near the line of the ball. That changed with the introduction of 'length' bowling – tossed-up deliveries which bounced, and therefore required the bat to straighten, and so necessarily to bring the batsman's person nearer the line of fire. It was only a matter of time before someone saw the possibility of a new line of defence – the boot.

Tom Taylor, the dashing Hambledon stroke-maker, is credited with the dubious distinction of being the first batsman to systematically use his feet to stun or trap the ball. Silver Billy Beldham, the most brilliant of the Hambledon cricketers, described

Taylor's ploy as 'shabby', a view endorsed by the next revision of the code in 1774. This outlawed such unsporting behaviour, but demanded the judgement of Solomon from umpires by stating that the batsman should only be given out if he 'puts his leg before the wicket *with a design* to stop the ball, and actually prevents the ball from hitting the wicket' (my italics).

Being dismissed lbw was regarded as the most shameful way of losing your wicket. Indeed, the batsman's legs generally were a potential source of embarrassment. It was despicable to use them to defend your wicket, and the older players simply howled with derision when the first attempts at protection were introduced, in the modest form of shin pads.

But as it became clear that the batsman's legs were here to stay, the umpires were at least excused having to guess his intention regarding their deployment. In the 1788 code, the first issued by the Marylebone Club, the batsman is out if hit by a ball which 'pitched in a straight line to the wicket, and would have hit it'. How simple it sounds, but in practice the lbw law has always been a huge burden for the umpire. This was especially true when the official at the bowler's end was also responsible for determining the fairness of delivery. Not only did he have to determine that the feet were legally positioned, but during the interminable controversy over round-arm bowling, he was responsible for judging the height of the arm. With a March of Intellect bowler virtually spread-eagling himself on the point of delivery, the umpire must have had his work cut out getting an unimpeded view of the ball's flight.

And of course, like a straight stick bent in a pond's still waters, the umpire's judgement could be distorted in the prism of self-interest – or simple incompetence. The appeal system, which injected a rush of passion and aggression into the proceedings, increased the pressure and could easily result in the disappointed appellants nursing a sense of injustice that might in turn breed dissent. Nor was it just the fielding side that could be left feeling aggrieved. In 1839, *Bell's Life* noted a match between Rochdale and Denton in which one batsman was given out lbw 'to a ball which hit him on the shoulder'. The report went on, 'the game ended in dispute'. But then, some umpires never gave decisions on principle. The great Kent batsman Fuller Pilch simply didn't believe in lbw, and would turn down appeals with a reproving 'None 'o that. Bowl 'em out. Bowl 'em out.'

A man of Pilch's standing in the game would not expect to have his decisions challenged, even at their most idiosyncratic, but most umpires did not have the natural authority conferred by greatness. In August 1829, the *Sheffield Mercury* reported a particularly blatant piece of umpire bullying in the match between Nottingham and Sheffield. One of the Sheffield players was given not out, both umpires agreeing on the decision. But, said the paper, 'several of the Nottingham players, headed by Denis, declared that they would leave the field if he did not go out. The umpires at length gave way to the clamours of the Nottingham players, and thus they had one whom they dreaded out of the way.' And they won the match by 18 runs. In 1833, Richmond's last man was given out by Reigate's umpire, and the batsman's brother was so incensed that he encouraged the crowd to throw him into the Thames. He was only saved by prompt action by his own team and their supporters.

The single biggest headache for umpires during the nineteenth century was the interminable wrangle over the height of the bowling arm. The gap between what was practised and what was allowed by the laws became too great to be bridged, and most umpires simply turned a blind eye. Every so often a new explosive charge was detonated by some brave or foolhardy official, with the result, in due course, of a further relaxation of the law. John Willes was driven out of the game in 1822, but William Lillywhite and James Broadbridge were soon raising their arms even higher. Their champion, Mr Knight, underlined how ridiculous things were when he pointed out 'at MCC itself the same bowler is allowed in one match and disallowed in another . . . everything is in the breast of the umpire; if he fancies you, he will let you bowl; if not, he will stop you'.

In 1835, round-arm bowling was made legal, but that could only be a staging post to the full liberty to deliver the ball from any height the bowler pleased. It certainly did nothing to rid the game of unseemly altercations. In 1838, the *Sunderland Beacon* reported a local match which 'ended abruptly because the Darlington bowlers began to throw and were no-balled by the

Bishop Wearmouth umpire. Darlington refused to play on unless their throwing was allowed.'

While most umpires endeavoured to keep a low profile, a tiny minority positively relished the opportunity to seize the limelight. William Caldecourt – or 'Honest Will Caldecourt', as the press sometimes called him – took a very public stand against illegal actions, whatever the embarrassment it caused. In 1839, he no-balled another Sussex bowler, James Hodson, for raising his arm above elbow height, even though, as one of the Sussex newspapers indignantly insisted, the other umpire considered his action quite legitimate:

> Had Mr Caldecourt no regard for the opinions of Mr Good, his colleague? [T]he interference was ill-timed and manifested a hostile feeling to the Sussex players. Not one of the spectators approved of this decision, and it was repudiated by 9/10 of the Marylebone Club – not the young players, but the veteran players, whose judgement Caldecourt, we are persuaded, will not be bold enough to question!

And so it went on, with umpires and players placed in an impossible position by the dithering of the law-makers, who continued to tinker with Law X without either accepting the inevitable or making a stand and insisting on the law being maintained by all umpires at all times. Finally, after yet another failed holding operation in 1859, when it was wearily conceded that the bowler's hand might be at shoulder level on delivery, and after the famous no-balling of John Willsher at Lord's in 1862, the MCC gave up the unequal struggle, and from 1864, the law governing the fairness of a bowler's action made no reference whatsoever to the height at which the ball should be released.

The new law, or rather, the cancellation of the old one, ushered in a relatively halcyon period for umpires. Their next major headache would be the wave of real, bent-arm throwers that infested the game in the last decade of the century. In the meantime there were plenty of individuals to watch and incidents to judge. Inevitably, W. G. was the most notable of the individuals, and scarcely a year went by without some *contretemps* involving him. The season after his piratical tour to Australia, during which he had treated his fellow professionals very poorly while making a pretty fair fortune himself, he duly turned out for the Gentlemen against the Players, and, while batting with his brother Fred, deliberately obstructed the bowler as he made to accept a straightforward return catch. The pros appealed vociferously to both umpires, G. Keeble and A. Luff, but in vain. This was one of the rare occasions when the players transcended their near-Buddhist acceptance of Grace's behaviour as something beyond their influence and protested strongly against what they felt was a conspiracy. *Wisden* seemed to agree with them: 'Nearly every appeal by a gentleman was decided affirmatively, and the players' appeals were mainly met with NOT OUT!'

Teresa McLean has called Grace 'the umpires' single biggest problem . . . He inspired a whole generation of cricketers in every class of cricket to dream of dominating cricket as he did, overwhelming players and umpires alike.' As she says, there are accounts of Grace's involvement in harassing umpires and 'overriding the rules in all sorts of matches throughout the 1870s and 1880s; if anything, more in humble matches, since smart players had learnt from experience to view his behaviour with slightly qualified admiration'.

Though Grace was by a clear margin the most difficult player to have in a match if you were umpire, he was not the only Victorian cricketer who made life difficult for officials. The great Surrey stonewaller Harry Jupp was notoriously difficult to dislodge from the crease. He once played in an exhibition match at his birth place, Dorking, and was bowled in the first over. Jupp reassembled the wicket and resumed his stance for the next ball. To the plaintive enquiry from slip, 'Ain't you going out, Juppy?' he replied briskly, 'Not at Dorking.'

But dealing with recalcitrants like W. G. or Jupp was easy compared to combating the chuckers. For the most part, the umpires chose discretion over valour, but even that did not guarantee a quiet life. In 1873, at the height of the furore over John Crossland's action, Edmund Peate, the Yorkshire slow left-armer, turned up for a Roses match at Old Trafford determined to expose the umpires' weakness. George Wootton, the old Nottinghamshire and MCC fast bowler, was standing at Peate's end. According to Edward Roper, a Lancashire amateur who was batting at the time, Peate said to Wootton, 'Look here, George, you umpires are not worth twopennorth of gin, you daren't call anybody. The first ball of next over I declare to you I will throw at Mr Roper, and I'll bet you anything you like that you daren't no-ball me.' And when the time came, he took an obvious shy at the stumps. Hearing no call, Roper hastily improvised a defensive stroke, later recording (suitably censored) Peate's words to the impassive Wootton: 'There, that shows what you umpires are all worth.'

Peate proved his point, but the vast majority of umpires would have followed Wootton's example. Most were old professionals, and they had an understandable sympathy for their successors, whose livelihoods they would be jeopardising if they called them for throwing. But self-interest played its part as well. In the intensely hierarchical structure of Victorian cricket, umpires were a long way down the pecking order, well below the amateur county captains and committees. And to call a man like Crossland, a regular member of the Lancashire team, would in effect be to call into question the judgement, if not honesty, of the men who picked him and the captain who bowled him. As Bob Thoms, England's leading umpire, explained when questioned on his and his colleagues' inaction: 'We're not going to do anything, the gentlemen must do it.'

Lord Harris tried, with some success, to rid the game of throwing; but then club self-interest swung the pendulum back again, so that by the late 1890s the problem was even more serious than before. The solution this time came in the form of a self-appointed Wyatt Earp from Australia, James Phillips. He was no respecter of rank, as his calling of C. B. Fry in 1899 showed; and he went on to prove the nemesis of the unfortunate Arthur Mold of Lancashire. But he came in for a great deal of criticism from people who thought his stand against chuckers was a publicity stunt. Many journalists either couldn't see the problem or couldn't see the fault in a particular bowler's action. In an interview with one such, Phillips asked, 'Where were you sitting? In the press box? Right, I'll come and umpire there next innings.'

The umpire's position in the game gradually improved. In 1883, a flat rate of £5 per match was established for those standing in a county game, and in 1892, the MCC issued *Instructions to Umpires*, giving their authority a further boost. But the game, as always, was on the move, with players on either side of the great bowling–batting divide constantly seeking ways to tip the balance in their favour. From the 1880s the two great Nottinghamshire professionals Shrewsbury and Gunn pioneered a new technique – the use of the pad to minimise risk.

Pad play was widely deprecated. Thoms, answering a *Wisden* questionnaire in 1888, was forthright in condemning it: 'This very unsightly play cannot be termed batting,' he wrote; ''tis simply scientific legging.' Once again it put the umpires in the spotlight, as the bowler responded vocally to the new 'scientific' mode of defence. The shift in the importance of the lbw law can be judged from the fact that, up to the 1880s, it accounted for only one in forty first-class dismissals, but by the 1920s, this ratio had changed to one in nine.

Various avenues were explored to reduce pad play, but tinkering with the lbw law was deemed potentially more damaging. The law remained as it was, with the ball having to pitch wicket to wicket to secure a dismissal. This – along with vastly improved wickets – was one of the foundation stones of modern batting which saw far heavier scoring than the Victorians could have dreamt of. Jack Hobbs, the greatest run-scorer ever in first-class cricket, would temper praise with the reflection that 'he made his runs when the lbw law was framed more kindly to the batsman'.

Hobbs's great career straddled the First World War, and he emerged from the blood-letting having lost only four seasons' worth of aggregates and centuries. Among the many who were less fortunate was a young player of huge promise, who had won his Worcestershire cap at the age of sixteen, but who now surveyed life from the ranks of the disabled, having lost his right arm in the fighting.

Rather than abandon the game he loved, Frank Chester studied to become an umpire and was admitted to the first-class list in 1922 at the tender age of twenty-six. Overcoming the natural prejudice against one so young and relatively inexperienced – a gateman at Northampton refused him entry to the ground in his first season; he simply thought he was having his leg pulled – Chester went on to establish a reputation as the greatest umpire of his generation, whose authority was unquestionable. Once, when someone asked him why he hadn't given a batsman the benefit of the doubt, he retorted, 'Doubt? When I'm umpiring, there's never any doubt!'

It was a measure of Chester's integrity that in his first ever first-class match, he gave decisions against both captains – Johnny Douglas (Essex), lbw, and John Daniell (Somerset), stumped. His older partner warned him, 'You'll be signing your death warrant if you go on like that,' and he was certainly going against the trend. Douglas relinquished the Essex captaincy, but kept playing – only to find friends commiserating with him for his apparent loss of form. That wasn't how he saw it. '"Loss of form be hanged!" When I was relieved of the captaincy of Essex it cost me thirty wickets and two hundred runs a season. The bloody umpire couldn't say anything but "Not out" when I appealed, and they only said "Out" when I was appealed against.'

Having refused to show favours to county captains, Chester went on to establish a formidable reputation, becoming one of the most widely respected Test umpires of the twentieth century. His standing was such that after the Second World War he was given a national testimonial – a unique honour for an umpire. Towards the end of his lengthy career, however, there were whispers that he was getting above himself. According to *Wisden*, he once responded to an appeal by 'a very famous bowler on an international occasion at Lord's' with 'Not out, and that was a very bad appeal.'

Although Don Bradman declared him 'the greatest umpire' he ever played under, not all Australians were fans. In 1948, Chester took a public stand against what he saw as their general aggression and the strength and frequency of their appeals, and by the time of the next Australian tour in 1953, it was felt in the visitors' camp that his attitude had hardened into discernible bias. At the start of the series he was the veteran of an astonishing fifty Tests, and left no one with any doubt that he was going to run the show his own way.

Things came to a head in the fourth Test at Leeds, when controversial reprieves for Simpson (run out) and Denis Compton (caught slip) brought a protest from the Australian captain

Lindsey Hassett to the MCC. The case was accepted, and Chester stood down for the final, and deciding, Test at the Oval, in which England won back the Ashes for the first time since 1932–3. As we shall see, this courtesy was not always extended to visiting teams.

The 1950s were a quiet time for umpires – quiet, that is, apart from the constant sound of frustrated bowlers appealing for lbw. The law-makers had finally come up with an experiment that seemed worth persisting with when, in 1937, the lbw law was extended to allow dismissal by a ball that pitched outside the off stump but which struck the pad between wicket and wicket and would, in the opinion of the umpire, have hit the stumps. This amendment was adopted into the Laws straight after the Second World War.

While obviously fairer to the bowler, the new law introduced more imponderables for the umpire (as well as breeding a generation of in-swinging and off-cutting seamers who did not necessarily increase the game's aesthetic appeal). Paradoxically, it also seemed to produce more of the 'scientific legging' identified as a problem by Thoms the previous century. Batsmen made sure they got their pads outside the line of the off stump, often elaborating the 'leave' with bat raised high above the ball in balletic disdain, or stretching so far forward as to scotch any chance the umpire might have had of determining the delivery's final destination.

Dependence on the pad was probably never better displayed than in the Edgbaston Test of 1957, when England faced the wiles of Sonny Ramadhin who, with Alf Valentine, had caused a terrific upset when they bowled the West Indies to an unexpected first ever Test victory at Lord's on their previous tour in 1950. 'Those two little pals of mine,' as the victory calypso had it, had woven a terrible net of self-doubt around the leaden-footed English batsmen, and there was no great confidence that the home side would be better qualified to play them seven years on.

That lack of confidence seemed well founded when England were bowled out for 186 in their first innings. History seemed to be repeating itself, with Ramadhin taking 7 for 49 in 31 overs, and although his calypso partner was not playing, it appeared a safe bet that he would be sufficient to bowl West Indies to a use-ful 1–0 lead in the series. Set 289 to avoid an innings defeat, England started badly, and at 113 for 3 on the third day, the writing was on the wall. The team had booked out of their hotel. It seemed only a matter of time.

Time certainly came into it – enormous amounts of time, as the match was painstakingly first saved and then nearly turned round completely to produce a miraculous victory. England's saviours were the two Oxbridge amateurs Peter May and Colin Cowdrey, who had come up with a strategy for dealing with Ramadhin. According to May, '[we] agreed that we must keep going forward'. And they stuck to their task quite as deter-minedly as the great professional progenitors of pad play, Gunn and Shrewsbury, ever did.

The partnership began shortly before noon on the fourth day, Monday, and lasted well into the fifth, resulting in a stand of 411 – the highest partnership for England, and the third highest Test partnership ever. And throughout this marathon of concen-tration, Ramadhin wheeled away with his sleeves buttoned to his wrist, trying to engineer the breakthrough which would have opened up one end. Over after over his flighted venom would be met by the extended fortress of bat and pad, and in most overs there would be at least one appeal for lbw. *The Times* reported that 'the inscrutable Ramadhin would half-turn his head, raise his eyebrows, and look questioningly at the umpire out of the corner of his eye. But the gentlemen in the white coats must have seemed to him like Russian diplomats as they vetoed his requests.'

The men in white coats were Charlie Elliott and Emrys Davies, and they remained impervious. Ramadhin bowled 48 overs on the fourth day, and his ill luck was widely noted. The West Indian cricket writer Tony Cozier told his readers, 'the ball repeatedly beat the forward defensive stroke and hit the front leg . . . Soon throats became sore from appealing to the umpires. As is cus-tomary in England, they were reluctant to uphold them with the point of contact so far from the stumps.' Another West Indian, Michael Manley, conceded the umpires' right to their doubts when the ball made contact outside the line or when the pad was stretched well forwards, but claimed that 'much of the time the left pad was in line with balls that seemed to be perfectly directed at the wicket'. There were some English sympathisers too. Peter Richards thought 'Colin had to be out so many times', while Tom Graveney, who was twelfth man, said, 'Colin kicked him to death. He never tried to play with the bat.'

Ramadhin himself is quoted by Peter May's biographer, Allan Hill, as saying that his treatment at the hands of the English umpires was 'unbelievable'. He went on, 'Most of my wickets were either bowled or lbw because I bowled more off-breaks than leg-breaks.' Of Cowdrey he said simply, 'Colin always played with his pads,' but after Edgbaston, everybody else did too. He was utterly disillusioned; in fact, 'I was so disgusted I refused to tour England with the West Indies in 1963.'

By the end of the England innings, the mystery spinner was side-lined. May was piercing the field at will as he accelerated to a personal score of 285 and a declaration which put a badly demoralised side under considerable pressure. The exhausted Ramadhin walked off straight into the record books. He had bowled more balls than anyone else in a Test match – 774 in 98 overs – and more deliveries – 588 – in a single innings, which was also a record for all first-class cricket.

West Indies saved a match they felt Ramadhin should have won for them, but not without an undignified collapse against the English spinners Lock and Laker which brought them to their knees at 72 for 7. In the final rearguard, Goddard, the captain, played the Surrey pair more or less exclusively with his pads, as if daring the umpires to give an lbw decision. Although Ramadhin avoided the final indignity of having to go out to bat to save the match, he must have had to put his own pads on and sit anxiously waiting for the final overs to be bowled. He recollected that, at the end of that terminally frustrating day, 'when I got on to the bed, I was aching all over. I couldn't sleep.'

May and Cowdrey had effectively ended the West Indian spin threat for the rest of the tour. Ramadhin took only 14 wickets in the series, and as Peter May said, 'he was never the same force again'. When Alf Valentine came back into the side to resume their once lustrous partnership, he seemed, in *Wisden*'s words, 'to lose all faith in himself when he faced an English batsman'. With his length gone, he bowled only 26 overs in the two Tests he played in, and West Indies lost the series 3–0. The treatment Ramadhin received at the hands of the English umpires caused considerable resentment in the Caribbean, and one West Indian umpire developed a series of experiments involving bowlers aiming at a wicket through a pad-wide gauge set up where a batsman's front foot would be. Based on a nearly 100 per cent success rate, he claimed it should be possible to give front-foot lbw decisions. A similar trial was conducted at Lord's from which the opposite conclusion was drawn.

For most of the twentieth century, umpires could be confident that whatever the players thought of their decisions, they would accept them. This was part of the iron discipline imposed at every level of the game. Lingering at the wickets was always considered the height of bad form, as a story from the post-First World War period shows. Frank Lee, a young member of the Lord's ground-staff, was batting at headquarters one day and was given out lbw. He hesitated a moment at the crease, and, on his return to the pavilion, was summoned by the MCC secretary, Sir Francis Lacey, who demanded an explanation. Lee produced a sliver of wood from his bat which had been dislodged by the ball from which he was adjudged leg before. He had simply paused to pick it up. He still left the secretary's office with a flea in his ear and a warning that if he did it again he would be sacked. When Frank Woolley in his glorious prime once hesitated after being given out by Frank Chester, he hastened to apologise, explaining that he wasn't doubting the decision, just wondering how he had managed to get out to such a poor bowler. This unquestioning acceptance of the umpire's decision was expected – and forthcoming – from all: from men like Hobbs, Woolley and Bradman (whom Keith Miller cited as exemplary in this respect) down to the humblest member of the Lord's groundstaff. That was the accepted code, and transgressions against it were not tolerated.

Erosion of confidence in umpires and the end of unquestioning assent is easy to lump with everything else that changed as a result of Packer in the 1970s. But this would not be accurate. The Australian umpires' refusal to make a stand against throwers in 1958–9 was a low point for the men in white coats; and the notion of home umpires' impartiality had further doubt cast on it when, in the controversial series in the West Indies in 1965,

Gerry Gomez, a West Indian selector, was draughted in at very short notice to umpire the Guyana Test. As the Australians reasoned, a man who helped pick Charlie Griffith was hardly likely to call him for throwing (a view possibly confirmed when Gomez joined in an appeal for a run out against Bill Lawry before raising his finger to send him on his way).

As we have seen, England's tour to South Africa in 1964–5 put the home umpires in the spotlight and generated a great deal of bad feeling. A columnist in the *Daily Rand* said of Mike Smith's team, 'they've made more appeals than the Salvation Army in Self-Denial Week', and went on to suggest a radical solution: 'There is only one way to stop the nonsense. It is to banish "Owzat?" from the vocabulary of cricket . . . and allow umpires to adjudicate strictly according to their judgement and eyesight.' While conceding that mistakes would still occur, he insisted that abandoning the appeal system would save the game from being plunged 'neck deep in bad blood'.

Within a decade, things had got considerably worse. In 1973, for the first time in a Test match, an umpire felt angry enough to refuse to continue standing. Arthur Fagg, the former Kent batsman and a first-class umpire of high repute, finally lost patience when the West Indian captain, Rohan Kanhai, swore and gesticulated in response to one of his decisions on the second day of the Edgbaston Test. Fagg had turned down an appeal against Geoffrey Boycott, and Kanhai spent the rest of the session making his feelings clear. Fagg made his feelings just as clear when he came off the pitch, refusing to continue to officiate on the following day, and explaining why in his press statement:

> If they will not accept decisions, there is no point carrying on. Why should I? I am nearly 60. I don't have to live with this kind of pressure. I've had to live with it for $2\frac{1}{2}$ hours out there. People don't realise how bad it has become. I don't enjoy umpiring in Tests any more.

In the end, after persuasion from his fellow umpire, Dickie Bird, and an apology from the West Indian manager on behalf of his captain, Fagg did resume his duties, but only after Alan Oakman, the Warwickshire coach and ex-first-class umpire, had taken his place for the first over of the third morning. The atmosphere remained poisonous, with the West Indies slowing the over-rate, bowling bouncers and deliberately running down the pitch. Bird and Fagg called both captains to them at lunch and issued a warning that unless things improved the match was in serious danger of being called off. This seemingly had the required result.

Other Test matches have been jeopardised by players' responses to adverse decisions. In the third Test between India and Australia in 1981, Sunil Gavaskar was given out lbw to Dennis Lillee. Quite certain that he'd got a measurable amount of bat on the ball, the Indian captain first lingered at the crease, and then ordered his batting partner, C. P. S. Chauhan, to accompany him from the field. They were met at the pavilion gate by the Indian manager who persuaded Gavaskar on into the changing-room while sending Chauhan back to continue his innings. Gavaskar was unrepentant: 'I was infuriated at the injustice of it all. Mr Whitehead has stood in all three Tests, and we have lost count of the bad decisions we have had from him.'

A bad umpire, or one who has forfeited the respect of one or other side, is a problem for both camps. No team has addressed the difficulty more dramatically than the MCC 'A' side sent to Pakistan in 1955–6 to play four unofficial 'Tests'. The first was drawn; the tourists lost the second, and so needed to win the third to square the series and set up the fourth as the decider. On the first day there were four lbw decisions against the visitors. Not content with making some undiplomatic asides within the hearing of the offending official, Idris Begh, some members of the team lured him back to their hotel, where he was subjected to what *Wisden* described as 'the water treatment', before going on to explain, 'one of the standing jokes on the tour between the MCC players themselves had involved the use of cold water much in the same way as students might do in a rag. Unfortunately, some of the players did not realise that the type of humour generally accepted by most people in Britain, might not be understood in other parts of the world.'

The incident caused huge embarrassment, and Lord Alexander, the MCC President, sent two cables of apology and also telephoned offering to recall the team and reimburse Pakistan for loss of revenues. In the event, the tour continued, and the tourists won the fourth 'Test' by the narrow margin of 2 wickets – though not, according to the Pakistanis, without subjecting their batsmen to systematic verbal abuse.

On their return home, the manager, C. G. Howard, issued a statement on the dousing incident, claiming that it 'was actuated by nothing more than high spirits and a sense of fun. It had no connection whatsoever with umpiring decisions made by Mr Idris Begh.' All the same, someone's head was obviously required to roll, and the MCC Committee that sat in judgement singled out D. B. Carr, the team captain, 'who was present at the time, [and who] should have recognised at once that this "ragging", although initiated by nothing more than high spirits and with no harmful intent whatsoever, might be regarded, as it was in many quarters, as an attack upon an umpire. The Committee are satisfied that this was not the case.'

The Committee may have been satisfied, but there were lingering doubts in Pakistan. The next time a Pakistani umpire felt that he had been insulted, he let the whole world know about it, and brought a delicately balanced Test match to an abrupt halt. The time and the place remain fixed in the game's communal memory, but before looking at Mike Gatting's famous finger-wagging confrontation with Shakoor Rana in Faisalabad in December 1987, it is necessary to look at a string of other events which preceded it.

By some unhappy quirk of the international fixtures list, Pakistan had been in England earlier in 1987 for what proved an acrimonious series. One of the causes of friction was umpire David Constant. Pakistan had had a low regard for Constant since their previous tour in 1982, when they blamed one of his decisions for the loss of the Headingley Test, and with it the rubber. They now requested that he not be picked for the current series. Despite the precedent of Lindsey Hassett's request that Frank Chester be stood down in 1953, Pakistan's protests against Constant were ignored, and he stood in the first two matches. As John Crace said in his book *Wasim and Waqar*, 'at the very least this was high-handed; the Pakistanis took it as a sign that they were treated as an inferior touring team, with all the implied racist overtones' – an attitude all too powerfully confirmed by the remark made to Matthew Engel, the

Guardian's cricket correspondent, by one of the English officials: 'we couldn't let the fuckers get away with it'. As Gatting sagely observed in his memoir, *Leading from the Front*, 'Unfortunately the bad feeling engendered here may well have lit a very long fuse that went all the way to Faisalabad.'

However, umpire Constant may not have been the only blue touch-paper leading to the Faisalabad powder keg. England and Pakistan had met in a meaningless one-day game in the Perth Challenge Cup in Australia. Rameez Rajah had been caught off a no-ball, failed to hear the call, walked, and then been run out by the fielder, Bill Athey. Wasim Akram noted, 'Mike Gatting was captaining the side at the time, and he could have recalled Rameez, but chose not to, and in so doing he, albeit unwittingly, defined his approach to the Pakistanis. He was a captain who was not above sharp practice, and therefore not to be trusted.'

Gatting and the new Pakistan captain, Javed Miandad, had also had a run-in during the 1987 World Cup. When Miandad lingered after an lbw decision, Gatting had put an arm round his shoulder in mock commiseration and told him, 'Come on, you've been given out, on your way.' Miandad says Gatting swore at him. Gatting denies that he did, and says that even if he had, it wouldn't have justified Miandad taking a swing at him with the words 'I kill you!' [*sic*].

Quite apart from the explosive personal chemistry between the two captains and a great deal of previous suspicion between the two sides, Pakistan were in the doldrums after their abject failure in the World Cup. The players were in virtual disgrace; the crowds were poor; the atmosphere grudging and vengeful. Things got off to a bad start in the first Test at Lahore. The umpiring was, by general consent, very bad. For reasons no one could divine, three umpires who had stood in the World Cup were left on the sidelines. In Wasim Akram's view, those that were picked 'had been put under some kind of pressure' by the home authorities. If so, they certainly did not disappoint their masters. In the second innings, the temperamental Chris Broad refused to walk when given out caught behind off a delivery he swore he didn't touch. It took all his partner Graham Gooch's powers of persuasion to coax him out of the last ditch he'd established at square leg and shoo him on his way back to the pavilion. Gooch himself went the same way – with rather better grace – adjudged caught behind off a ball which in Gatting's view, from the other end, he had missed 'comfortably', adding the gloss, 'Comfortably, in cricketing terms, is a very long way indeed.'

The leg-spinner Abdul Qadir took 9 wickets in the first innings and four in the second, but in addition to producing a fine bowling performance, he multiplied the pressure by persistently appealing, and when denied, turning vocally on the offending umpire. (He also lost his temper when his own innings was terminated by a poor decision, exchanging words with the umpire and the England captain on departure.) After the game, both England's tour manager, Peter Lush, and Gatting made public criticisms of the umpiring, though they appeared reluctant, in *Wisden*'s words, 'to acknowledge that the batting had been woefully substandard'. Javed Miandad kept the pot bubbling by declaring that all the umpiring decisions had been '100 per cent correct'.

Things were to get even more acrimonious at Faisalabad. Having been 254 for 4 overnight, England were disappointingly all out for 292, and felt once again that they had been the victims of some poor decisions. This led to the first regrettable incident on the second day, when an English appeal for a bat–pad catch was turned down by Shakoor Rana. Enough disappointment was evinced by the England players for the umpire to walk down the pitch to confront them and have a word with Gatting, who was standing at slip. Something had obviously already been said – perhaps by the umpire in defence of his decision – when Bill Athey remarked, 'The sooner we get out of this fucking country, the better.' Gatting, seemingly in response to Rana's further reaction, said, 'No, no, off you go. One rule for one and one rule for another.' He claimed later that neither remark was intended to be heard by Rana, but in that case it's hard to tell who the 'No, no, off you go' *was* addressed to. The stump microphones picked his words up loud and clear (Gatting alleged that they had been turned up unusually high).

Despite the deteriorating atmosphere, England were doing well, at one stage reducing Pakistan to 77 for 5. Gatting kept the pressure on, and runs came at a trickle. Further aggravation was caused as the sun began to set and the close catchers' shadows presented a potential distraction for the batsman. Rana intervened with several warnings, which were not well received by the England captain. The end of a long, hot and fractious day was in sight when the simmering antipathy finally boiled over. Eddie Hemmings, the off-spinner, was bowling what should have been the day's penultimate over. Gatting decided to bring David Capel up from deep square leg, telling the batsman, Salim Malik, that this was what he was doing. Then, seeing that Capel was coming in too close, gestured for him to stay back saving one. Hemmings had hesitated in his run-up, gone back and started again, and had just delivered the ball when Rana intervened from square leg, calling out, 'Stop, stop!' The other umpire, Khizar Hayat, had the presence of mind to call 'Dead ball', and Gatting turned to find out what the matter was.

According to his own account, Rana said, 'It's unfair play.' To which Gatting replied, 'What's unfair play?' 'You're waving your hand – that's cheating. You're cheating!' he was told. This Gatting denied, saying he'd informed the batsman of the field change (taking place behind his back), and had only signalled to Capel to stop him coming up too far. He then advised the umpire to return to square leg and let them get on with the game. Rana apparently started to comply, but then perhaps feeling that the intervention had not quite achieved its desired object, decided to get things off his chest once and for all, and told Gatting, in earshot of all the other close fielders, 'You are a fucking cheating cunt.'

A deaf ear at this point would have consigned the incident to a footnote, saved Gatting's position as captain of England, and, most likely, produced a rare Test match victory in Pakistan. But Gatting was at the end of his tether, and with one shake of his bull-like neck, was tossing and goring in the verbal arena with a vengeance. What the world saw was the England captain practically jabbing the umpire in the chest, and it wouldn't have taken Desmond Morris to interpret his body language as hostile. The actual language was hostile and abusive as well, although an exact transcript does not seem to have come down to us. But the pictures, which even appeared on the front pages of German newspapers, told their own story. It was an own-goal of similar proportions to Gatting's disastrous reverse-sweep in the recently lost World Cup final, and the consequences were immense.

The immediate upshot was that Rana refused to continue standing in the match unless Gatting apologised. This the England captain was prepared to do, provided he got an apology in return. This was being brokered behind the scenes when Rana decided not to apologise after all. Most accounts of the affair blame Miandad, who could recognise a lifeline when he saw one, and who persuaded the now world-famous umpire that the honour of Pakistan was at stake and that he should stick to his guns. With no apology from Rana, none was forthcoming from Gatting, and the stalemate cost the entire third day's play. The England team took the field, but the home side stayed in the pavilion, happily ensconced behind the barricade of Rana's injured feelings.

The England team took a leaf out of the bodyline side's book and issued a statement of support for their captain, and Gatting only backed down under the most intense pressure from the TCCB (themselves under pressure from the Foreign Office), who ordered Peter Lush to ensure the impasse was resolved 'at any cost'. In the end, Gatting delivered his famous and much photographed scrap of paper, which looked, for all the world, like a hastily written note for the milkman. It consisted of the tersest apology 'for the bad language used during the 2nd day of the Test Match at Fisalabad [sic]'; and the game continued.

However, the lost day was not replaced, and with rain costing more time, the match petered out into a draw, and England's best chance of winning a Test in Pakistan until December 2000 was wasted. The third Test, played under another cloud of controversy after the home authorities had insensitively chosen Shakeel Khan, who had stood at Lahore, to officiate and only withdrawn him after vigorous protests, also fizzled out in a draw, so giving the series to Pakistan, 1–0.

As a surprising coda, the England players were each awarded a 'hardship bonus' of £1,000. Many of them, on hearing the sum, assumed it was a fine, and were astonished to discover they were being given it on top of their contracted fees. As Mike Selvey, who covered the tour, said, 'It was widely interpreted as conscience money.' Looking back on the affair, Gatting described it as 'strictly a one-off thing in which we were in my opinion set up, and we were made to pay for the Pakistanis' feud with umpire Constant which was nothing to do with me, and perhaps, too, it arose out of their frustration at not having done very well in the World Cup.'

Unfortunately, it proved anything but a one-off thing. The two sides next met in 1992, again in the aftermath of a World Cup, but this time England had succumbed disappointingly in the final to Imran Khan's 'cornered tigers'. The series – the first five-Test series between the two countries – developed just as hostile an atmosphere, and produced some equally unedifying scenes as the Gatting tour of 1987, though this time it was the Pakistan captain Javed Miandad locking horns with an English umpire.

The incident took place at Old Trafford, when Roy Palmer intervened to warn Aqib Javed, the youngest of the Pakistani fast bowlers, for intimidatory bowling against Devon Malcolm. This incensed the Pakistanis, who claimed that Malcolm had dished out the short stuff to Aqib in the previous match, and was now simply being served some of his own medicine. That was no justification for Aqib shouting at the umpire, still less for his captain to come steaming in to add to the fracas. It was the end of the over, and Palmer had difficulty pulling Aqib's sweater out of his belt, and when it came it looked as though he might have thrown it at him in disgust. According to Wasim Akram, that was clearly not the case (though the manager Intikhab Alam was to tell the press it was). In Wasim's view, 'it was basically Javed Miandad's fault. He ought to have stepped in straight away when he saw that his young excitable bowler was losing his rag at the end of a tiring day. He should have told Aqib to get back to his mark and stop harassing the umpire . . . But that wasn't Javed's style; he looked for confrontation.'

There were more confrontations in the next Test at Headingley, when England struggled hard to score the 99 runs they needed to square the series. They got them, but not before the visitors had been 'flabbergasted' by some of the umpiring decisions. Graham Gooch should have been run out on 13. The television replays showed him out of his ground by yards, but Ken Palmer, brother of Roy, said 'Not Out', while David Gower, according to Wasim, 'was plumb out twice, lbw and caught off bat and pad at short leg', but survived to steer England closer to victory. 'Keep fighting, boys – but we'll have to hit the stumps to get them out!' was a cry that could have been lifted straight from the script of the Gatting tour of 1987.

But the 1992 tour will be remembered longest not for the *contretemps* between Pakistani players and umpires but for the highly emotive issue of ball tampering. This was something that could not be defused with a handwritten note; in fact, it led some of the protagonists, including the umpire Don Oslear, to the witness box in the High Court.

CHAPTER 12

Ball Tampering

———

Ball tampering has been around since time immemorial. The first recorded instance of a bowler deliberately changing the condition of a ball occurred in 1806, when Beldham, Robinson and Lambert played Bennett, Fennex and Lord Frederick Beauclerk in a single-wicket match at Lord's. It was a closely fought match, but Beauclerk's last innings looked to be winning the game. As Pycroft recalls in *The Cricket Field*:

> His lordship had then lately introduced sawdust when the ground was wet. Beldham, unseen, took up a lump of wet dirt and sawdust, and stuck it on the ball, which, pitching favourably, made an extraordinary twist, and took the wicket. This I heard separately from Beldham, Bennett, and also Fennex, who used to mention it as among the wonders of his long life.

If there are few other known instances of interfering with the ball during the nineteenth century that is because bowlers simply didn't see the need. For the most part they were playing on wickets which gave them all the help they could want. Charles Kortright summed up the science of fast bowling in the Victorian period with touching simplicity: 'Personally, I didn't worry a great deal about how I held the ball in relation to the seam as long as I got a firm grip on it, and I think most of my contemporaries felt the same.' Bowlers, in fact, were quite often seen rubbing the ball in the dirt to remove the shine to improve their grip, and this was perfectly legal until the law changed in 1980.

Things changed in the twentieth century. With George Hirst

developing such prodigious swing that he needed all the canni-ness of his Yorkshire team-mate Wilfred Rhodes to help him control it, a whole new school of bowlers came into being, who saw the virtue of keeping one side of the ball shiny to assist its movement in the air.

The only aids to shining allowed in the Laws were sweat, spit and elbow-grease, but it wasn't long before bowlers and fielding sides generally started resorting to other ploys. And these were not limited to aiding the swing bowlers. Seamers like a proud seam, and spinners need a good grip, so in time seams were picked and resin smuggled on to the field. In fact, it soon became generally accepted that the ball was the preserve of the fielding side, and that provided they didn't actually bring a boot-boy out on to the field to polish the thing under the umpire's nose, no one was going to worry too much. Arthur Mailey, the great Aus-tralian leg-spinner, cheerfully admitted to carrying resin in his pocket, and when that ran out, to getting bird-lime off Bert Old-field's wicket-keeping gloves. He was also happy to pick the seam for the fast bowling duo, Gregory and McDonald.

In the Test at Adelaide in 1932–3, Maurice Leyland, acting 'under orders', accused Bert Ironmonger of using resin. Jack Fin-gleton describes the bowler's reaction:

> Ironmonger snorted. A look of injured virtue flitted over his face.
>
> 'As if I would use such a thing,' he barked.
>
> He dived his hand into his pocket, took out a handkerchief, waved it furiously and defiantly – and clouds of something that looked like resin floated in the atmosphere.

The tradition of suiting the ball to the bowler's requirements continued unbroken after the Second World War, passed down from one generation to the next. Keith Miller, playing in the 'Victory' Tests of 1945, was taken in hand by George Pope, the Derbyshire seamer, who told him, 'I never go on the field bare-headed.' And he showed Miller why: despite the fact that he was bald, the inside of his cap was heavily greased with hair oil. Miller turned to Brylcreem.

Miller also became adept at lifting the seam. As he confided in *Cricket Crossfire*, 'If you can do this without being spotted by the umpire and you can get the ball to pitch on the seam it will fairly fizz through.' Everybody knew this went on, but it was rare for any action to be taken, though Miller recalled one occasion during the Headingley Test of 1953 when he attracted unwelcome attention. The players were leaving the field after an appeal against the light, and

> without thinking, I threw the ball to umpire Frank Lee. I had been bowling and had made the seam stand up. Unfortunately I had forgotten to press it down again before tossing the ball to Frank. When he looked at it, he called out to me, 'The seam is rather high today, isn't it, Keith? How did it come about?'
>
> 'Oh,' I replied, trying to sound ever so casual, 'I suppose it's these cheap balls we are getting nowadays. You know how it is, Frank. Craftsmanship is not what it was.' I thought I had struck just the right tone of carelessness in my tone. But Frank gave me what is known as an 'old-fashioned look'. He didn't believe my explanation but he had to accept what I said.

Other bowlers have been subjected to 'old-fashioned looks', sometimes when it was hardly justified. On the MCC tour to South Africa in 1948–9, Doug Wright was reprimanded by an umpire for licking his fingers. Shortly afterwards the following verse appeared in *The Times*:

> As finger-bowls would be denied
> To cricketers (fastidious souls),
> So Wright claims right upon his side
> And having licked his fingers, bowls.

Three decades later, on the MCC tour to India in 1976–7, Bob Willis and Peter Lever came under suspicion. Both applied gauze strips to their foreheads with Vaseline in order, they said, to stop sweat running into their eyes; but Bishen Bedi, the Indian captain, accused them of using the resultant substance to shine the ball illegally. After consultation with the manager and the team captain, Tony Greig, Lord's rejected the allegation.

Ball tampering only became an issue with the rise of a new phenomenon in fast bowling, reverse swing. This was a Pakistani invention, and is generally regarded as being the only genuine innovation in seam bowling for nearly a hundred years. As its name suggests, reverse swing is when the ball moves in the opposite direction to that expected by the batsmen. Other features are the exaggerated movement and the lateness of the swing, and the fact that it can only be achieved with an old, well-worn ball. For normal swing bowling, the shine is paramount, and all sides jealously preserve it, keeping the ball off the ground as much as possible and polishing it vigorously in between deliveries. But playing conditions in Pakistan mean that the new ball loses its shine very quickly. With slow, grassless wickets offering little or no movement off the seam, and with the traditional aid to swing, the original lacquer, going so early, Pakistani seam bowlers cast around for a new method of getting the ball to move and ended up making a virtue of the fact that the shine goes fast. In the words of one of the leading practitioners, Wasim Akram:

> We started to avoid the usual method of keeping one side polished, hoping that would aid the swing. Instead, we kept one side smooth and the other rough. The idea is to weigh down one side of the ball so that it acts as a bias against the other, leading to unexpected and late swing. We would weigh down the smooth side with sweat and spit, earth or mud, so that it would be heavier than the dry, rough side.

So far, so ingenious. But the question was whether the work put in on the ball was legitimate or did it constitute ball tampering?

Sarfraz Nawaz is generally credited with being the father of reverse swing – 'Yes, Lambie, I am the king,' he once crowed on bowling an unplayable banana at his Northamptonshire colleague and future High Court opponent – but the bowler who attracted the most attention for his power to extract dramatic movement from the old ball was Imran Khan. Imran has been quite open about his methods, claiming that all seam bowlers like to tailor the ball to their needs and always have done. He has gone on record as saying: 'I have occasionally scratched the side and lifted the seam. Only once did I use an object. The ball was not deviating at all, so I got the 12th man to bring on a bottle top and it started to move around a lot.' This was in a county match between Sussex and Hampshire in 1981, and on that occasion the ploy went undetected.

A year later, when Pakistan toured England, people did begin to take notice. One of these was Allan Lamb. In the Lord's Test of 1982, he noted how Imran and Mudassar Nazar 'swung the ball so much throughout . . . in conditions where our bowlers hardly got it to wobble, we even wondered whether they had found some ingredient to help make the ball swing'. At the end of the match the balls were taken away for examination, but the report on them 'showed that no unusual substance had been used'. Imran supplied 'a simple answer' – Pakistan bowlers were 'more dedicated polishers of the ball than any others in the world because of the hard wicket conditions in Pakistan'.

Imran's dedication to bringing the ball's condition into harmony with his own ambitions for its movement in the air was brought to the attention of the umpire Don Oslear in 1983 when Sussex played Warwickshire at Edgbaston. With an old ball, Imran took 6 wickets for 6 runs in 23 deliveries, including a hat-trick. Alvin Kallicharran, watching from the security of the bowler's end, commented, 'How Imran did what he did in that spell of six for 6, I will never know. It was easily the most astonishing spell of bowling I have ever seen in my entire career.' Others were less impressed. Chris Old told the *Daily Mirror*, 'I saw the ball [Imran] had tampered with, and it looked like a dog had chewed it'; while for Oslear,

> This was the first time I had seen one side of the ball scratched and torn, with pieces of leather ripped out. The quarter-seam had been opened up at a point where it meets the stitched seam and it appeared that some of the stitches had been cut. This allowed a triangle of leather to be pulled up from the surface of the ball; it was a piece large enough to be gripped between forefinger and thumb, and by which the ball could be suspended.

He sent a report to Lord's.

A decade later, Imran's protégés, the amazing Waqar Younis and Wasim Akram, backed up by Aqib Javed, also started producing devastating late swing with the old ball, and cricket was running literally hell for leather into yet another controversy. The first concerted murmurings against the pair came in the 1990–1 season, when Pakistan played host to New Zealand and the West Indies. The New Zealanders in particular were convinced that balls had been tampered with, and on their return home, the manager, Ian Taylor, said, 'I'm not sure how they did it – whether they used fingernails or sandpaper. *I would not have been surprised if they used knives.*' He also admitted that one of his seam bowlers, Chris Pringle, had experimented with the same tactics in the third Test at Faisalabad, and ended up taking 7 for 52 as the home side were dismissed for 102. The New Zealand accusations received some support from an unexpected quarter. Mudassar Nazar, now Pakistan national 'B' coach, declared: 'The outlawed practice of roughing up one side of the ball to enhance swing must be eradicated in Pakistan. It's got to stop; it will be hard to enforce, but we will be firm.'

There were more murmurings during the West Indies series that followed, especially when Pakistan won the first Test at Karachi by 8 wickets. Imran Khan, who had felt it beneath his dignity to play an obviously inferior New Zealand side, was back at the Pakistani helm, conducting bowling operations at one remove. Wasim and Waqar took 8 wickets between them in the first innings and another 7 in the second, which prompted a response from the West Indies manager, Lance Gibbs. However, the secretary of the Pakistan Board said that on being shown the evidence at the end of the match, 'the manager agreed that the ball used by the West Indians was in a much worse condition than the one used by Pakistan'.

As a once-great spin bowler, Lance Gibbs may not have been party to the fast bowler's new necromancy. Certainly, Mudassar Nazar thought the West Indians were 'worse than us' in this respect. One member of the visiting party had confided to him that they had been ball tampering for the last two Tests against England in the Caribbean the previous year. As John Crace put it, 'both sides realized that if there was anything untoward going on, then both sides were at it, and no one was gaining an appreciable advantage'.

By this time, the triumvirate of young Pakistani stars were playing county cricket in England, Wasim for Lancashire, Waqar for Surrey and Aqib for Hampshire. In 1991, all did well, especially Waqar, who took 113 wickets. To say that no eyebrows were raised by their methods would not be true. As Don Oslear noted in *Tampering with Cricket*, 'reports were received by the TCCB from a number of their contracted umpires about illegal interference with the ball by two or three sides, all of which contained a Pakistan Test bowler'. The counties involved were Lancashire, Surrey and Hampshire. According to Vic Marks (then of Somerset), when 'an abused ball' was handed round at the county captains' meeting at Lord's in 1991, there were signs of recognition from some around the table. David Hughes, of Lancashire, 'gulped' at the evidence, and 'passed it on to Ian Greig of Surrey who, adhering to the forthright tradition of the family, blurted out, "This looks like one of ours"'. But the general run of English cricketers seemed to have accepted that here were three exceptionally talented young fast bowlers making their mark with sensational performances. As for their methods, the general attitude can probably be gauged from the relaxed exchange between Imran Khan and Robin Smith outside a wine bar in St John's Wood before the start of the Lord's Test against the West Indies in 1991. Allan Lamb reports that Imran asked the Hampshire captain how Aqib was doing: 'Robin said, "Very well – he was doing a good job for us but had got warned on numerous occasions for tampering with the ball." Imran replied, "Yes, I've told him to be more discreet when he does it."'

Three talented young fast bowlers trying it on in county cricket was apparently one thing; but when the trio emerged as the difference between the two sides when Pakistan played England in five Tests and a one-day series, attitudes hardened. 1992 generated quite as much acrimony as Gatting's 1987 tour, and cast a far wider radius of fall-out.

Ian Botham summarised the situation in *The Botham Report*:

At the heart of the controversy lay the conviction of myself, Allan Lamb and several other England players, not to mention Micky Stewart [the England manager], that the Pakistan bowlers Wasim Akram, Waqar Younis and Aqib Javed tampered with the ball throughout. I remain convinced to this day that all three of them cheated by contravening the laws of the game.

Botham cites *Law 42.4: Lifting the seam* – A player shall not lift the seam of the ball for any reason . . . ; and *Law 42.5:*

Changing the condition of the ball – . . . No one shall rub the ball on the ground or use any artificial substance or take any other action to alter the condition of the ball . . . before returning to the charge:

> In my opinion the actions of Wasim, Waqar, and Aqib Javed were in clear and direct contravention of those laws. Using their fingernails they made such an unholy mess of the ball at times that a ball that had been in use for 40 or 50 overs looked as though a pack of dogs had chewed it.

Suspicions were voiced throughout the five Tests, and on one occasion the ball was submitted by the umpires to the match referee, but no action was taken. The series was a close one, but what turned it in Pakistan's favour were England's cataclysmic middle-order collapses. At Lord's their last 6 wickets managed 42 runs in the first innings and 38 in the second; at Headingley they lost their last 8 wickets for 28 runs; and at the Oval they declined from 182 for 3 to 207 all out and in the second innings from 153 for 5 to 174 all out. In those five collapses, 221 runs were accumulated for the loss of 36 wickets, of which Waqar and Wasim claimed 24. It was after the fifth and deciding match at the Oval that Micky Stewart, the retiring England manager, declared darkly that he knew how they did it. He bit back any further comment, but the implication was clear.

The only time the umpires took action over the condition of the ball occurred in the one-day international at Lord's in August. Because of rain, the game had gone into the second day, the Sunday. England were batting in the morning session, and as the players came off for lunch, Allan Lamb was seen talking to the two umpires, Ken Palmer and John Hampshire. During the lunch interval the two officials, backed up by the third umpire, Don Oslear, decided to replace the ball, and informed the match referee, the former West Indian wicket-keeper Deryck Murray, accordingly.

In the view of Don Oslear, 'What followed that decision by the umpires was a shambles or a cover-up and most likely both, with neither the TCCB, which appointed the umpires, nor the ICC, which appointed the match referee, prepared to state why the ball had been replaced . . .'

An embarrassed silence fell over Lord's like an untidily draped tarpaulin. This enraged the England dressing-room, and, rather like Bradman leaking Woodfull's remark at Adelaide in 1933, Botham tipped off the press corps. Lamb followed this by writing up his version of events for the *Daily Mirror*. The article appeared on 26 August under the headline 'How Pakistan Cheat at Cricket'.

In the absence of any official announcement, the Pakistan coach, Intikhab Alam, replied to press speculation by saying that the ball had been replaced, as the Pakistanis themselves had wanted, because it had gone out of shape. It was also pointed out that when the breakthrough came, and England succumbed to yet another collapse – from 172 for 5 to 201 all out (to lose by just 3 runs) – the damage was done by the replacement ball. A further technical point was that while Law 42 (5) governing changing a ball because it had been tampered with states that the replacement should be of markedly inferior quality (an irony, given that reverse swing depends on the rapid deterioration of the ball), in actual fact the replacement ball at Lord's was not markedly inferior, so the change could not have been made for that reason.

The authorities' silence was resented by both sides. Wasim Akram later wrote: 'What really fanned the flames was the reaction afterwards of the ICC referee, Deryck Murray. He refused to make any comment, other than confirming that the ball had been changed. That gave our detractors an open goal to aim at.' It was a case of 'no smoke without fire'. Meanwhile, for Lamb there was plenty of fire, and he found himself roasted on it. First his county, Northamptonshire, suspended and fined him for breaking his contract, and then the TCCB 'bounced' him with an even stiffer £5,000 fine. When they followed this up by giving Surrey a suspended fine of a mere £1,000 for ball-tampering offences the previous season, the disparity in treatment was too obvious to overlook. Under the headline 'Silencing the Sacrificial Lamb', Donald Saunders wrote in the *Telegraph*: 'Now we are left to conclude that talking to the newspapers about controversial incidents in an international match is a far deadlier sin than cheating in the County Championship.'

Lamb decided to appeal against his fine, but while attracting popular support for his go-it-alone, Charles Bronson-type vigilante stand, he was also coming under intense pressure to drop it. With scenes of enthusiastic book-burning on the streets of Bradford an all too vivid recent memory, it was hardly surprising that the authorities were keen to prevent any further affront to the sensibilities of the Muslim community. As Lamb wrote in his *Autobiography*, a senior Northamptonshire figure tipped him off that

> he had been speaking to someone in Anglo-Pakistani diplomatic circles who had just come back from Pakistan, and he thought that things could get heavy. I asked him in what way, and he hinted at threats . . . to me and my family. He even said that there could be race riots in the Midlands if I went ahead with the appeal, and told me that it was such a sensitive issue that it would be better for everyone concerned if I let it go without any further action.

The TCCB expressed the position more formally during the interminable exchanges in the build-up to the first of the libel cases Lamb was involved in over the next three years: 'there is a serious risk that the court hearing and more particularly the press reports of it will serve to exacerbate relationships with the Pakistan Board of Control and with the Pakistani community in England as a whole. These are both matters of legitimate and serious concern.'

If Lamb felt himself increasingly under the *fatwa* of the TCCB, he was also on the receiving end from those he had accused. Waqar and Wasim responded to Lamb's initial article with a statement in the *Telegraph* in which they said, 'We are amazed that a fellow professional has stooped so low as to make such unfounded comments in the papers. We can only guess at Allan Lamb's motives for his article in the *Daily Mirror*, but we hope that they are nothing to do with money or even worse our nationality.'

For Imran Khan the question of motives was uppermost, and would eventually lead him to the High Court to defend (successfully) a libel case brought by Botham and Lamb. In his view, the ball-tampering controversy simply confirmed what he had felt about English cricket and society for a long time. All through the 1980s cricket relations had been strained, as much by off-the-pitch events as on: racist taunts from sections of the Edgbaston and Headingley crowds at Test matches; campaigns in the tabloid press, culminating in the infamous *Sun* headline from 1987 – 'Paki Cheats'; and, of course, the equally notorious remark by Botham, which might have been lifted straight from the *Bernard Manning Joke Book*, that he would not even send his mother-in-law to Pakistan. In May 1992, Imran had delivered a pre-emptive strike in an article headlined 'Cheats Tag Rooted in Colonial Attitudes', but exposed himself to the charge of trying to have it both ways. 'They accuse us of doctoring cricket balls, with one side of the ball apparently scratched by the bowlers. Why should it be such a crime to do that?' he asked. To which Don Oslear replied in *Tampering with Cricket*: 'Because it is against the Laws of Cricket.' The umpire added, 'In my remarks to Lord's about Imran in 1983, I did not accuse him of cheating, although the weight of evidence pointed that way and is now endorsed by his own admission.'

Oslear was the key witness in the first of the two libel cases that arose from the 1992 series. This was brought against Allan Lamb by Sarfraz Nawaz, who claimed that he was libelled in Lamb's original article in the *Mirror*. It was widely suspected that Sarfraz, who had retired the previous decade, was really a stalking horse for Waqar and Wasim. Whatever the truth of that, the case ended up focusing on the events of 23 August 1992, and the reason why the ball was changed. The climax came when Oslear was asked on oath, 'Was the ball changed under Law 42 (5)?' and he replied, 'Most certainly, sir.' At that point Sarfraz threw in the towel, later claiming that the case was not 'serious' because there were 'nine young girls on the jury who didn't know the difference between a football and a cricket ball. We should have had a multi-racial jury, instead we had 11 English people.' Costs were awarded to Lamb.

The wider fall-out was considerable and the press had a field-day, just as the TCCB had feared. And to compound their fears, most fingers were pointing at the game's administration and its instinctive culture of secrecy. Alan Lee in *The Times* reflected on the key revelation that the ball had been changed under Law 42 (5):

That it had not been made public before is a matter for the conscience of the ICC. Its appointed officers chose to remain silent, inviting the worst and most prolonged form of speculation which eventually led to the High Court. It was a silence which spoke of fear and weakness, provoked by the belief that Pakistan would either take legal action or abort the tour, maybe both if the truth was told.

Martin Johnson in the *Independent* wrote scathingly:

As always, the 'sit tight and say nothing' approach by the ICC and TCCB has merely made things worse. As far as Pakistan are concerned, cricket in England is run by arrogant racists. As far as England are concerned, Pakistan cheat. Today the two countries are as far apart as ever.

Many felt that tougher action sooner would have prevented the whole sorry business. The law governing ball tampering had been strengthened in 1990 – the umpires being given the power to replace a ball with one 'of inferior condition' – but there was no point in giving them more powers if they were not then supported when they tried to act. Oslear for one felt that the umpires had been let down by 'a weak and inept cricket administration'.

The whole thing was a sorry mess, and a libel case was the least satisfactory way of resolving it. Not that it did. As we have seen, Sarfraz did not accept defeat, and certainly those originally accused of ball tampering refused to plead guilty to cheating. In his cricketing autobiography, published in 1998, five years after the High Court case, Wasim Akram devoted an entire chapter to denying the charges. He called it 'England's Bad Losers', and declared, 'I'm certain that the English camp tried to catch us out in 1992 because they failed to understand that they had been undermined by a radical new bowling technique. The new art of swing bowling had passed them by and they were found out.'

As to his own methods, he writes,

At no stage in my career has an umpire said, 'Stop that! You're tampering with the ball.' It would be virtually impossible to do that in front of umpires, especially in England where they have become very jumpy about this issue. At various stages we all do little things to help the ball along. When I want it to get drier to aid the reverse swing, I've thrown the ball on the square, into a rough patch . . . I've taken mud off the seam and raised the seam with my finger, but so has many another bowler. Sometimes, when my grip isn't too good, I'll put mud or earth on the seam and wet my fingers, but I don't call that ball-tampering.

Of course, what the bowler calls ball tampering and what umpires and opponents think may be very different things. There are parallels with the ancient controversies over the March of Intellect style of round-arm bowling in the first half of the nineteenth century. Just as in the early debate over whether round-arm constituted an obvious affront to the laws of the game or an inevitable step in cricket's evolution, so reverse swing and the means employed to achieve it divided the cricket community.

The Essex and England seamer Derek Pringle was more intrigued than outraged. He was playing in the final Test at the Oval, and so was in a good position to assess what happened.

Pakistan defended with the new ball until it started to reverse swing. The methods by which they achieve this are against the rules, yet while it was obvious after the end of the innings that the ball had been tampered with – I happened to have a good look at it – it is virtually impossible for the umpires to detect the process as it is under way.

The slight hint of admiration is confirmed in Pringle's admission that he tried something similar when playing for Essex against Australia in 1985. Although he had not been personally discovered, the umpires had known something was up and changed the ball. He concludes, 'Some English bowlers who try it are usually doing it for themselves only, but Pakistan's entire match strategy is based upon getting the ball to reverse swing.'

Ted Dexter too saw the positive side: 'For the first time it seems that somebody had found that, by damaging [the ball], they can make it swing. That could be a good thing because it makes the bowlers pitch the ball up and, if the ball swings more, maybe not so many bouncers will be bowled.' Two more former

England captains, David Gower and Bob Willis, were for a gentle relaxation of the law. For Gower the subject was not really 'an item' until he moved to Hampshire and started playing with Aqib Javed – 'and he knew the theory'. All the same, according to Gower,

> It still comes down to skill, and the authorities will have to face up to it because it is not going to go away. It needs a high-quality bowler to use it properly, and personally I would support a liberalisation of the Law. I would not go all the way and allow bottle tops and such like, but a reversion to the pre-1980 change of law to allow rubbing the ball into the ground is more easily controllable by umpires.

Willis would also support change – 'to allow fingernails to help roughen one side' – but again would draw the line at artificial aids.

Graham Gooch, England's captain in 1992 (though not in fact for the particular match in which the ball was changed), played ultra-safe in his cricketing memoirs, saying the charges of ball tampering remained 'unproven'. In signing up with the 'Hear no evil, see no evil, speak no evil' party, he did put the question interestingly into context:

> Down the century in cricket there has always been a fine line between accepted gamesmanship and cheating. Gamesmanship has been part and parcel of county cricket since the championship began. For instance, what batsman hasn't 'inadvertently' scuffed the pitch with the studs on the soles of his boots when he's batting just before a declaration? Or what wicketkeeper hasn't 'accidentally' made a practice of running down the track to take a throw from the boundary and so scuffed up the pitch 'on a length' for his bowlers? As for ball tampering, perhaps the answer is for the umpires to throw the new ball to the fielding side at the beginning of an innings and say, 'There you are, it's yours for 100 overs, shine or mutilate it as much as you want'.

If roughening up the side of a cricket ball is morally no better or worse than scuffing up the pitch to aid your own bowlers, then perhaps batsmen deserve what they get and everybody should be left to get on with it. Jack Bannister, co-author with hardliner Don Oslear of *Tampering with Cricket*, thinks that the authorities need to loosen the Law, recognising that for bowlers from the subcontinent there is 'little, if any, difference' between on the one hand 'doctoring the surface of one side of the ball by roughening it' and, on the other, 'producing a high polish . . . with illegal substances', which 'has happened in English cricket for years'.

Christopher Martin-Jenkins, writing in the *Daily Telegraph*, offered some judicious conclusions:

> Certain truths need repeating: that ball tampering is no greater cricketing crime than seam-lifting, which has been endemic in the game at all levels for decades; that if certain Pakistani bowlers are, or have been, pioneers in the dubious art of ball tampering, they are not the only ones to have tried it; that Pakistan have in Waqar Younis and Wasim Akram – and formerly had in Imran Khan – brilliant exponents of the fast, swinging yorker with an old ball; that these men would have been emulated by other bowlers of their own and other nationalities if only they had possessed the necessary skill; that batsmen defeated by swinging deliveries of full length have less reason to complain about the broken spirit of the game than those whose bones have been broken by bouncers; and that, despite all this, the law is explicit and needs to be enforced.

1992 was not an isolated year for ball tampering. Indeed, at the end of the previous season, umpires in the last Test against the West Indies had told Gooch that they suspected his bowlers of breaking the rules. Two years later, his successor as England captain, Michael Atherton, found himself hauled over the tabloid coals for the 'dirt in the pocket' incident.

This occurred in the first Test match of the short series between England and South Africa on the latter's readmission into the international fraternity. What happened was that on a hot and slightly sticky afternoon Atherton was seen repeatedly dipping his hand into his trouser pocket and then seemingly applying something to the ball when he brought it out. When challenged by the match referee Peter Burge over this 'unusual action', he denied having anything in his pocket, but as *Wisden* noted:

> . . . the following day, after further television pictures were shown that looked even more sinister, and England's batsmen had crumbled to a humiliating four-day defeat, Atherton admitted publicly that he had not told Burge the truth by saying that he had nothing in his pocket. In fact, he said, he had some dirt there that he picked up to keep his hands dry and prevent moisture getting on the ball while Darren Gough was trying to reverse swing it; the second set of pictures clearly showed some dirt falling off it.

After the furore of 1992, it was obviously paramount that the England captain should be above reproach, and in being 'economical with the truth' Atherton put himself in a much more difficult position. He was saved from dismissal by the prompt, if draconian, fines levied by the new England supremo, Ray Illingworth. Later, in his book *A Test of Cricket*, Atherton wrote, 'I am not alone in thinking that the Laws should be changed to allow certain action[s] which the players tacitly accept as part and parcel of the game.' There's no evidence that the South Africans minded much, except insofar as the whole thing distracted attention from their thoroughly well-earned victory.

After their years in the wilderness, they were finding many new developments, but fundamentally Test cricket was just as competitive as before, with teams and individuals as determined to gain the last ounce of advantage over their opponents as they ever had been.

CHAPTER 13

Turf Wars, Time Bandits and Space Invaders

Just as tinkering with the condition of the ball to gain an advantage over your adversaries has been around for a long time, so too has skewing the turf in favour of your team. The groundsman has always had the potential to swing a match or a series, and all countries tend to produce wickets that help their own side – if only because their own players have grown proficient in their own conditions.

Far back in the game's history, it was indeed the prerogative of bowlers to choose the pitch, and the great Hambledon bowler David Harris was a past-master at selecting the wicket most advantageous to him, not always to the entire satisfaction of his own side's batsmen. The art of preparing a pitch came surprisingly late in cricket's evolution. Thomas Lord took his turf with him on both occasions that he moved his ground, but although that might argue some reverence for the 'hallowed' playing surface, the actual wickets were so shoddily cared for that it probably indicated only a desire to cut costs. Attitudes were such that in the 1850s, when an agricultural grass cutter was purchased, one of the more reactionary members of the MCC committee conscripted a group of navvies to destroy it. This instinctive Luddism suffered a reverse with the death of George Summers in 1870, and that year a heavy roller was at last employed on the notorious Lord's square.

Despite being able to bat better than anyone on bad wickets, W. G. Grace was passionate about their improvement. He was appalled at the state of the Australian wickets he found on his first tour in 1873–4 – one up-country pitch was so bad it would have been preferable to use the road outside the ground; a very slow ball simply refused to bounce and stopped dead in the dirt like an egg – and one of his lasting legacies was to lay down the rudiments of groundsmanship. By the time he returned eighteen years later, Australian pitches were well on the way to the perfection that would allow such heavy scoring in the twentieth century.

As the standard of wickets improved, so it made more sense to try to influence the way they would play. Rules regulating rolling and the covering of ends increased in number and detail, and with them the temptation to assist the natural processes of wind and rain. Grace was a stickler for such matters, and once nearly called off the friendliest of friendlies in Tasmania because he swore the pitch had been rolled before the start of play when it shouldn't have been.

More concerted pitch-fixing was a feature of twentieth-century cricket, both domestic and international. The Old Trafford wicket was so dangerous in 1901 that the Lancashire fast bowler Jack Sharp took 100 wickets in the season, and on one occasion C. B. Fry extracted a collection of pebbles or foreign bodies which were later displayed in the window of Johnny Tyldesley's sports shop in Deansgate. Suiting the ground to your bowlers was by no means universal. Harold Larwood and Bill Voce, for instance, slaved away on the featherbed of Trent Bridge, described by Neville Cardus as 'A lotus land for batsmen, a place where it was always afternoon and 360 for 2 wickets,' and by common consent there was less of it before the Second World War than after it. One professional whose career spanned the war years said when interviewed in the late 1970s:

I think the game is farcical compared to what it used to be. I was brought up on the finest ground in England – they played bowls on the outfield – and I had to learn my craft on it . . . Today, there is so much fiddling of wickets that a lot of good bowling performances are fictitious. When they come to play on good test wickets, they haven't learned their craft . . . Since the war, counties have prepared wickets to suit their bowlers. The celebrated story on one ground during the 1950s was of a visiting captain who, on being asked which roller he would like, replied, 'I don't want a b. . . roller: I need a s. . . vacuum cleaner.'

Writing in 1959, Bill Bowes told readers of *The Cricketer*: 'The spectator is fed up with seeing Laker and Lock, on helpful pitches, winning the County Championship for Surrey seven times in succession and making all international games in England a near farce.' The editor of *Wisden* took the same line in his Notes for 1959, pontificating on the 'Fallacy of "Sporting" Pitches', which he said had been 'in vogue in this country since the war. It was very satisfactory to outplay our visitors on these uncertain surfaces, but the fallacy has been revealed in our most recent tours to West Indies, South Africa and Australia, where England failed each time to win the rubber.' A case in point was the Old Trafford pitch on which Jim Laker took 19 wickets against Australia in 1956. It was perhaps fortunate that this sporting triumph coincided with the Suez crisis, a point acknowledged by the groundsman, Bert Flack, after the match.

The West Indians of 1957 fared no better. At the conclusion of the final Test at the Oval, which England won by an innings thanks to their two spinners taking 16 wickets between them, Peter May said, 'I don't know if there is an answer to Lock and Laker on a wicket like this.' Clyde Walcott's response in *Sixty Years on the Back Foot* was: 'I know there isn't, but there must be a better way of preparing pitches. Three of the five in the series were suspect and each time we came off worse.'

In 1972, the Australians again found themselves on the wrong end of a helpful wicket against a home side with the best bowler in the world to exploit it – by coincidence making his first appearance in the series. Tony Lewis, writing his diary of the season for *The Cricketer*, wrote, 'The Leeds wicket has turned from the start, the ball has kept low. Certainly there was rain all over the square only the day before the match started, but before they even bother to strap the pads on for the second innings I give Australia no chance in these conditions.' He went on, 'I concede that world-class players have to cope with the most bizarre conditions without complaint but I believe in even contests. This one at Headingley is definitely not that.' His next entry reads: 'Oh dear! I was right . . . England (Underwood six for 48) won this Test match in three days and therefore retain the Ashes . . . Much has been written and spoken about the wicket. It is bound to be reported to Lord's.' And he concludes:

The Australian manager, Ray Steel, was quoted as saying that his camp were 'surprised and disappointed' by the pitch. With Lillee and Massie in peak form I am not surprised. Yet when MCC play abroad they have to face sticky dogs, bouncy Perth strips and all sorts. It is an argument that Test matches could be played on ash-tips if the players have the all-round quality. It is not an argument that appeals to me. The game of cricket is best played with both sides having a near even chance at the toss-up. Only one side could win this one.

Not everyone has shared Tony Lewis's concern. Ian Botham, for one, sees no reason to bend over backwards to be helpful to visitors. In his *Botham Report* he condemns the sort of wickets prepared for the Australians in 1993: 'By preparing in the main dry, grassless wickets, which, thanks to a roaring hot summer merely got drier and more bare as the series went on, the Test match groundsmen . . . more or less handed the Ashes to Shane Warne on a plate.' To prepare wickets with more grass on to help the home seam bowlers might have given rise to accusations of 'pitch-doctoring', but Botham questions why England 'alone among Test playing nations' should deny themselves home advantage.

There can be a serious conflict of interest between the groundsman, whose reputation is, after all, on the line, and the home side, whose main interest is a favourable result. Ron Allsop was in charge of Trent Bridge during the 1980s when Nottinghamshire had an exceptionally strong seam attack, led by Richard Hadlee. The Nottinghamshire captain, Clive Rice, another overseas star and a seamer in his own right, was reputedly always eager for the wickets to be left well grassed. Allsop resisted the pressure, on one occasion prompting the enquiry from Rice: 'What's the matter? Have you gone bloody religious?'

Allsop was his own man, and put the groundsmen's case eloquently when he explained the difficulty of producing a fair wicket which gives something for both batsman and bowler:

> If they want pitches that do bugger all, that's easy. If they want pitches that are dangerous, that's easy, too. Good cricket pitches, the sort we think we produce more often than not, are difficult. The dividing line between a flat pitch and a dodgy one is very thin, and occasionally you miscalculate. If the TCCB aren't careful, they will frighten groundsmen into being responsible for producing exactly the sort of cricket they used to moan about before.

The two most awesomely ill-prepared Test wickets of recent times have both involved hapless England sides facing the fury of the West Indies all-pace attack. At Edgbaston in 1995, the first ball of the match bowled by Curtly Ambrose rose like a jump jet and sailed over both batsman and wicket-keeper to clatter ominously into the hoarding at the far end of the ground. Once a few early sighters had established the relevant drop zone, England were doomed, and the match was over in just two and a half days.

Three years later in 1998, England went out to bat on an even greater minefield of a pitch in Jamaica. Alec Stewart managed one of the bravest 9s in the history of the game, while his fellow opener Mark Butcher, forced into the firing line as a late replacement, got a duck for his extra cap. It was quite clear the pitch was unfit for first-class cricket, and the two umpires bravely but sensibly abandoned the match.

While the groundsmen at Edgbaston and Kingston had no doubt done their best, the fate of the Headingley track in 1975 was determined by a desperate group determined to do their worst. Protesting the innocence of an armed bank robber (who, on release, was soon apprehended with stocking mask and gun in hand again), protesters broke into the ground, dug up parts of the wicket and poured oil on the grass, thus making the last day's play impossible and sabotaging a finely balanced match.

Although members of the public have on occasion been useful – most notably at the Oval in 1968 when they helped mop up the outfield, allowing Derek Underwood in turn to mop up the Australian tail – cricket has always been subject to unwanted interference from the popular seating, whether taking the form of vocal abuse, the hurling of missiles or straightforward pitch invasion.

Even after the game had grown out of its 'Wild West' phase and reached the maturity of the modern game, there were still plenty of incidents involving the paying public. Once, before the First World War which cost him his life, Colin Blythe was bowling to C. B. Fry during Canterbury Week. The sun was going down, and bowling from the west end of the ground, Blythe was tossing the ball up so the batsman was dazzled as he searched for its flight. This was apparently a well-known dodge of Blythe's at the end of the afternoon, but well-known or not, Fry didn't like it and demanded that stumps be drawn. The umpires demurred. Nor did the crowd think much of a batsman appealing against the light when the sun was bathing the St Lawrence ground in a beautiful warm evening glow. They started to boo. Fry eventually lost patience and set off from the square towards the crowd, telling them pretty plainly what he thought of them. The crowd retorted in kind, hurling abuse at the Sussex captain. Things only calmed down when his Kent counterpart appealed for a more sportsmanlike attitude, and the day's final overs were played out in stony silence.

This was not the only time that Fry's hauteur and free tongue had roused a county crowd to indignation. In 1894, just down from Oxford and playing his first season for Sussex, Fry appeared at the new county ground at Bristol. It was the August Bank Holiday, and a large crowd was disappointed when a heavy shower caused play to be abandoned for the day. In order to give them some amusement, W. G., the Gloucestershire captain, proposed a game of soccer on the practice ground. But this was not well received. If the ground was fit enough for football, it was fit enough for cricket.

The confrontation was perfectly good-humoured until Fry responded provocatively to one particular sally, and the mood turned hostile. Giving up any idea of football, the players tried to leave the ground, but were mobbed and heckled as they retreated, while a splinter group of outraged spectators headed for the square with the intention of wreaking havoc with the pitch. However, Ted Spry the groundsman, sensing trouble, had roped off a decoy strip, so the real one remained unscathed and the match could resume the following day.

The Bristol groundsman had better luck than a colleague in Kent. Sir Charles Igglesden, for many years the cricket correspondent for the *Kentish Express*, recalled an occasion when the umpires decided the Tonbridge ground was too wet and abandoned play for the day. 'This decision outraged the spectators, who, rushing up to the pitch, deliberately broke up the turf with the heels of their boots. A solitary policeman arrived, and they threatened to mob him.' They were finally persuaded to leave the ground, but the match could only be resumed in the morning once a new pitch had been cut.

In between the two world wars, the main issue involving crowds was barracking. Barracking had long been a tradition in Australia. W. G. was regularly barracked, and by the end of his second disastrous tour of 1891–2, was subjected to concerted mock applause every time he got near the ball. Forty years later, Douglas Jardine was the focus of the Australians' impotent fury during the Bodyline tour. It is often overlooked that, as far as the tourists were concerned, the constant vocal barrage was just as serious an infringement of the spirit of the game as the barrage of short-pitched bowling dished out by Larwood and Voce.

When the Australians came to England in 1934, some English crowds decided to retaliate. There was a particularly hostile atmosphere at Trent Bridge because of the way Larwood had been treated. Jack Fingleton remembers rhythmic hand-clapping as the bowler came up to bowl, and Don Bradman, now Australia's captain, sending out a message that if it continued, the batsmen were to 'withdraw from the wicket'. 'I told Hammond and he agreed with the orders. I therefore drew away. Next time I drew away and stopped Verity in his run-up, Verity squatted on his haunches and I went one further and sat on the turf.' Fingleton strongly disagreed with *Wisden*'s assessment of the barracking as 'never more than mild, certainly not hostile, and from only a small proportion of onlookers'. On the contrary, 'It came from around the ground, was continuous and loud, and, if I may say so, in execrable taste.' Bradman himself later drew away from the wickets when these tactics were directed at him.

The domestic post-1945 crowds were large and docile,

thrilled simply to bask in sunshine and the thrilling batsmanship of Bill Edrich and Denis Compton, but gradually, as society changed and cricket set itself deliberately to attract a new and less constrained audience, standards changed. In 1980, even members of the MCC disgraced themselves, during the Centenary Test at Lord's, when they mobbed umpires David Constant and Dickie Bird for their decision that the ground was unplayable after rain. In 1985, Mike Brearley could write without much fear of contradiction:

> Cricket crowds are getting more unpleasant. Policemen have been beaten up at drowsy Taunton; a pint of beer was thrown from the balcony of the pavilion at Old Trafford, narrowly missing Mike Smith and myself as we walked off for bad light during a Gillette Cup match; police dogs were brought into the ground at Headingley after fighting broke out between England and Pakistan supporters during the World Cup match in 1979.

There was more trouble when the two sides faced each other in a one-day international in 1987, with fights between 'gentlemen with white and brown faces', as a red-faced TCCB chairman Raman Subba Row put it. Pakistan's 1996 tour also witnessed more racially motivated trouble, which was not always policed either sensitively or fairly. A publication called *Inside Edge* noted that 'while racist chanting went on unchecked, spectators were treated to the surreal sight of a pantomime cow being ejected from the ground for parading up and down while play was in progress'.

While no England Test match has been subjected to a serious pitch invasion, let alone a full-scale riot,* England teams have had their share of excitement playing away from home. In India in 1961–2, the second Test was marred by crowd trouble. Mirrors were used to dazzle batsmen, fires were lit and fights kept breaking out, though despite these distractions, England managed a draw. When, at the end of the decade, the MCC tour to South Africa was abandoned due to the Basil d'Oliveira fiasco,

---

*However, the proposed South African tour was abandoned in 1970 because of the threat of just such action.

an alternative trip was hastily arranged to Ceylon and Pakistan at the beginning of 1969. While the former was a haven of peace, the latter was in political turmoil. The first Test at Lahore was played against the backdrop of a continuous riot. The captain, Colin Cowdrey, made a century out of a total of 306, with what Michael Melford described as 'a political pantomime' going on in the stands. Play was regularly interrupted by demonstrations among students 'who saw the series as a perfect soap box for their grievances'. Tom Graveney made a few air shots at invading spectators, commenting later, 'They weren't very hard, but I think they were my only decent strokes up until then.'

The second Test at Dacca could only be played by permission of the students, who had superseded the more usual agents of law and order. On an under-prepared wicket, and with something of a siege mentality prevailing, England held their own in an undistinguished draw. The third Test only got as far as the third day. Colin Milburn, flown in from Australia, scored an exhilarating century. Graveney was another centurian, and Alan Knott would almost certainly have made a third, but just as he was approaching three figures, the riot that had been threatening for some time finally exploded and discretion dictated a hasty retreat to the pavilion. Even there they did not feel safe as the adjacent VIP lounge was totally wrecked by the mob. Eventually the decision was taken to abort the game and withdraw from the tour. It was the first Test match to be abandoned because of a riot.

There were more riots on England's tour of 1977–8, which provided Mike Gatting with his first experience of Pakistan. He had vivid memories of the trouble sparked 'when Bhutto's daughter turned up to sit in the big covered stand' on the third evening:

> The rival faction on the other side started throwing chairs on to the canopy, and when the police waded in, all hell broke loose. There was teargas fired into the 35,000-strong crowd, and the players were rushed off the pitch under a hail of rubbish and seats. Some bricks that had marked the boundary were turfed up and thrown at police, the law made a stand in the middle of the pitch before being forced back, and the wire

fencing and gate to the dressing room enclosure came crashing down under the weight of seething Pakistani bodies trying to get in.

It was quite frightening waiting for the police reinforcements to come and rescue us. We'd barricaded ourselves in, putting chairs against the doors as bricks and rubble rained down on the dressing room, smashing the windows. We'd left one window slightly ajar for air and there we stood, with bats in our hands, listening to the crowds chanting and swarming outside. 'It's all right,' they shouted, 'we're not after you. We're after those nasty policemen.' Fortunately, when the cavalry came, they got them in overwhelming quantities.

But the subcontinent reserves its most ferocious crowd disturbances for encounters between India and Pakistan. These tend to be few and far between because of the political friction between the two nations, and more often than not the two sides meet on neutral ground – at Sharjah or even in Canada (though even in the anodyne atmosphere of Toronto a one-day match in 1997 was halted when a heckler with a megaphone incited Inzamam-ul-Haq to leave the field for the stands, bent on violent retribution). When a tour does take place it imposes huge strains on the visiting team. Wasim Akram recalled the Pakistan tour to India in 1987: 'At Ahmedabad and Nagpur, three of our fielders on the boundary resorted to wearing helmets, because they were being pelted with stones. It's incredibly tiring being put under that kind of pressure, but you can't complain because exactly the same thing happens to the Indians when they tour Pakistan.'

At Karachi, during the first Test of India's tour to Pakistan in 1989, a Pakistani supporter scaled the twelve-foot perimeter fence to attack Kapil Dev as he walked back to his bowling mark. This triggered a wider conflagration, during the course of which Srikkanth was also attacked and had his shirt ripped. Earlier in the same year, the Pakistanis had come under attack in the Punjab from fellow Muslims outraged that they had consented to take part in the Nehru Cup. They spent a miserable time being helicoptered around by the Indian army and pelted with stones when they appeared on the field. They were similarly hampered by their supposed supporters in a one-day series in

1997–8 at Karachi. Stone-throwing interrupted their innings four times, and when the fifth Indian fielder was hit, the umpires agreed with Sachin Tendulkar that things were becoming too dangerous and the Pakistan innings was halted mid-over, resulting in a much easier target for the visitors. A year later, in India, a Test match was seriously disrupted when Tendulkar was given out by the third umpire after being clearly impeded by Shoaib Akhtar from making his ground.

The other part of the cricketing world with a bad track record for crowd behaviour is the Caribbean. Len Hutton's unpopular tourists experienced trouble in the third Test at Georgetown in 1953–4. After going 2–0 down in the series, England badly needed a win, and with a first innings of 435 built around Hutton's 169, they achieved a commanding position. A West Indian collapse on the fourth day led to frustration in the crowd, but then the eighth-wicket pair put on 99, only to trigger a shower of bottles from the popular side when one of them was needlessly run out. Hutton kept his players on the field, albeit grouped around the pitch for safety, while Johnny Wardle produced some clowning antics to appease the crowd. Yorkshire phlegm was rewarded by an eventual resumption of play and the fall of further wickets that evening, leading to a crushing England victory.

The next official MCC tour of the West Indies took place in 1959–60 and was captained by Peter May. The manager, R. W. V. Robins, was mindful at all times of the diplomatic dimension. He wanted batsmen to walk and the captain to make sporting declarations. When Colin Cowdrey, deputising for May, failed to set a getable target on the last day of the fifth Test, preferring to play safe and retain the 1–0 lead won by hard graft, Robins gave him a dressing-down in front of the whole team.

But for all the efforts to ensure that the tour went off without trouble, trouble there was. The first Test was drawn, and the two sides resumed battle at Port of Spain, Trinidad. As ever, the internal politics of the West Indies contributed to an uneasy atmosphere, with two Jamaicans excluded from the final twelve flying home and alleging hostility from the locals who had thronged the net sessions. Meanwhile, C. L. R. James, journalist, Marxist and cricket theorist, was beating a familiar drum to the effect that the West Indies should shake off the old colonial tradition of having a white man as captain. He told his readers that 'the idea of Alexander captaining a side on which Frank Worrell is playing is to me quite revolting'.

England won the toss (as they did throughout the series) and scored 382 over the first two days. The home side started the third day with all 10 wickets standing, but were reduced to a parlous state by an astonishing performance by Fred Trueman and Brian Statham. The Yorkshire fast bowler took 4 for 32, including Rohan Kanhai, Gary Sobers (for a duck) and Worrell. On 98 for 7, Sonny Ramadhin called his fellow tail-ender Singh for a short single and Ted Dexter ran him out from cover. The umpire, Lee Kow, was in no doubt, and raised his finger. 98 for 8. Then, in the words of Alan Ross, 'it started':

> First an ugly, growing roar of protest, then a storm of boos, finally, from far back in the open stand to the right of the pavilion, the bottles.
>
> Lobbed like hand-grenades the opening volleys bounced separately along the boundary edge. Within seconds these had grown into thick showers, not from this stand only, but from all round the ground. May called his boundary fielders in, and in no time at all only a tiny island round the pitch was free of bottles.
>
> Gerry Alexander ran out through swarms of people who had now jumped the boundaries and were advancing menacingly on the middle. He talked briefly with May who had no alternative but to lead his players off the field. Flanked by police officers and with Trueman and Statham holding a stump each they managed to get safely through, the umpires, also with police escort, just behind them. A ricocheting stone struck Pullar on the elbow: otherwise they miraculously got through unscathed.

In an attempt to restore order, a fire-hose was turned on the rioters, but the pressure was low and the water 'merely sputtered out in pools at the firemen's feet like an elephant urinating'. This 'provoked a renewed frenzy of bottle and stone throwing', and the trouble subsided only with the arrival of mounted police. Thirty casualties needed hospital treatment, while a further sixty were treated for minor injuries. No more play was possible and the teams were escorted back to their hotels by the police.

Various dignitaries from the Governor down queued at the microphone to broadcast appeals for calm, coupled with denunciations of the 'disgraceful behaviour' which had disfigured Trinidad's 'good name for sportsmanship', and a telegram of abject apology was sent to the MCC. The wider public took a rather less solemn view of the incident, and were soon humming along to a new calypso by 'Lord Brynner'. The chorus went:

> It was bottle and stone riot in Queen's Park Oval,
> The whole test match turn to a carnival,
> I had to hide me clean head inside a canal,
> To get away from the big scandal,
> Right in the middle of the Federal Capital.

The song concluded:

> Anyhow I'm sure,
> These kind of things won't happen no more,
> Because I'm sure everybody understand,
> West Indian back-bone of cricket is England.

As it turned out, Lord Brynner was wrong. Seven years later there was trouble at Kingston, Jamaica. In 1967–8, the tourists were again regarded as underdogs, especially given that the first-choice captain had been replaced at short notice and under controversial circumstances by Colin Cowdrey, widely regarded as not tough enough for the job. In the event, England narrowly, but deservedly, won the rubber, 1–0. However, in *Wisden*'s words, the series was marred by 'sub-standard umpiring and unruly crowds':

Such is the pressure from supporters desiring success for the home side that even an efficient umpire is apt to be influenced. Umpiring and crowd behaviour are, therefore, closely associated. Quite the most professional of the umpires was Sang Hue, but he was never so efficient after as before his correct decision against Butcher in the second Test, which sparked a bottle-throwing riot by his fellow Jamaicans.

This was an instance of crowd misbehaviour materially influencing the outcome of a match. England batted first and, led by Cowdrey (101), posted a total of 376. John Snow then took 7 for 49 as the home side were rushed out for 143. Invited to follow on, the West Indians were hardly out of the woods at 204 for 4 when Butcher was dismissed by a diving catch by Jim Parks off Basil d'Oliveira. 205 for 5, and the abyss of defeat opening before them. On came the bottles, and off went the players. It took seventy-five minutes to restore order, and, once resumed, the game was transformed. From looking as though they were cruising to victory, England were suddenly rocked on to the back foot, first by brilliant batting from Sobers (113 not out, though dropped on 7), and then in their final innings by extraordinary umpiring.

As a very sporting gesture to the visitors, who were so clearly in the ascendant when play was disrupted, it had been agreed to make up the time lost to the riot by extending the match into the sixth day, but by then England were on the ropes. As *Wisden* reported: 'The last innings was played in a feverish atmosphere, which seemed to unsettle the umpires. Cowdrey was lbw off his bat, and in forty-two minutes England were reduced to 19 for four. During the final seventy-five minutes on the extra day they barely held off the spin of Gibbs and Sobers.' They finished on 68 for 8, a mere 2 wickets short of losing a match they had looked to be winning on the third day.

Although that was the most serious instance of crowd trouble during the tour, it was not the only one. In Trinidad during the fourth Test, which England won, Cowdrey was subjected to sustained booing by the home supporters. His only crime was to have produced two excellent innings and to have captained England more skilfully than Gary Sobers had led the West Indies.

After the final test, in Guyana, when the draw had secured England's victory in the rubber, the tourists were attacked when leaving the ground. Tony Lock was hit on the head by a stone, and the captain, once again, was singled out. He had to wait in the pavilion until it was safe for him to be escorted back to the hotel. Nonetheless, the tour was a personal triumph for Cowdrey, who had proved that competing successfully at Test level did not mean sacrificing sportsmanship or diplomacy.

It was six years after Cowdrey's victory when the next incident involving England and a West Indian crowd took place, at close of play on the second day of the first Test match at Port of Spain in February 1974. After a dispiriting English batting performance on the first day – all out for 131 – the tourists' bowlers had removed the cream of the West Indian batting – Clive Lloyd, Rohan Kanhai and Sobers – cheaply. Only Alvin Kallicharran had stopped it being England's day with an undefeated century – undefeated, that is, until the last ball. Or, indeed, until after the last ball.

The delivery in question was bowled to his partner Bernard Julien, who played it gently past Tony Greig at silly point and set off to the pavilion, Alan Knott helpfully pulling up the stumps for the umpire. At the other end, Kallicharran was also on the move, and by this time Greig had caught up with the ball. With his back to the players, he was the only person in the ground who hadn't realised hostilities had been suspended for the day, and, seeing Kallicharran out of his crease, winged in a direct throw to the stumps, instinctively appealing as the ball hit. The hapless umpire, Hang Sue (again), reluctantly, but correctly, raised his finger, and Kallicharran was indeed on his way – run out. Predictably enough, the home crowd were not pleased. The pavilion was soon besieged by an angry mob, and it was quite clear that no one was going to get back to the hotel without calling upon serious degrees of force, and that the continuation of the match, and possibly even the series, was in the balance.

Two hours later, after a lengthy discussion with the English party, the West Indies Board issued a statement which announced that 'in the interests of cricket generally and this tour in particular' the appeal had been withdrawn and Kallicharran would resume his innings next morning. In order not to undermine the umpire, who had bravely made what he must have known would have been an unpopular decision, it was stressed that the decision had been the correct one.

Over the years other teams from around the world have felt the oppressive power of West Indian crowds. Sunil Gavaskar pulled no punches in his appraisal of the home support: 'To call a crowd "a crowd" in Jamaica is a misnomer. It should be called a mob. The way they shrieked and howled every time Holding bowled was positively horrible. They encouraged him with shouts of "Kill him Maan!", "Hit him Maan!", "Knock his head off, Mike!"'

Even the indomitable Australians have found the heat too much on occasion. Their 1998 tour to the Caribbean produced one of the greatest Test series ever played, but the one-day games provoked bad crowd trouble, witnessed, among others, by Henry Blofeld:

> Drunkenness on its own causes bad enough problems; empty bottles as missiles quite another . . . one, at Kensington Oval, Barbados, thrown at great velocity, missed the Australian captain Steve Waugh's head by no more than a foot . . . This incident was seen on television and this particular bottle was apparently propelled by someone sitting in the most expensive seats in the house, in the Sir Garfield Sobers pavilion.

The match at Georgetown ended in scenes that could have been lifted from the 1700s. The crowd streamed on to the pitch at the end of the penultimate over, with Australia needing 4 runs to win. The ground was cleared and play resumed. Keith Arthurton was bowling to Steve Waugh, and managed five consecutive dot balls, leaving four still required off the game's last delivery. Waugh drove to long-on, but even as he and Shane Warne embarked on their unlikely mission, the playing area had been swallowed up by a sea of spectators, one of whom even tried to steal Waugh's bat. The match was abandoned and the referee, Raman Subba Row, later declared it a tie.

The last game of the one-day series was played at Bridgetown. West Indies were cruising at 138 for 1 when Shivnarine Chanderpaul pushed Brendon Julian to mid-on, and Sherwin Campbell set off for a quick run – only to be rammed by Julian and knocked over. When an appeal for run out was upheld, the stadium erupted, and the ensuing riot led to Campbell's reinstatement. (He went on to 62 and West Indies won the game.) Waugh said that the decision had been taken 'in the interests of cricket', but a contributory consideration was probably the fact that the police said they could not guarantee the Australians' safety if play was abandoned. Waugh later said, 'We are risking our lives again for a game of one-day cricket. If it keeps on like that, there's no point in us playing.'

Though less volatile, Australian crowds are no less partisan. Ray Illingworth's ultimately triumphant team of 1970–1 met with great hostility, most of which was directed at the captain and his leading strike bowler, John Snow. After going one-up after a handsome victory in Sydney, the visitors found the spectators at Melbourne for the fifth Test in belligerent mood. When Ian Chappell reached his century on the first day, at least 2,000 people rushed the ground, stealing the centurian's cap, Cowdrey's white hat and a stump, while during the last forty minutes of play, Geoffrey Boycott and John Edrich had to bat against what *Wisden* called 'a continuous background of booing, handclapping in unison and the banging of empty beer cans'. This cacophony sent the umpires into conclave, but nevertheless play was allowed to continue.

John Snow was subject to close scrutiny by the umpires throughout the series, though when he was warned against short-pitched bowling at Melbourne, the England camp were convinced he had offended less than the Australian Alan 'Froggy' Thomson. This continued to be a source of friction. As the visitors had the only really quick fast bowler, it put the home umpires in an invidious position when it came to adjudicating on intimidatory bowling. In the final test at Sydney, Australia's number ten, the leg-spinner Terry Jenner, ducked into a short ball from Snow and was hit in the face. Snow was warned by umpire Rowan, which in turn brought Illingworth into the piece, wagging his finger with Gattingesque vigour. This went down badly with the crowd, and when he returned to his post at fine-leg, Snow had his shirt pulled by an angry spectator. Although the photograph of the incident shows the assailant, if he can be so termed, acting alone – other spectators are sitting unthreateningly nearby rather than standing on their feet – the gesture, with Snow's understandably brusque response, seems to have broken the illusion of inviolability, and soon the sky was darkening with beer cans.

Such interactive incidents where players and spectators have become embroiled have been on the increase. With a regular stream of pitch invaders and outfield trespassers – normally over-lubricated males, but occasionally bra-shedding females – the players' patience has on occasion snapped. In the opening

Test of the England tour to Australia in 1982–3, Terry Alderman decided to apprehend a member of the crowd who was holding up play, and who had also tried to steal his hat. Unfortunately his Australian Rules tackle was imperfectly executed, and the flying fast bowler damaged his shoulder and was out for the rest of the series.

As we have seen, a spectator with a megaphone eventually goaded Inzamam-ul-Haq into invading the stands in Toronto, brandishing his bat. No blood was shed, but the enraged batsman was suspended for two matches. Others, including the equally uncompromising Viv Richards, who once surprisingly turned up in the press box bent on exacting redress for a perceived injustice, have pursued their quarry beyond the boundary, but most cricketers have kept their retaliatory gestures within the bounds of the playing area – if only just. A decade before the Inzamam incident, his compatriot, the fiery leg-spinner Abdul Qadir, turned on a persistent heckler near the fence during Pakistan's tour to the West Indies in 1988. The injured party settled out of court.

He could consider himself lucky compared to the spectator hit by a brick thrown by Sylvester Clarke on New Year's Eve 1980. Clarke was patrolling the boundary at Multan, Pakistan, when he found himself the target of a barrage of oranges. His response was to tug a loose brick out of the boundary wall and hurl it into the crowd, causing personal injury and igniting public fury. In a novel method of crowd control, Kallicharran went down on his knees in supplication and thereby narrowly averted a riot. Clarke was suspended for three matches.

Even when not actively involved with the players, modern crowds have witnessed a spectacular array of bad behaviour. Clarke's mindless aggression may have been among the worst individual acts seen on a Test ground, but the West Indies as a team had produced a much worse impression on their New Zealand tour of 1979–80. As unofficial world champions, they were exasperated to lose a three-match series to cricket's supposedly weakest national side. They convinced themselves that the umpiring was not only bad but biased, and they had to dismiss a home batsman 'nine times' before getting a decision. Their manager even suggested that New Zealand were 'determined to do something' to mark fifty years as a Test-playing country and that the visitors were 'set up'.

The players made their feelings clear out in the middle. When Michael Holding had an appeal for caught behind turned down in the first Test he took his anger out on the batsman's wicket, scattering the stumps with a gracefully executed kick. Though the press photographs dramatised this breach of the game's spirit, more worrying was the fact that he received no obvious reprimand from his captain, Clive Lloyd, and only a 'talking to' from his manager. Half a century earlier, J. A. Newman performed a similar feat playing for Hampshire against Nottinghamshire at Trent Bridge. His captain, the Hon. L. H. Tennyson, sent him off the field.

When the New Zealanders scraped home by the narrowest of margins – one wicket – Gordon Greenidge gave a similar display of ill-temper as he left the field, and only Desmond Haynes attended the award ceremony. Richard Hadlee criticised the West Indies for their lack of sportsmanship, while the visitors reflected bitterly that the great bowler's match-tipping 11-wicket haul contained seven lbws.

There was more controversy in the second Test at Christchurch. The New Zealand captain Geoff Howarth made an unbeaten 141, but a confident appeal for caught behind was turned down by umpire Fred Goodall when he was on 68, as a result of which the West Indians refused to take the field again after the tea interval. They demanded that Goodall be replaced, but were eventually persuaded to continue with the match without their demand being met. Goodall later claimed he was abused by Colin Croft, who protested against being no-balled by knocking the bails off and, more forthrightly, by deliberately barging into the umpire as he approached the wicket. Goodall then had to walk the entire length of the pitch to talk to the West Indies captain Clive Lloyd, who would not budge an inch from slip to meet him.

Physical clashes out on the field are so rare that they are always shocking. In 1969, John Snow deliberately collided with Sunil Gavaskar after some aggravation between them. A big man knocking over a small one is never going to look very sporting, and Snow can't have been surprised at the hostile attention he received, especially as he had apparently compounded his insensitivity by flinging the Indian's bat at him after he'd picked himself up.

An even more explosive incident occurred in Perth in 1981. In the opening Test of a series against Pakistan, Dennis Lillee clashed with the visitors' captain Javed Miandad. Like Gavaskar, Miandad had gone for a quick single, but found his way blocked by the towering pace bowler. Rather than take a fall, he 'brushed the Australian aside with his bat' according to one journalist, at which Lillee took a swing at him. This missed, but a subsequent kick, placed with some skill around the legs of the intervening umpire, did not. Miandad's response was to raise his bat above his head in the time-honoured posture of the public executioner. Both teams subsequently backed their man. The Pakistan manager said Lillee had been instrumental in raising the temperature and cited his 'mimicking, clapping and antics of sitting on the pitch' before declaring that he should never play Test cricket again. Ian Chappell, the Australian captain, blamed his opposite number: 'Javed provoked the incident, and we are very strong in our condemnation.'

While the bowler generally has the advantage – he has a potentially lethal weapon in his hand for a start, and is surrounded by team-mates – the batsman is also equipped to exact retribution. A bat does not have to be brandished like a two-edged sword to make an effective point. Many batsmen have been adept at more rapier-like thrusts, finding the bowler's unprotected shin a particularly rewarding target. When, shortly after their readmission to international cricket, Kapil Dev ran out one of South Africa's batsmen who was backing up out of his crease, Kepler Wessels expressed his team's feelings with a tidily administered crack of the bat.

There's no point in pretending that such incidents are not enjoyed by at least some sections of the crowd. The same cannot be said of time-wasting, though that too has a long history. As far back as 1767, a correspondent to the *Reading Mercury* denounced Sonning Cricket Club for cynically preventing Reading winning a game by wasting the last hour of the match 'throwing the ball about, out of the way'. Few sides have been as blatant as that, but there are a lot of things a fielding side can do to impede the progress of the game, including constant field changes, long conversations between captain and bowler, painfully slow returns to the bowling mark and excessive attention to the condition of the ball. Time-wasting is most obviously employed as a tactic to stop the other side winning, but it can also be used strategically to ensure that the game is played at the preferred tempo of the fielding side. Under Hutton in Australia, the England over-rate reached a nadir of 54 overs in a full day's play. A decade later, Colin Cowdrey bemoaned the fact that Worrell's West Indians managed only 13 overs an hour, and, of course, through the years of their world domination, the system of rotating four fast bowlers endlessly had a predictable effect on over-rates.

This is an obvious affront to the spectators, who are liable to express their feelings accordingly. In one of the most notable cases, at Edgbaston in 1967, the Yorkshire team, led by England captain Brian Close, were left in no doubt as to how the home crowd viewed their tactics as they ran the gauntlet of jostling, jeering Warwickshire members. It was reported that Fred Trueman had been attacked by a man with an umbrella, and the popular press later blew up an incident that occurred at lunch to portray the England captain 'seizing a spectator by the collar' and 'shaking him angrily'.

At the end of a fiercely competitive game – Yorkshire were pressing hard for the County Championship – Warwickshire needed 142 runs to win the match, and had 102 minutes in which to make them. The light was poor and the ball wet, and Yorkshire bowled only 24 overs in that time, and only 2 in the last eleven minutes. Even so, Warwickshire scored 133 for the loss of 5 wickets from the 144 balls they received, and their supporters felt that they had been cynically deprived of a well-deserved win. The match assumed a wider significance, partly because the two points they snatched for the draw took Yorkshire to the top of the championship table, but more importantly because Close was the current England captain, and the side for the West Indies tour was about to be announced.

Aggrieved at what he saw as a concerted campaign to oust him from the England captaincy, Close devoted much space to the incident in his cricket memoir *Close to Cricket*. The alleged assault on the spectator, which caused him as much damage as the time-wasting, was revealed as a press fabrication. Someone had made a deeply wounding personal remark within earshot as he had come off at the interval. He decided to confront the culprit, but couldn't find him. The member he did accost, by laying a hand on his shoulder as he asked whether he had made the remark, denied it, and Close immediately apologised to him and left it at that.

As for the time-wasting, Close was adamant:

> At no time during our match with Warwickshire did I instruct my bowlers deliberately to take their time in the bowling of an over. The conditions were such that with a wet ball, a greasy pitch and the run-saving field-setting, a normal over-rate was impossible. Had the fieldsmen not wiped the ball we might have bowled two or three more overs, but wiping and cleaning the ball is accepted in all normal regular day-to-day cricket as being in all fairness to the fielding side. If we had continued without wiping and our bowlers had bowled with a wet ball this would have made a mockery of a first-class fixture.

Close even questioned whether it was entirely fair that the Warwickshire batsmen were allowed to run in to the wicket from the pavilion: 'Is "quickening up" the game by the batting side not even more unfair on the bowling side than is a refusal to be "rushed" by the side in the field?'

This quixotic speculation fell on deaf ears, as did Close's extenuating claim that 'Yorkshire played no differently at Edgbaston from the way hundreds of county cricket teams have done'. He was carpeted at Lord's and then sacked as England captain, and had to watch the captain he had pipped to the County Championship, Colin Cowdrey, take the team out to the Caribbean.

As for the game itself, the consequences of that dark afternoon at Edgbaston were dramatic. The Laws were changed so that it became mandatory to bowl a minimum of 20 overs in the last hour.

Nearly twenty-three years later, another England captain, Graham Gooch, found himself on the receiving end of some expert time-wasting in the Caribbean. Having won the first Test against all expectations, the England party was delighted when the winning streak continued in Trinidad. They required 151 on the final day to take a 2–0 lead in the series. At 73 for 1 at lunch, even with Gooch himself out of the game (and series) with a broken hand, it looked a formality.

A short shower delayed the restart and left the equation standing at 78 runs from 30 overs. The West Indians were also without their captain, and Desmond Haynes, standing in for Viv Richards, was determined not to have the disaster of a second defeat associated with him if he could possibly avoid it. What followed was a masterclass in delay, as described by Allan Lamb: 'What with sending for sawdust and some of their bowlers – Ian Bishop was one – getting halfway through their run-up and then stopping because they said it was too slippery – we only got eight overs in the first hour.'

Lamb eventually got to the wicket himself, but then could only 'watch helplessly as the umpires were powerless to stop what was now little less than cheating'. The only sanction at their disposal was to report Haynes to the ground authority after the match,

> and by then he'd have saved the game. Which he did. Of the supposed minimum of 30 overs, we got 17, and the last four of those were in light that was unplayable. When Jack Russell and David Capel finally had to come off, we only wanted 31 from 13 overs with five wickets left, but someone might have got killed if we'd stayed on.

England got even closer to a deserved victory in December 1996. In fact, they couldn't have got any closer, as the scores in their inaugural Test match against Zimbabwe ended tied. The home team's tactics triumphantly combined a slow over-rate and far-flung fields with bowling wide outside the leg stump, and produced such a pressure of frustration in the England camp that their coach, David Lloyd, exploded with his 'we flippin' murdered them' outburst. Clearly a job well done.

A happier outcome – from England's perspective – came four years later when their tour of Pakistan was capped with a surprise victory in the dying moments – and light – of the third and final Test at Lahore. Despite strenuous efforts by Pakistan's captain Moin Khan to deprive England of enough overs to reach their target, the visitors were within reach as darkness began to fall. Ignoring all protests, umpire Steve Bucknor insisted on play continuing, and with fielders standing like statues as the ball sped past them in the gloom, Graham Thorpe and Nasser Hussain hustled home to a spectacular, if unlikely, victory.

No doubt had things been the other way round the England over-rate would have been similarly grudging. Nothing is sweeter than winning, but there is great satisfaction to be had in denying opponents victory. Something of the same competitive, not to say confrontational, spirit is discernible in the unfolding story of the attempt by players, promoters and administrators to carve up the expanding cake of cricket's revenues.

CHAPTER 14

Money Again: Packer and After

As far as English cricket was concerned, the onset of the twentieth century heralded no immediate changes. The class divide between professionals and amateurs was as great as ever, and the game was firmly under the control of the establishment at Lord's and run locally with patrician high-handedness by the various county committees. Even the great W. G. was still playing first-class cricket.

However, chill blasts from the outside world soon made the prospect bleaker from the amateur perspective. Lloyd George's 1909 budget, with its increase in death duties and introduction of super-tax, chipped away at the privileges of the wealthy. The 1914–18 war cut swathes through a whole generation of young men from all backgrounds, but the toll on young commissioned officers was particularly appalling. And after the heady days of the 1920s came the depression, which meant even fewer talented young men could idle their summers away as amateur cricketers.

But those who ran the game were so obsessed with the amateur ideal, and in particular, amateur captaincy, that everything possible was done to enable the right individuals to continue the tradition. In addition to expenses, the amateur could claim compensation for losses incurred by his business; while for those with no business but the right level of talent, a niche could be found as 'assistant secretary' to their county club.

One new way of making money from being a cricketer was journalism. Amateur nabobs like C. B. Fry and Plum Warner sustained their position in the amateur ranks by writing copiously about the game. Warner continued to do so even when he was a selector, and as founder editor of *The Cricketer*, he had a huge influence on how the game was perceived. More junior figures also took the journalistic route. On the 1920–1 tour of Australia, two young English amateurs, P. G. H. Fender and E. R. Wilson, augmented their meagre expenses by filing copy for papers back home. This caused friction when their remarks were 'quoted back' in the Australian press, especially when Fender was critical of crowd behaviour and umpiring during the fifth Test. He was fiercely barracked, sections of the crowd picking up on his initials to chant 'Please Go Home, Fender'. The MCC subsequently passed a motion 'deprecating' front-line journalism by those on active service.

Fender's typewriter got him into even more trouble three years later in 1924, by which time he had become captain of Surrey. The South Africans were severely hampered by filthy weather at the beginning of their tour, and to help them get any cricket at all, some teams were prepared to cover their wickets. Strictly speaking this was against the Laws, and rumblings, believed to have been orchestrated by the arch rumbler Lord Harris himself, were heard from Lord's. It was at this point that the irrepressible Fender went public with a story of Lord Harris seeking his advice on covering the square at Scarborough to save a festival match a year or two before. This was a mistake. Fender had already been carpeted for bringing his professionals out with his amateurs through the same gate – 'We do not want that sort of thing at Lord's, Fender' – and now he was given an even more ferocious broadside: 'Don't you ever write anything about me, my views or MCC in print again, young man,' he was told, and he went to his grave convinced that Lord Harris had black-balled him from the England captaincy.

Professionals never had any trouble getting their views into print either, but they too inevitably paid a heavy price for any hint of dissidence. One of the earliest to fall foul of authority was the Lancashire spinner Cecil Parkin. Despite his reputation as 'Cricket's Comedian', Parkin did not take the game lightly. According to his son, who followed him into the county side, he was 'too forthright for his own good', and he pressed the self-destruct button when he went public with criticisms of Arthur Gilligan's captaincy against South Africa at Edgbaston in 1924.

Considering South Africa were bowled out for 30, England won by an innings and that Gilligan himself took 6 wickets for 7, a full-scale assault on the captain's handling of the bowling in the second innings was unlikely to gain a sympathetic hearing – especially as Parkin himself had a terrible match, dropping catches and bowling, when he did, well below par. He rounded off his column with a forlorn trumpet blast of defiance: 'I feel that I should not be fair to myself if I accepted an invitation to play in any further Test match.'

There was very little danger of that. Parkin's outburst prompted universal condemnation, expressed in varying degrees of intensity. *The Times* tut-tutted, more in sorrow than in anger, but in *The Cricketer*, Pelham Warner demanded 'a frank public apology . . . otherwise the cricket world will regard him as the first cricketing Bolshevist, and will have none of him'. Parkin did apologise, and let it be known that he blamed the journalist who was ghosting the piece for exceeding his brief. But he never pulled on an England sweater again.

The authorities were just as quick to pounce on professional indiscretions after the Second World War. Johnny Wardle was another individualistic English spinner who brought about the end of his own career by an ill-judged foray into print. Wardle's clowning may have diverted bottle-throwing West Indians during Len Hutton's tour in 1953–4, but his antics were not so well received at home. Yorkshire had a grim time watching Surrey take the championship year after year, and in a demoralised and divided dressing-room, Wardle was seen as the main disruptive influence.

Things came to a head at the end of July 1958, by which time Wardle had been selected for the forthcoming tour to Australia under Peter May. On the eve of the Roses match, Wardle withdrew from the Yorkshire team because of a series of articles that would appear under his name in the *Daily Mail* during the game. In these he set out to answer criticisms and point the finger at those he held responsible for the sorry pass the county had come to. 'I don't intend to hide anything and I am not going to pull any punches for my heart is still with Yorkshire cricket,' he wrote, adding, 'I'm going to get it all off my chest. The truth will do the game a ton of good.' Just how much good it did is arguable. It certainly didn't do Wardle any good, as the only measurable ton of anything was the ton of bricks that rained down on his head. The most poignant sentence in the entire series of articles reads, 'I don't think Yorkshire will ask me to play for them again this season – and frankly I don't care a hoot. I'll have plenty of time to think about the future before I get to Australia in September.' But not only were Yorkshire to make it plain that they wanted to have nothing more to do with him, the MCC also withdrew his invitation to tour. It was the end of his career.

Wardle was not the only discontented senior pro on the circuit in 1958. Jim Laker was also gearing up for a display of bolshiness that nearly deprived the MCC of a second spinner. Relations with his Surrey and England captain Peter May deteriorated badly, and when May accused him of not trying in a match against Kent, Laker immediately told Lord's he would not be available for Australia. Someone leaked the story to the papers, and so the protracted peace process whereby Laker was lured back into the fold was played out against a background of excited press speculation.

Laker eventually got the form of words from May that allowed him to retract his withdrawal from the tour, but he then caused more waves by threatening to turn amateur. He went to see Gubby Allen and told him 'that I thought I would be better off in financial terms playing as an amateur in the England team in Australia with expenses rather than drawing professional pay. I knew that this was true because Trevor Bailey had told me he would receive £1000 and I was due to get £800.' Trevor Bailey, he added, 'had been working a flanker for years as the supposed secretary of Essex'.

Laker remained a professional but retired the following year. His parting shot was a ghosted memoir, *Over to Me*, which was forthright in its criticisms of May and Freddie Brown, captain and manager respectively of the touring party, as well as his own county, Surrey. The MCC withdrew his honorary membership, while Surrey stripped him of his pavilion privileges, telling Laker, 'There have been other books recently which lovers of cricket have regarded as harmful and in bad taste, but in the opinion of the committee yours has done a greater disservice to cricket than any of them.'

Laker was probably getting the brunt of the backlash against the professionals as a whole. Although many blamed the loss of the Ashes on May's tour to Australia's chuckers, there were dark mutterings that pride had predictably preceded a fall, and that the professionals had been getting above themselves. But the old dispensation could not be sustained for much longer. Although an MCC committee under the chairmanship of the Duke of Norfolk decided at the start of the 1960s that the distinction between Gentlemen and Players should continue, two years later the Advisory Committee for County Cricket judged that it should be abolished. From the start of the 1963 season all those who played the game would simply be known as 'players' and paid for their services.

But by whom? Gates had been steadily falling, and from a strictly business point of view, the first-class game was teetering on the brink of bankruptcy. In addition to abandoning amateurism in the dressing-room and on the field, the authorities wearily conceded that it would have to go in the board-room as well, and in addition to seeing all cricketers credited with their initials before their surnames, 1963 witnessed the start of cricket's relationship with sponsorship.

Initially, this meant Gillette giving their name to a cup for a one-day knock-out competition. Limited-overs cricket was not new, but the combination of the sudden-death finish and vigorous promotion aimed at attracting new audiences produced what was virtually a new game. It was very successful. Sponsorship plus huge crowds plus television fees produced a life-saving upturn in the game's finances. In Christopher Brookes' words, 'a nineteenth-century game [had] become a twentieth-century business'. But how were the profits to be shared out? The players addressed the question by forming a union, the Cricketers' Association, in 1967, but while their counterparts on the shop-floor made 1970s Britain a byword for industrial unrest, strike action on county cricket grounds was not a serious option.

The challenge to cricket's board of directors, when it came, emerged not from the shop-floor but in the guise of a hostile take-over bid. The Packer Affair, or 'Conspiracy' as many viewed it, arose out of Kerry Packer's frustration with the Australian

Cricket Board. Packer wanted to cover cricket on his television station, Channel 9, but just as Lord's always gave the English rights to the BBC, so the Australian Board favoured the Australian Broadcasting Corporation. Packer decided to challenge this cosy relationship between the ACB and ABC. If he couldn't buy into Test cricket, he would invent a rival to it.

And so, 130 years after William Clarke conceived the All England Eleven, Packer's World Series Cricket was born. And just as Clarke's entrepreneurial revolution was driven by money, so was Packer's; lots and lots of money. For Test players who had long been the paupers of a sporting world inhabited by millionaire boxers, fabulously wealthy tennis players and golfers, and flashy footballers, the pennant of Mr Packer's cheques provided a sufficient flag around which to rally.

The first the world knew of the Packer revolution was in May 1977 when it was announced that thirty-five of the world's leading cricketers had signed up to play a series of one-day games during that Australian cricket season. They had been recruited in strict secrecy – many by none other than the England cricket captain Tony Greig, who had started his treacherous business, as his detractors saw it, under cover of the Centenary Test at Melbourne in March 1977.

The Australian Board were no less shocked than the MCC, especially as they had begun to recognise that things were going to have to change. Concessions to 'player-power' were in the air, and the new contracts were worth £12,000 for an Australian player fulfilling the 1977 programme. They had also put in place a three-year sponsorship for the Test team; but it all proved too little, too late. Four senior players – Greg Chappell, Australia's captain, along with Rodney Marsh, Richie Robinson and Doug Walters – jumped ship and signed up with Packer; and more followed.

Tony Greig continued to act as Packer's recruiting officer, flying from Melbourne to the Caribbean, where his affable salesmanship soon had players signing generous contracts, including a hefty advance on signature.

Astonishingly, the whole campaign was conducted in total secrecy, and when he was ready to go public, Packer was able to announce an impressive list of the world's leading cricketers, all recruited without the cricketing authorities anywhere suspecting a thing: Asif Iqbal, Imran Khan, Mushtaq Mohammed, Eddie Barlow, Mike Proctor, Barry Richards and Graeme Pollock, Alan Knott, Derek Underwood and John Snow (plus Greig), followed by Dennis Amiss and Bob Woolmer, and Viv Richards, Clive Lloyd, Michael Holding, Andy Roberts and Deryck Murray. The weeks that followed saw more or less the whole of the West Indies side sign up, while all but four of the 1977 Australian touring party finally joined Packer.

The announcement triggered the biggest news story generated by cricket certainly since the war, if not in the entire century. High horses were saddled and ridden up and down the newspaper columns, and a positively Old Testament deluge of invective was aimed at the blond and unbowed head of Tony Greig for his perfidious betrayal of trust. John Woodcock delivered what he intended as the stake through the heart when he reminded readers of *The Times* 'that Greig is English only by adoption, which is not the same as being English through and through'.

Greig was immediately sacked as England captain and replaced by Mike Brearley. Freddie Brown, the chairman of the Cricket Council, announced, 'The captaincy of the England team involves close liaison with the selectors in the management, selection and development of England players for the future and clearly Tony Greig is unlikely to undertake this as his stated intention is to be contracted elsewhere during the next three winters.' Greig himself said, 'I knew I was putting my captaincy on the line. The only redeeming factor is that I have sacrificed cricket's most coveted job for a cause which I believe could be in the interests of cricket the world over.'

Packer posed a multitude of problems which different countries handled in different ways. Greig was sacked as captain, but England still played their 'Packer' players; Greg Chappell retained the Australian captaincy, and brought with him a more or less full Australian side for the scheduled Ashes series in the English season of 1977. In the event, the tourists proved insufficiently focused, and England, under Brearley, soon got the upper hand, greatly aided by the Test début of Ian Botham and the end of Geoffrey Boycott's self-imposed exile from international cricket. The Ashes were won almost as conclusively as they had been lost two years before by Mike Denness.

Behind the scenes, the two sides sparred with each other. At a meeting in June, the ICC seemed conciliatory, offering some changes to the Australia vs India programme and the promise of first-class status for a limited programme of Packer matches. Packer then raised the stakes by reintroducing his demand for exclusive television rights. This was the issue that had precipitated the crisis in the first place, but the Australian representatives were no more inclined to grant Packer's demand than they had been at the beginning. The hardliners won the day, and Packer, as they thought, was sent packing.

The hardline hardened as the summer went on. In July, the ICC's Annual Meeting produced talk of declaring 'open war' on Packer, and the bullish tone was emphasised when the chairman remarked, 'wars are not won by appeasement'. The players' 'defection' to Packer was seen as a breach of trust that had to be punished. The ICC got its retaliation in first, declaring that the matches in the Packer 'Circus' would not count as first-class nor appear in the official records. Furthermore, those who took part in them would forfeit their right to play official Test cricket. Member countries were also urged to extend the same sanctions to domestic first-class cricket.

This was in effect an ultimatum to the players to rescind their Packer contracts or be cast into the wilderness. In coming out so clearly and so aggressively the ICC certainly conveyed their disapproval, but, as cautious voices (mainly from the West Indies' representatives) suggested, they were in danger of being hauled before the courts for both restraint of trade and for inciting the players to break their contracts.

And so it proved. The case came to the High Court in London in September 1977 and lasted seven weeks. The game's authorities based their defence on the higher interests of cricket, arguing that it would be seriously damaged if a rogue promoter was allowed to cream off the best players. Packer's lawyers simply produced the various statements already on the record to show this position up as 'dictatorial and penal and an infringement of the liberty of the individual'.

Mr Justice Slade was persuaded. Indeed, he expressed surprise that there had been no previous challenge to the cricket establishment. Although he expressed sympathy with those in charge of international cricket, their fears for the revenues from Test cricket were not sufficient justification for their actions, and although he could see the reasons for the force of criticism levelled at Tony Greig, the other players were simply pursuing legitimate self-interest:

A professional cricketer needs to make his living as much as any other professional man. It is straining the concept of loyalty too far for the authorities to expect him to enter into a self-denying ordinance not to play cricket for a private promoter during the winter months merely because the matches promoted could detract from the future profits of the authorities, who were not themselves willing or in a position to offer him employment over the winter or guarantee him employment in the future.

He accepted that the authorities had acted in good faith and in what they saw were the best interests of the game, but that was not sufficient to justify their actions. The ICC not only lost the case, but had to find a quarter of a million pounds to pay the costs.

It was some consolation for them that the first Packer season was a flop. His three teams, 'Australia', West Indies and the Rest of the World, simply played an endless round-robin of matches and did not catch the public imagination. The official Tests between India and Australia, on the other hand, were closely fought and followed with interest.

Although the High Court had prohibited any blanket ban, its ruling did not mean that WSC-contracted players were immune from the usual selectorial processes. However, when the West Indies selectors dropped a Packer player during the series against a new-look Australian XI, whose oddest look was the return of Bobby Simpson as captain after a thirteen-year break, Clive Lloyd, the West Indies captain, led a walk-out on the eve of the third Test in Guyana. This caused maximum embarrassment, and it was only with the greatest difficulty that the Board got a new team together and flew the players to the South American mainland to fulfil the fixture. It was thought that the walk-out did not come as a complete surprise to Packer; it showed he could flex his muscles in Australia and cause upsets on the other side of the world. The situation was reversed when the English side touring Pakistan after their rout of the Australians refused to play a Test if three Packer stars were brought back into the home side's team. The threat worked and the triumvirate were not called upon after all.

Although, after the smoke from the legal battle cleared, both sides claimed they wanted peace, it was a long time coming. The turning point was the Ashes tour of 1978–9. Various factors played their part. For one thing, WSC, with the full weight of Channel 9 behind it, was proving more successful. It appealed to a family audience, and the day–night matches played under floodlights were an exciting innovation. And then there was the fact that Mike Brearley's team were beating the 'official' Australian team hands down. Suddenly the WSC Aussies, who after all would have been the Australian first choice, looked altogether more attractive and started gaining the support they had failed to attract the year before. Revenues from the official Tests started to fall, and from being advocates of the hardline, the Australian Board now became rather more concerned about the bottom line.

All Packer had ever wanted to do was to sit down round a table and negotiate television rights, and this the Board now agreed to do. Fortuitously, the contract with the ABC had expired, and the ACB now agreed a multi-million-dollar deal with Packer, giving him pretty well everything he had asked for in the first place. Only after the two-year war, he was now in a position to demand rather than ask for what he wanted. As Gordon Ross ruminated in *Wisden*: 'Throughout the debate, the sixty-four thousand dollar question was "Why has the Australian Board done this?", and the sixty-four thousand dollar answer can be succinctly given in one word – "Money".' For the first time ever, an Australia vs England series had lost money. Faced with a tour by India – which was bound to lose money – the Australian Board could see the spectre of bankruptcy approaching fast. It was left with precious little bargaining power.

Ross concluded:

Packer had all the cards in his hand. It could be said that, in the circumstances, Australia had come out of it pretty well. Financially, of course they may have, but time alone will tell whether the Australian Board – a very small dog, with Packer as a very large tail – will find that the tail wags the dog on any issue of divided opinion. It easily could.

The deal was not only about rights and money; it also ceded to Packer a degree of control. A tour by an India team for 1979–80 was abruptly cancelled to be replaced by a triangular series involving England, Australia and the West Indies. The *volte face* was shocking – some described it as 'capitulation' – but when it came down to it, the cricket world was ready for a truce, and at the end of June 1979 the ICC met and approved the deal struck by Packer and the Australian Board.

The war was over, but peace could not turn the clock back. Cricket was irrevocably changed. What natural deference the game subtly encouraged evaporated on the steps of the High Court. Packer had done much more for player-power than any Cricketers' Association, exposing long-standing assumptions about the divine right of boards and committees to rule the game. At the same time, cricket's commercial horizons were extended unimaginably. From now on, it could command big money, albeit at the cost of aping such American sporting spectacles as 'World Series' baseball. That cost may have been far too high for the purists and traditionalists, but the players weren't complaining. In 1978, Cornhill Insurance made its first massive injection of funds into the English game, starting a sponsorship regime that would last until the end of the century. Countless other firms followed suit, and as they climbed into their logo-festooned cars and scrutinised their improved bank statements, post-Packer cricketers could reflect that Packer had placed them on a pinnacle of power and importance that their predecessors could not have dreamt of.

Being set on a high place often goes hand in hand with temptation, and the post-Packer period has been notable for the central role money has assumed in the game. A clear example is the various rebel tours to South Africa during the apartheid years. These were undertaken by players from England, Australia and even the

West Indies in contravention of the Gleneagles Agreement which put South Africa out of bounds as far as sporting links were concerned. The rebels and their supporters put up a defence based on the progress the South African Cricket Union had taken to desegregate the game. As they also pointed out, businessmen were not barred from trading with South Africa, while sportsmen and women were also free to compete against nations with equally unsavoury human-rights records. However, the way Geoffrey Boycott and his backers went about recruiting for the first rebel tour of 1982 was strongly reminiscent of Greig's recruitment for Packer. Boycott's position was particularly inglorious. As a sportsman blacklisted for his links with South Africa, he posed a threat to the scheduled England tour to India in October 1981. The tour hung in the balance and only went ahead when Boycott publicly condemned apartheid. The Yorkshireman was particularly keen for the tour to be saved, as it gave him the opportunity of breaking the England record for Test runs. This achieved, he returned home suffering from fatigue. It was not long afterwards that it became clear that all the while he had been scheming to set up the South African tour which followed with indecent haste.

As Asif Iqbal wrote in *The Cricketer* in 1982, it was 'the height of hypocrisy to condemn apartheid [with whatever degree of sincerity], but to have no qualms about fraternising with those who perpetrate it'. Poet Kit Wright satirized the mind-set of those who were prepared to take the tour sponsors' money in his 'I Found South African Breweries Most Hospitable':

Meat smell of blood in locked rooms I cannot smell it,
Screams of the brave in torture loges I never heard or heard of
Apartheid I wouldn't know how to spell it,
None of these things am I paid to believe a word of
For I am a stranger to cant and contumely.
I am a professional cricketer.
My only consideration is my family.
. . .
They keep falling out of the window they must be clumsy
And unprofessional not that anyone told me,
Spare me your wittering spare me your whimsy,

Sixty thousand pounds is what they sold me
And I have no brain. I am an anomaly.
I am a professional cricketer.
My only consideration is my family.

One man who by his own account agonised at length about joining the tour was Graham Gooch. When he did finally make up his mind to go, he ended up being talked into captaining the team, thus firmly linking his name with the venture ('Gooch's Dirty Dozen', etc., etc.). Although Gooch managed to persuade himself that he and his companions were doing nothing wrong, their united front was shattered on their return to Britain. He recalled the scene at the airport when Boycott and his companion, Ann, were seen

> scuttling through the cameras towards the exit. Ann was holding a newspaper in front of her face, and Geoffrey his coat to cover his, like crooks coming out of court and into a Black Maria. At a stroke, every TV news bulletin had its top feature and dramatic pictures – the most famous one of us all coming home like a criminal, admitting his 'guilt'.

While many of the rebels, such as Alan Knott, Mike Hendrick, Wayne Larkins, Peter Willey, Derek Underwood and John Lever, had come to the end of their England days and saw the tour as one last pay bonanza, younger men like Gooch and his close friend John Emburey were still Test regulars and knew that they were jeopardising their England places. But when they were banned from playing for England for three years, they felt hard done by. That their places were taken by South African-bred cricketers like Allan Lamb and Robin Smith was perceived as a bitter irony.

Their three-year sentences served, the 'traitors', as they were sometimes termed, were welcomed back with open arms, going on, in the case of Gooch, to serve England as captain, manager and selector. After 'rebel' tours by Australian and West Indian sides, a second England tour was arranged in 1989 under the captaincy of Mike Gatting. Gatting belligerently refused to acknowledge any connection between sport and politics, but the blindest of blind eyes could not protect him and his squad from the flood tide of change that was beginning to sweep aside the old apartheid regime. With angry crowds presenting a threat that even the most enthusiastic of police forces could not contain, the tour was called off in a blaze of bad publicity and bad feeling. This time those handed out Test match bans were reprieved by the coming to power of Nelson Mandela and the reacceptance of South Africa into the world's sporting fraternity. Gatting, like Gooch before him, played again for England and, after he had retired, went on to join his fellow rebel as a national selector.

By the end of the twentieth century, Test cricketers at least could look back on a significant change in the balance of power. In contrast to their predecessors at the turn of the previous century, they were in the box seat and fully aware of their worth. When push came to shove, it was the game's supposed authorities that had to climb down. There were two instances in 1998. For the first time ever West Indies were due to tour South Africa, but on the eve of this truly historic event, there was a Caribbean *coup d'état*. While the majority of the team flew to South Africa from the Far East, where they had been taking part in yet one more round-robin of one-dayers, Brian Lara and Carl Hooper, the captain and vice-captain, suddenly refused to join them, flying instead to London, where they set up camp in a hotel near Heathrow.

Both were immediately sacked, but Courtney Walsh, the previous captain, and Clive Lloyd, the manager and veteran of the Packer revolution, supported them, and so did the rest of the team, who left South Africa and flew to Heathrow. Pat Rousseau, the president of the West Indies Board, was forced to climb on to a plane himself and enter negotiations. An appeal was made by Nelson Mandela, and given the enormously high stakes, there could only be one outcome. With new terms agreed, and Lara and Hooper reinstated, the team flew back to South Africa. But this was no way to prepare for a Test series and they were thoroughly trounced, enduring a humiliating 5–0 whitewash.

There was no possibility of the Australians allowing anything to distract them from the task of beating the Poms, but on the eve of England's forlorn 1998–9 Ashes quest, their hosts did flex their considerable muscle in order to ensure a higher rate of remuneration for completing this by now routine job. The hint of strike action was enough to see their demands met, and in contrast to the West Indians, the Australians returned to the field of battle not one whit less effective for having won a major battle off it.

Everything during that Australian summer was going according to plan, with a super-confident home team satisfactorily dismissing the puny challenge of the visitors, until a piece of investigative journalism revealed that Shane Warne and Mark Waugh had been fined – in secret – by the Australian Board for accepting money from an Indian bookmaker. This revelation stoked an inferno of speculation into the actual extent of the corruption scandal that had been brewing ever since the same pair, with Tim May, had alleged they had been offered bribes by the then Pakistan captain, Salim Malik, to underperform. As the century approached its close, cricket suddenly appeared to be wobbling on the edge of yet another abyss.

CHAPTER 15

The Root of Evil

On 7 April 2000, the cricket world was shaken by what many took to be a belated April Fool: rumours of match-fixing allegations against Hansie Cronje ran through the world's media, sparking a bush-fire of speculation and incredulity. The story originated in a police inquiry in Delhi, and the evidence took the form of taped telephone conversations during which Cronje mentioned three other players who had agreed to help him influence matches. In South Africa the accusations were met with total disbelief. Assured by the captain and the three other players named – Herschelle Gibbs, Pieter Strydom and Nicky Boje – that there was no truth in them whatsoever, the United Cricket Board (UCB) issued a strong denial, concluding: 'Cronje is known for his unquestionable integrity and honesty.'

It seemed inconceivable that South Africa's favourite cricketing son could have compromised his position as the leader who took the national team to the number two slot in the international rankings, while seemingly representing all that was best in Nelson Mandela's colour-blind Rainbow nation. As an individual, Cronje seemed the epitome of Afrikaans probity: unbending, focused and puritanical. Indeed, as a born-again Christian, he was publicly committed to the highest standards of personal morality, though there was no perceptible softness of approach in his cricket captaincy. He was a man at the top of his game, on a pinnacle of national respect, and at the peak of his earnings potential. There was surely no chance that he would have risked all this for a few backhanders?

Incredulity hardened into outrage when the veteran South

African cricket journalist Trevor Chesterfield pronounced the tapes as fakes – and bad ones at that: the supposed Hansie Cronje spoke with an unmistakable Indian accent. (This was explained later when it emerged that Chesterfield had heard a reading of the transcript, not the original recording.) On 9 April, Cronje and his co-accused, along with Ali Bacher and the President of the UCB, Percy Sonn, called a press conference where the players protested their innocence and Bacher and Sonn yet again denounced the charges. What looked like an attempt to embroil South Africa's leading light in the toils of subcontinental corruption appeared to have been foiled. Not for long. In the small hours of 11 April, Cronje's conscience – or the conviction that there was no way of continuing the cover-up – prompted him to phone Bacher to admit that he had 'not been entirely honest' in his denials, and that in fact he had taken between US$10,000 and 15,000 from an Indian bookmaker called Sanjay. He also wrote a confession in which he claimed 'the devil made me do it'.

The UCB's response was swift and unflinching. Cronje was withdrawn from the national side, the government was asked to convene a judicial inquiry, and a public apology for defending the corrupt captain was issued. This sudden *volte face* stunned South Africa and took the rest of the world by surprise. Cronje released a statement on 13 April in which he acknowledged the damage he had inflicted on himself, his family, his team, his sport and his country. However, while accepting the 'awful predicament brought about by my own foolishness and naivety [in taking money from Sanjay]', Cronje went on to deny more serious allegations: 'I was not involved in fixing or manipulating the results of cricket matches. I always played to win.'

In the days following, two of the other players named, Strydom and Gibbs, wriggled uncomfortably on the hook of media attention, and the probing enquiries of the cricketing authorities. Strydom, who had several inclusive phone conversations with Cronje, at first denied participation, then admitted it. Under instruction from Cronje, Gibbs also denied that he had been approached, a line he stuck to in order to 'protect' Cronje. Others who admitted to being approached were Mark Boucher, Lance Klusener and Jacques Kallis, who had previously laughed off the suggestion that they take money to underperform as a joke.

The government set up the requested judicial inquiry with exemplary speed, and a retired judge, Edwin King, was invited to preside over it. The first hearing, in Cape Town, was on 7 June, and the proceedings began with an account of betting on a game: spread-betting – wagering on a spread of runs that a team (e.g. between 230–240) or an individual (e.g. between 25–35) will make; betting on the number of runs in the first 15 overs of a one-day international (ODI); and line betting, where the punter bets a batsman will make less than a given score. As the *Interim Report* noted: 'The opportunities for malpractice are self evident; if e.g. the bookie or punter knows that a particular batsman will contrive to get himself out on a score of less than that stipulated which has been agreed in advance.'

The key witness was, of course, Cronje. He first revealed the initial snare. Hamid Cassim, a familiar figure around the fringes of the South African team, approached him at the start of the tri-angular one-day competition between South Africa, Zimbabwe and England in January 2000. He said he could have made money had he known of the controversial declaration in the fifth Test against England at Centurion Park a few days before. Cronje foolishly and provocatively responded, 'Why didn't you ask?'

The next time they met, he did. He and Sanjay were staying at the same hotel as the South African team in Durban during the next ODI. Cronje told the inquiry how things progressed:

> Hamid and Sanjay indicated that Sanjay wanted me to supply them with information, but did not specify what information. They also said that I could make a lot of money if we would lose a match. I said that I was not prepared to do it unless we were assured of a place in the final of the triangular series. I was spinning them along as I did not think that I had any real intention of throwing a match. Sanjay handed me a cell-phone box containing US dollars in case I changed my mind.

Sanjay must have returned to his hotel room to congratulate himself and his confederate on how easy it had been to 'turn' the South African captain. Cronje continued his evidence, mention-ing in passing that the 'fee' offered for deliberately losing a match was a round US$100,000:

It was not initially my intention to throw any games or to fix results: driven by greed and stupidity, and the lure of easy money, I thought that I could feed Sanjay information and keep the money without having to do anything to influence matches. In fact there was no manipulation of games or results in South Africa, and I supplied no information in respect of the matches in South Africa.

According to Cassim's evidence, however, if there was no fixing, there was certainly some well-informed forecasting, as Cronje guided Sanjay through such topics as the pitch, the conditions, team selection and likely batting order. And under cross-examination, Cronje was made to face the implications of the first 'bung'. Did he really think he could return it and resume life as though nothing had happened? The examining advocate, Ms Batohi, returned to the theme:

I am not going to belabour this point, Mr Cronje, but what I am putting to you is that when you took that money, at that point, the thought never occurred to you that you would give the money back? You must surely have realised, the money was given to you just to make sure that you don't change your mind, that you knew, that is in your statement. You must therefore have realised that when you accepted that money, you were effectively hooked, because the thought of returning it never crossed your mind.

Cronje reluctantly admitted, 'I know the money that he gave me was a sort of deposit for maybe speaking to the players and helping to influence players and that there would be a further sum if in fact I was able to predict the result, not predict, to give him a result in the right way.'

Ms Batohi: Did you think or did he say that to you?
Mr Cronje: He said that to me.
Ms Batohi: I see. So this was just a deposit and if you delivered then there was going to be more?
Mr Cronje: That is correct.

The inquiry also revealed that, prior to Cassim's approach, Cronje had allowed his judgement to be swayed over the final day's play of the fifth Test against England at Centurion Park. The match had been ruined by rain, with no play possible on days two, three and four. On the fourth day, talks were held to see whether the game could be rescued if play was possible on the fifth day. South Africa had already run up a reasonable total, and discussions focused on a declaration and then the forfeiture of England's first innings and South Africa's second to give the visitors an agreed target. However, no agreement could be reached, so it looked as though the game would peter out into a meaningless draw. From a South African point of view this would be perfectly acceptable. They had won the series decisively already. Chasing a target on a contrived final day offered England the only possibility of winning a Test, so why give them the opportunity?

The answer lay in a phone call Cronje received from a man called Marlon Aronstam urging him 'to make a game of it'. Aronstam's motives were quite clear. By backing both sides at long odds to win, and covering himself by backing a draw, he reckoned he could turn in a profit of 40–45 per cent on the substantial sum he was prepared to invest (an anticipated R300 000,00–500 000,00). If Cronje could contrive a result, Aronstam offered to give a sizeable donation to a charity. Aronstam testified that Cronje promptly took the discussion a step further and started talking about the possibility of 'throwing a match', though he added that this would require the help of at least some of the team.

As far as the final day of the fifth Test was concerned, Cronje was obviously highly motivated to set up a result. He returned to the negotiating table to offer 270 runs in 73 overs, and when England captain Nasser Hussain turned that down, came back with 255 in 73 overs. This too was rejected, and all the while time was ticking away. Finally, and dramatically, the England captain was given an offer he felt he couldn't refuse: 249 runs in 76 overs. The deal was struck, and the declaration and two forfeitures (whose legality was questioned by such experienced umpires as Don Oslear) were made, and England went on, with a characteristic wobble towards the end, to secure a historic victory, making 251 for 8 with just five balls to spare.

Though this was a happy outcome for the spectators and the

England party, the South Africans were less content. Kallis testified that 'a lot of the guys were very upset'. Lance 'Zulu' Klusener declared himself 'a little bit astounded' by the decision. Ironically, because of the protracted negotiations in the morning, Aronstam had not been in time to place his bets. This meant that the 'charitable donation' was not forthcoming; but Cronje was not left unrewarded. With an eye to the future, Aronstam gave the South African captain R50 000,00 – and a leather jacket for his wife.[*]

It is quite clear from the Aronstam incident that Cronje was corruptible; indeed, looking to be corrupted. Sanjay and Cassim were pushing at an open door. As the team prepared to fly to India, he was, by his own admission, hooked. Once there, Cronje came under increasing pressure to produce results – for his backers rather than his own side. Cassim denied that he was any more than an intermediary or facilitator, though Cronje clearly regarded him as a co-participant with Sanjay. Whatever his true role, he was regularly on the phone to the South African captain, as was Sanjay, increasingly frustrated at the lack of a positive outcome for his investment.

Not that Cronje was not trying. On the eve of the first Test against India he approached the new cap, Strydom, with the offer of R70 000,00 if the side was bowled out for under 250. Although Cronje made his pitch in a 'very lighthearted manner', it was an extraordinary way to be welcomed into Test cricket. Strydom refused, but Cronje had not entirely misjudged his man, as the débutant said that if he had played eighty or ninety Tests he would have thought about it seriously. In the event, South Africa did make less than 250, and Strydom acknowledged to Cronje afterwards that they could have made a lot of money.

Cronje cast his net wider next time. A few days before the second Test, he raised the question of throwing a match with three stalwarts of the team, Klusener, Boucher and Kallis. The topic came up in the room Boucher and Kallis were sharing, and was introduced with the same jokey lightheartedness that Cronje

[*] According to Pieter Strydom, on the hectic last morning of the Test, Cronje had asked him to place a R50, 00 bet on South Africa winning; he had been unable to get the bet accepted.

had adopted with Strydom. All three senior players assumed that that was all it was, a joke. These rebuffs left Cronje in a difficult position. Sanjay was constantly on the phone demanding results, and though he would subsequently claim that he was only stringing the bookie along, Cronje was clearly motivated to get some sort of match-fixing started.

With the Tests out of the way, the pressure to influence the ODI series increased dramatically. The first match was played at Cochin on 9 March 2000, and Cronje assured Sanjay that he had willing recruits, naming Herschelle Gibbs, Nicky Boje, Hayward and Williams, and that South Africa would get less than 250 and lose the match. In the event, South Africa scored just over 300 runs, which obviously made a nonsense of betting based on Cronje's promise. Sanjay was understandably furious and refused to pay up. Cronje apologised but still demanded the money, using Sanjay's failure to produce it as the reason he could not get cooperation to fix the second ODI at Jamshedpur on 12 March. In fact, at this stage he was simply stringing Sanjay along, and the 'results' he promised in the third and fourth ODIs were no more than forecasts. He approached no members of his side, and tried his best himself, wanting, he claimed, to win the series.

However, by the fifth ODI at Nagpur on 19 March, South Africa had lost the series 3–1, and now at last Cronje agreed to recruit accomplices to deliberately throw the game. He was successful to the tune of getting Gibbs and Williams on side. Gibbs agreed to score less than 20 and Williams to concede in excess of 50 runs in his 10 overs.

Having targeted two of the youngest members of the squad, who also happened to be non-whites, Cronje also planned to cheat them of their ill-gotten gains. He negotiated a bung of US$25,000 for each with Sanjay, but actually offered them US$15,000, with the vague suggestion that he might be able to get it 'bumped up' if things turned out well.

But they didn't. Gibbs, greatly to his credit, found the exhilaration of batting for his country outweighed any mercenary considerations. He slammed his first two balls for four, and carried on, in his own words, 'like a steam train', making a glorious 74 off 53 balls. South Africa piled on the runs, reaching 320 for 7, and when they came to bowl, Williams failed to deliver his side of the bargain, breaking down at the end of his second over, having taken 1 for 11. The visitors won by 10 runs. As an attempt at match-fixing, it was farcical.

However, even though their contributions to the attempted fix had been non-existent, Gibbs and Williams were to pay a heavy price for countenancing Cronje's suggestions. Both were banned for six months from 30 June 2000 and fined, Gibbs R60 000 and Williams R10 000. Many thought they were let off lightly, in view of the new ICC ruling that 'contriving or attempting to contrive the result of any Match or the occurrence of any Event' should result in a life ban. However, although agreed in October 1999, delays had meant that the ICC regulations only came into force in April 2001 – after the misdemeanours took place. The UCB president Percy Sonn acknowledged that the pair were 'beneficiaries' of that delay. In reaching the sentences that they did, the UCB disciplinary committee accepted that there were mitigating circumstances. The conspiracy had come to nothing, and both young players were heavily under the influence of Cronje.

The disgraced South African captain was, of course, the main villain of the piece, and the longer the King commission sat, the more horrifying were the revelations that came out. It became apparent that far from suffering a sudden aberration in 2000, Cronje had in fact been approached as early as January 1995, and had shown an unhealthy interest in the possibilities of match-fixing then.

The approach came from a man who called himself 'John' during the Mandela Trophy tournament between South Africa and Pakistan, which consisted of a couple of ODIs played in Cape Town and Johannesburg. Cronje took John's offer sufficiently seriously to discuss it with one of his most senior players, Pat Symcox, who thought it a bad idea, adding, according to Cronje, that the money wasn't sufficient anyway.

Much to Cronje's discomfort, the opposing captain, Salim Malik, was obviously aware of John's approach, asking whether they had spoken. Cronje said he felt 'ashamed and embarrassed' and tried to avoid any further discussion of the matter. He turned down a second offer from John on the eve of the second

ODI. However, as the King Report noted, 'the first time Cronje was approached to fix a match, he was prepared to and did entertain the suggestion'.

A year later, in 1996, he got in much deeper. Firstly, at Sharjah, he was befriended by a man called Sunil, who casually enquired whether he was interested in match-fixing. He said he was not, but not only did he not distance himself from his new acquaintance, he supplied information which, as he admitted later, 'would have been handy to him if he wanted to make a bet on a game'. However, he claimed not to have been paid anything. Sunil was understandably very ready to resume their relationship when the South Africans toured India in December 1996, but it seems the first person from whom Cronje accepted money corruptly was a new figure, Mukesh Gupta, or 'MK'.

Gupta would prove the arch match-fixer, who had devoted several years of his life to getting inside knowledge of the game in order to corrupt players and influence the course of matches. But the most dramatic aspect of this part of Cronje's confession was the identity of the man who introduced him to Gupta. He was none other than the former Indian captain, Mohammed Azharuddin. The introduction took place at the end of the third day's play in the third Test at Kanpur. MK at first claimed to be a jeweller wanting business contacts in South Africa, but soon revealed himself to be a match-fixer. MK was prepared to pay money if the South African captain could persuade his men to throw their wickets away and ensure that they lost the game. As the South Africans were doing very badly and seemed bound to lose the match comfortably, this seemed an irresistible deal, and Cronje accepted the US$30,000 on offer and then let events take their natural course. He spoke to no one, and India cruised to a 280-run victory. This was easy money, and there was more – a lot more – to come. According to the King findings, in addition to the initial US$30,000, Cronje received a further US$80,000 when the Indians were in South Africa in January.

After the opening freebie, which had involved no action on his part, Cronje did show that he was prepared to get his hands dirty. Towards the end of a gruelling tour in which the South Africans had logged twenty-three internal flights across India, there was a benefit match for the former Test player Mohinder

Armanath. According to wicket-keeper Dave Richardson, this was a match 'no one really wanted to play'. Nor, as it turned out, was it a match that large numbers of people wanted to watch. With ticket sales low, the South African Cricket Union agreed to an Indian request to upgrade the game to full international status. Having a full ODI foisted on them at short notice greatly upset the exhausted players, and Cronje decided to harness this mood of disaffection: he called a team meeting to discuss the possibility of throwing the match. The whole squad was present, apart from Allan Donald and Jonty Rhodes, who had gone home. According to Symcox's testimony, the money on offer was US$250,000, and there was no doubting that the offer was seriously made and seriously considered. Cronje's stance was that everyone had to be involved or it was 'no go', and when several players, notably Andrew Hudson, Derek Crookes and Daryl Cullinan, spoke out against it, he seemed to abandon the idea.

However, after the meeting broke up, he was left with a handful of (presumably) sympathetic players, and as if to show that he had not been bluffing, he telephoned MK and asked for the offer to be bumped up by another US$100,000. MK complied, though it was still not taken up. Even so, Gupta did not despair of achieving his ends. When India followed their visitors back to South Africa for a return series during December 1996 and January 1997, MK transferred US$50,000 into Cronje's building-society account and offered him a further US$300,000 to lose the third Test. This the South African captain declined to do, but he was by this stage hopelessly compromised.

He was not, of course, the only rotten apple in the barrel. That was why the ICC – belatedly so many commentators thought – had introduced the new and draconian measures against those caught involved in match-fixing. It had become clear that cricket had a problem akin to that of the eighteenth and early part of the nineteenth centuries. As the twentieth century drew to a close, match-fixing was reaching epidemic proportions.

According to some, the rot set in as far back as 1981, when Dennis Lillee and Rodney Marsh found odds of 500–1 against England at the low point in their fortunes at Headingley irresistible. One of the entourage was sent off to place a couple of small bets, and then, according to the players themselves, the whole thing was forgotten until well after the most famous reverse of modern Test history had been achieved. No one has ever suggested that Lillee or Marsh withheld an ounce of effort in opposing Ian Botham's extraordinary counterattack. Cricketers, and in particular Australians, have long been renowned for having a punt. Keith Miller was a famous betting man, as often summoning the twelfth man to take betting instructions as to add to his sweater count. It would be worth a small bet that, had he been present at Headingley, he too would have put a tenner on England. The bets laid by Lillee and Marsh were an instinctive response to ridiculous odds, a gesture completely separate from their commitment to the Australian cause. All the same, some thought the lack of an official reprimand an opportunity missed by the authorities.

Certainly, in the post-1990s climate, such behaviour would attract strong condemnation, fines and the possibility of suspension. Back in the early 1980s it seemed innocent enough. The debate on whether to allow the bookies back into the cricket grounds after their long exile had thrown up various predictions of corruption, but in the event, the move proved harmless. The problem, when it came, occurred in countries where betting on cricket was illegal. The really big money, and the corruption that followed in its wake like a vast oil-slick, was generated on the subcontinent.

There were rumblings about match-fixing, bribery and corruption in the game from the end of the 1980s on, but something stronger than rumour and innuendo appeared to hit the headlines in 1995 when a trio of Australians – Mark Waugh, Tim May and Shane Warne – accused the Pakistani captain Salim Malik of trying to bribe them to underperform on their tour of Pakistan in 1994. Warne and May had been offered US$200,000 to bowl badly on the last day of the first Test at Karachi (2 October 1994), while Waugh had been approached a few days later to see whether he would be willing to recruit four or five others to sabotage Australia in the one-day international at Rawalpindi later in the month. All three rebuffed the advances robustly, though it was not until five months later that they went public with the story. They were also reluctant to return to Pakistan to give evidence in person to the judicial inquiry set up to investigate match-fixing. In the absence of a personal examination of the key witnesses, Justice Fakruddin Ebrahim found he had no option but to clear the accused of bribery.

This was an unsatisfactory outcome and hardly scotched the suspicions that match-fixing had been going on. Imran Khan was one of those unimpressed by the authorities' lacklustre approach to clearing the matter up. He recalled, 'when allegations of match-fixing surfaced, I went to the Board which at that time was headed by Arif Abbasi [chief executive] and told him in the presence of Javed Burki [chairman] that stern action should be taken against the culprits' – by which he meant 'bans for life and fines'. However, he suspected the Board allowed 'expedience' to sway them: 'at that time the Pakistan team was very strong and they did not want to disrupt it'. As Henry Blofeld put it, 'From a distance, it looks pretty obvious that the powers-that-be in Pakistan cricket over the last ten years have been keeping their fingers crossed in the hope that it would either all go away or that it would never come out.'

But it didn't go away, and in the end the government decided that the rumours, innuendoes and off-the-record allegations had finally to be addressed. In 1998, they set up a Judicial Commission in Lahore under the High Court judge, Justice Malik Mohammad Qayyum. A number of players were called before the judge and many stories aired. Javed Miandad reported that when he first got into the Pakistan team he had been warned of the culture of match-fixing. Aamir Sohail claimed he had been offered money by an Indian bookmaker while on tour in Australia and said he had been approached by the former player Saleem Pervez in Colombo. Pervez's response was to claim that 'most' Pakistan matches were fixed, and he admitted paying Malik and Mushtaq Ahmed US$100,000 for fixing a game in Sri Lanka. He also pointed the finger at Intikhab Alam, the Pakistan manager. Intikhab himself said that Basit Ali had confessed to match-fixing, while Ali said that was nonsense. Imran Khan claimed that fast bowler Ata-ur-Rehman had admitted being paid money by Wasim Akram. Sarfraz Nawaz said that Malik had been paid the equivalent of £12,500 to lose a match for Habib Bank vs Nation Bank of Pakistan, though offered no thoughts as to where he might have banked his bung. And so it went on, a veritable witness stand of Babel, with the strong suspicion that some, if not all, of those testifying were raking over the past to settle old scores.

It was against this background that the inquiry appealed to the Australians, who were touring Pakistan, for witness statements. Mark Taylor, the Australian captain, and Mark Waugh, one of the initial whistle-blowing triumvirate, agreed to give evidence in Lahore after the first Test had been played at Rawalpindi. There was little more they could add to the statements made in 1994, but Waugh did stress that he, Warne and May had been shocked by Malik's approach because they played the game for the love of their country and not for money.

What two of the trio – Waugh and Warne – had not seen fit to mention at the time was that there were some things they were prepared to do for money. In fact, on the tour to Sri Lanka preceding the trip to Pakistan in 1994, they had been approached by a man called 'John', and had agreed to swap seemingly innocuous information about pitches and playing conditions for small but useful sums of pocket-money – US$6,000 for Waugh, US$5,000 for Warne. Not only did the players not mention it; when the Australian Board found out, they also took the view that this shameful little secret would be better kept as just that – thus storing up a whole heap of embarrassment for themselves four years later when the story finally broke.

This it did, spectacularly, two days before the Adelaide Test of the 1998–9 Ashes series. Warne was out of the side with an injury, but Waugh was exposed in the full glare of publicity. Barracking and hostile banners met him when he made his way to the wicket, and perhaps not surprisingly his stay at the crease was short. But it was not long before attention shifted from the shamefaced stars to those who ordered the affair to be kept under wraps. Tim May was quite clear that the cover-up came from above: 'The ACB said: "Don't say anything, don't say anything, whatever you do, don't say anything."' So naturally they didn't. But that left a great deal of explaining to be done by those who had ticked the No Publicity box on their behalf.

ACB chief executive Malcolm Speed (who was not in office at the time) admitted the affair had 'damaged the high reputation of Australian cricket', and confessed that, with hindsight, disclosure would have been by far the more sensible option. The timing was particularly bad as the revelation of the cover-up came within days of Justice Qayyum making his report to the Pakistan president. After insisting for so long on Pakistan putting its house in order, the Australians suddenly found their own in danger of falling down around their ears as a hurricane of recrimination howled in from the subcontinent.

At a stroke, the testimony of Waugh and Warne lost its lustre as uncontaminated evidence. As Justice Qayyum wrote in his report,

> it cast some doubt on the credibility of the Australians as they had not been above board with the commission . . . In the light of John's offer and acceptance by these two it was clear why Malik approached these two only. Malik had possibly heard these two had some connections with bookies and so were approachable.

However, the commission were still keen enough to send a legal team to Australia to collect signed affidavits reaffirming the initial accusations against Malik. Malik himself poured predictable scorn on their standing as witnesses, and the Pakistan Board of Control was equally stiff in its condemnation of the ACB's cover-up.

But there was also a huge question mark over the ICC's role in the affair. By chance, the president of the ICC, Sir Clyde Walcott, and his chief executive, David Richards, were staying at the same Sydney hotel as Alan Crompton, chairman of the ACB, and Graham Halbish, his chief executive, on the night they took the decision to fine Warne and Waugh. Walcott and Richards were told the details, but in strict confidence, a confidence they respected for the next four years. Were they right to? The Warne and Waugh story surely had much wider implications for the rest of the game, and yet their senior administrators seemed concerned above all to limit the damage to Australia's reputation.

Waugh and Warne were not the only Test cricketers from outside the subcontinent with bribery stories to tell. Dean Jones revealed that he had been offered a large sum ('in a biscuit tin') by Gupta on the Australian tour to Sri Lanka in 1992–3, and the then Australian captain Allan Border claimed his Pakistani counterpart Mushtaq Mohammed had approached him to fix a Test match against England – an accusation Mushtaq laughed off as a joke. The New Zealand fast bowler Danny Morrison said that he had been offered US$1,000 merely to talk to an Indian bookie.

It wasn't long in most accounts before that particular phrase cropped up. The driving force behind the corruption in the game seemed to be the Indian betting industry. Betting is not wholly outlawed in India – backing horses is legal. But there's a catch: a 26 per cent tax on wagers and 40 per cent tax on winnings above Rs2,500. Because it officially doesn't exist, there are no taxes on cricket betting, and there is much, much more money to be made, by bookies and punters alike. The actual sums involved are staggering. According to the *Times of India*, 'Punters in India, it is believed, bet nearly one thousand crore rupees [approx. US$227 million] on each one-day game. This means between 30,000 to 40,000 crore [approx. US$6–9 billion] is bet in matches played by India alone in a year.'

That sort of money is inevitably going to attract a wider clientele than simply bookies and punters. There is a betting mafia with direct links to wider organised-crime circles. Pradeep Magazine, one of the Indian journalists working to expose corruption in the game, explains the connection between the underworld and betting syndicates in the case of Hansie Cronje:

> One of the main accused is Kishan Kumar, a small-time Bollywood actor and brother of Gulshan Kumar, who was murdered in 1997. His killers are suspected to be members of the Mumbai underworld which has been involved in extorting money, especially from businessmen and filmmakers. After Gulshan Kumar's murder, his younger brother Kishan came under police surveillance when he complained of receiving threats from the underworld. The Delhi Police had tapped his cellphone for that reason alone and it was sheer providence that they stumbled on to the 'match-fixing' story.

But this lucky break came against a background of extremely slow progress in the quest to clean up Indian cricket. Many, including Magazine, thought that the authorities were being criminally lackadaisical about the whole business. When, in 1997, he wrote up his own experiences of being approached by a bookie making extravagant offers ('I can give you a house in a locality of your choice in Delhi') simply for a personal introduction to Sachin Tendulkar, the story fell on deaf ears. As he wrote subsequently, 'The Indian Board's reaction was one of silence. Except for condemning me for bringing the "fair name of Indian cricket into disrepute" there was, as far as I know, no attempt to find out whether my story was true or not.'

Others were on the trail as well, and in the same year, the Indian periodical *Outlook* caused a stir with a report by Aniruddha Bahal and Krishna Prasad entitled 'Indian Cricket's Worst Kept Secret', which alleged that match-fixing was rampant. Their case was supported by an article signed by the former Test player Manoj Prabhakar, who claimed that he had been offered money by a team-mate to swing a match in Pakistan's favour. This was during the Singer Cup in Sri Lanka in 1994, a tournament mentioned in other depositions as a hotbed of shady dealing. But, as Prabhakar commented, 'in situations where money deals are made in the dark . . . no proof is available'. And there were many who disregarded his evidence as coming from a man disappointed at having fallen out of the national team and desperate for publicity. In the same issue of *Outlook*, Jagmohan Dalmiya, then secretary of the Indian Board and later ICC president, offered emollient reassurance: 'I don't think the players are involved at all and if it is proved it will be the shock of my life.'

However, *Outlook* had caused enough waves for some action to be taken, and the BCCI invited Y. V. Chandrachud, the former Chief Justice of India, to preside over a 'probe'. To those in the know this proved nothing more than a rubber-stamping of Dalmiya's complacency. It was, in Pradeep Magazine's view, 'a farce'. Despite being one of the whistle-blowers, Magazine was not initially called to give evidence; when, after lobbying, he did make it into the presence of the former Chief Justice, he was asked a few amiable questions and then told simply, 'Leave it.' It came as no surprise when Chandrachud's report exonerated the players of match-fixing and betting.

Despite this anodyne outcome (and the threat of a defamation case filed against him by the Board), Prabhakar would not be silenced. However, his refusal to name names made many sceptical. Pradeep Magazine quotes him as saying, 'If I name the player I might even get killed. I need protection. I need security. You don't know what kind of mafia controls this betting syndicate. They are dangerous people. Only if I am assured of foolproof security will I name the man.' Appearing on an Indian TV 'show trial', Prabhakar was found 'guilty' by the jury, a verdict that upset him greatly: 'How can I be guilty? Is this the reward for having spoken the truth? I have taken such a big risk and now I am being held guilty.' The jury had the grace to change their minds, but their initial response was indicative of the tendency to shoot the messenger rather than heed his warning (a syndrome Chris Lewis was to become familiar with when he did a bit of whistle-blowing in England). Prabhakar greeted the news about Waugh and Warne's involvement with bookies with understandable warmth. 'Will the people and the Board believe me now or will they continue to say I am "damaging Indian cricket"?'

Meanwhile, the *Outlook* team were still on the case, and persuaded the former Pakistani wicket-keeper Rashid Latif to give them a revealing interview in which he was prepared to name names. The names were those of prominent Indian players: the captain, Mohammed Azharuddin, along with Ajay Jadeja, Venkatapaty Raju and Navjot Singh Sidhu. As it happened, the Indian team were in Colombo preparing for a match, and Magazine was among the cricket journalists present. They were watching the players at practice when the news came through, and those covering the match immediately turned to the Indian manager, Professor Ratnakar Shetty. Shetty rubbished the report, but with the hungry eyes of the press pack on him, agreed to talk to the players concerned. He called them over to him and showed them the fax of the article. 'They looked like schoolboys being reprimanded for a prank by their teacher.' The outcome was a blanket denial, despite the suggestive body-language; and shortly afterwards, Latif retracted his accusations, saying that his words had been twisted. Hard on the heels of his exoneration, Azharuddin addressed the press, saying that allegations of match-fixing 'hurt' the players and also affected their performance, and he told the journalists: 'You should not be doing anything that would lower the prestige of the nation, which is celebrating the fiftieth anniversary of its independence.' When Magazine got the chance to talk to him privately, he noted that 'Azharuddin's conversations are always laced with words which convey a strong sense of morality and ethics' – a parallel perhaps with the soon-to-be-disgraced Hansie Cronje.

In due course the ambitious Dalmiya progressed from the Indian Board to presidency of the ICC. His initial statements indicated that he was continuing to take a complacent view of the game for which he now had global responsibility. By the end of 1998, however, the cat was too far out of the bag for anybody to pretend it didn't exist. Dalmiya called a press conference in December to announce that the 'guilty players' would not be allowed to get away with it, and that 'everything possible would be done to probe this sordid affair'.

The fact that even a man like Dalmiya was coming out of denial was indicative of the way things were going. Lord's was also waking up to the threat of match-fixing. If half the matches were rigged, who would bother to watch and, more importantly, sponsor the game? It was recognised that the problem was far too serious to be left to amateurs, and a task force to root out corruption was set up under the retired head of the Metropolitan Police, Sir Paul Condon. Pressure was mounting on those still intent on fixing matches, and the inviolability of the great names, past or present, could no longer be taken for granted.

If the Warne and Waugh revelations renewed Prabhakar's zeal for exposing corruption, the Cronje bombshell sent him into over-drive. Equipping himself with a hidden camera, he set off to find corroboration of his thesis that India's cricket was rotten to the core (or crore). The results, when shown on television in May 2000, were genuinely shocking. Names, the biggest names imaginable, were now revealed – even by those refusing to join Prabhakar in going public. Sidhu, one of those accused by Latif in his *Outlook* interview, told him,

I know you very well, but first listen to me. Even if you go to someone else, he will not go along with you. Nobody. After all, Kapil Dev is not an ordinary person. He is a respected man in this country. Highly respected. If you lift a finger against a respected man and you don't have proof, it's like inviting trouble. Secondly, I'm indebted to Kapil *Paaji*. He gave me an opportunity to play no matter what kind of person he is. I owe him a debt. I don't want to be dragged into this . . .

But Prabhakar's secret microphone ensured that he was.

The Indian authorities were at last spurred into action. As with Al Capone in the 1930s, the culprits were thought likely to be vulnerable with regard to their tax affairs. Raids on the homes of leading figures in the world of cricket, including Kapil Dev, Azharuddin and Dalmiya, followed, and the papers were soon publishing what Mike Marqusee called 'lurid accounts of the eye-popping wealth' uncovered by the investigating tax officials. As a result, the Central Bureau of Investigation (CBI) interrogated both previous captains, whose fall from grace in a culture of besotted hero-worship was of the same order of magnitude as Cronje's.

Towards the end of May 2000, Prabhakar finally broke his silence and did what he had long threatened to do. During an internet interview he was asked whether it was Kapil Dev who had offered him money 'to throw a match', and he confirmed that it was. He had given the same testimony to the CBI earlier in the day, and later went on national television to repeat his allegations. The pressure on the former Indian captain and record-breaking all-rounder was mounting, though he denied the charges and denounced his accuser in the strongest terms: 'I wish I could ignore these baseless and malicious allegations with the contempt they deserve, but I owe it to the nation to personally state that there is no truth whatsoever in these allegations. All I can say is that I am either being made the target of a deep-rooted conspiracy or personal jealousy or animosity.'

At the same time, Justice Qayyum's long-delayed report was finally published. This proved a meticulously detailed document, setting out the evidence taken from some seventy witnesses. (As far as Warne and Waugh were concerned, Qayyum was inclined to believe them despite the damage they had done to their own credibility.) The most notable judgement was that Malik had been guilty of match-fixing, and deserved nothing less than a life ban. Wasim Akram was clearly very fortunate to escape a similar condemnation. This had much to do with the retraction of evidence by the bowler Ata-ur-Rehman – characterised by Qayyum as 'perjury'. So far as Wasim was concerned, 'This Commission is willing to give him the benefit of the doubt. However, there has been some evidence to cast doubt on his integrity.' Qayyum recommended that he be stripped of the captaincy, 'censured' and 'put under strict vigilance', but not actually banned from playing.

There were others who had failed to cooperate with the commission: another former captain, Saeed Anwar, Waqar Younis and Inzamam-ul-Haq, and there were to be further investigations into Mushtaq Ahmed. In conclusion, Qayyum emphasised that his findings had to be based on the evidence before him: 'Various cricket experts like Imran Khan, Javed Miandad have stated that for a match to be fixed at least 5–7 players ought to be bought . . . [T]his commission could not find *conclusive evidence* [my italics] against as many players, thus on the whole the team is cleared of blame.'

The Pakistan Board found this a satisfactory outcome and gladly accepted the offer of a scapegoat. According to Lt Gen Taqueer Zia, 'Malik is the main culprit. He has brought the Pakistan national team into disrepute.' The notion that Malik managed to do this on his own caused many a lip to curl in derision, as did the punishments which followed. Malik was given a life ban, but that was no great loss to Pakistan as his international career was over. Ata-ur-Rehman was also banned for life – paying a heavy penalty for changing his mind about his evidence; but as he was by then playing for Nelson in the Lancashire League, that hardly represented a body-blow to Pakistan cricket. As for the others named in the report, their fines ranged from US$2,000 to US$6,000.

The mildness of the punishments meted out to members of the current Pakistan squad suggested a spirit of appeasement, and with its uncertainties and delays (some admittedly caused by outside factors like the Warne and Waugh revelations), the whole process left a lingering aroma of self-protection and a trail of unanswered questions.

For instance, doubts had been raised about Pakistan's World Cup campaign in 1999. There was something suspicious about their 62-run defeat by Bangladesh. As Henry Blofeld commented,

> . . . although this remarkable result may have had no bearing on the competition, it appeared to have made a few people much richer on the Subcontinent . . . It was said that bets were taken at 33/1 and then at 16/1 against Bangladesh and there were many people who felt that such an extraordinary result could only have been contrived. In other words, this was a match where the result must surely have been fixed.

Ali Bacher went one step further when testifying to the King Commission; he said that he had been told Pakistan had thrown not only the Bangladesh match, but the one against India as well. And then there was the final itself, which they lost in a humiliatingly short time to Australia. Blofeld pondered, 'Had the unscrupulous had a big chortle and decided to watch 30,000 at Lord's pay a hundred pounds a ticket to come and see a final which had already been decided?' Sarfraz Nawaz was one of those who claimed that the final had been fixed. The captain Wasim Akram seemed to take defeat with a Kiplingesque insouciance: 'I am not disappointed at all. We qualified for the final. We have got plenty of cricket ahead of us' – though this proved not to be so in his case as he was promptly suspended and had to spend an inconvenient amount of time shuttling to and fro between England and Pakistan to satisfy the Commission in Lahore that the defeat was not due either to match-rigging or to some of his team's extra-curricular activities in the days leading up to it.

It also struck many observers as strange that no official was ever cited as being even complicit in the corruption. Rashid Latif, who had played a similar role to Prabhakar, noted that no fewer than six Pakistan Cricket Boards had 'come and gone' since 1995 when he first raised the alarm and yet it had taken till the year 2000 for anything concrete to happen. He told *Gulf News* in an interview that he strongly suspected that some of the officials had also been given a share of 'the pie'.

Of course, an inquiry is very different from a police investigation, and India's CBI has the best track-record in terms of a forceful pursuit of the truth. Indeed, according to some, they used a little too much force. Indian film actor Kishan Kumar stated after he was released on bail, 'Crime branch detectives forced me to name some people falsely in the scandal or else they said they would show me as having links with underworld gangs.' He denied police charges that he had invested four million rupees (US$93,000) in match-fixing and said they had 'cooked up a false story to create an atmosphere of hatred and prejudice against me'.

The CBI's star witness was Mukesh Gupta himself, interviewed in October 2000. He seems to have made a clean breast of it, giving a long list of those he had corrupted over the years – including the leading whistle-blower, Prabhakar. He named four other Indians – Azharuddin, Ajaysinhji Jadeja, Nayan Mongia and Ajay Sharma – and then reeled off a list of nine élite Test players from around the world, including Brian Lara. Gupta said that he'd given Lara US$40,000 to underperform in two ODIs during the West Indies tour of India in 1994. It was a charge the batting superstar vehemently denied. The other eight players on MK's list were Cronje, Arjuna Ranatunga, Aravinda de Silva, Martin Crowe, Asif Iqbal, Salim Malik, Mark Waugh and Alec Stewart. It was almost impossible to believe so many highly distinguished Test captains could have been conscripted into MK's stable of nobbled thoroughbreds. Stewart had just arrived in Pakistan at the start of England's tour, and immediately found himself in the unwelcome spotlight. The former England captain denied all wrong-doing, adding that he had never 'knowingly' met 'MK'. After a few days' fevered speculation, Lord MacLaurin accepted his word and he was not withdrawn from the tour party.

Stewart's name had cropped up before. Chris Lewis, the former England all-rounder, caused a stir when stories about his involvement in a match-rigging scam appeared in the press. Lewis refused to name names, saying that he had said all he intended to say to the ECB. When press attention turned to Lord's, the matter was handled so ineptly that Lewis's credibility was undermined and he was mocked as a publicity-seeking fantasist, just like Prabhakar.

When the full story came out, Lewis was completely exonerated. In 1999, an Indian 'sports promoter', Aushim Kheterpal, called Lewis to a meeting and tried to get him to recruit members of the England team to underperform in the Old Trafford Test against New Zealand. £300,000 was apparently available for those taking part, and Lewis was specifically told to go after Stewart and Alan Mullally. Instead, he reported the matter to the ECB, and then, accompanied by one of their representatives, went to the police.

Kheterpal was an associate of, and possibly front man for, Sanjeeve Chawla, the Sanjay whose bungs to Cronje were revealed to the King Commission. In January 2001, detectives from the Serious Crime Group made a headline-grabbing arrest of Chawla at his home in north London: 'Scotland Yard Swoop to Arrest Cronje "Paymaster"'. The police said the arrest was in connection with the alleged attempts to suborn England for the Old Trafford Test against New Zealand. A further twist was given to the plot when it was revealed that the visitors' captain, Stephen Fleming, had also been approached by Kheterpal. Fleming rejected his advances out of hand.

The Serious Crime Group investigated the matter thoroughly, and despite England's very poor showing in the Old Trafford Test (all out for 199 to New Zealand's 496 for 9 declared), Scotland Yard cleared the entire squad of any complicity with the match-fixers. But still the stories keep coming. In January 2001, yet another ex-Pakistan player alleged that match-fixers in Australia had tried to lure players with call-girls. According to Qasim Omar, who played twenty-eight Tests for Pakistan alongside Imran Khan, Javed Miandad and Wasim Akram, there was a network of girls supplied to players from Brisbane to Perth organised by an Australian bookmaker eager to secure favourable match results. Sir Paul Condon's team of investigators, it was revealed, would be taking a list of the girls' names and telephone numbers when, in the course of their inquiries, they visited Australia.

Sir Paul's ICC-appointed team had already caused waves by raiding the ICC's own offices in both London and Hong Kong, and a high level of faith is invested in them around the world. Tarun Tejpal, who helped to produce a professional video out of the hours of footage shot secretly by Prabhakar, regarded the ICC squad as the game's best chance of redeeming its image. He told the *Daily Mail* in December 2000, 'I think everyone is much happier to have Sir Paul investigating and if he asked for all of our material we would pass it on quite gladly . . . The Cricket Board of Control in India showed a real reluctance to admit that there was a problem, initially – and the International Cricket Council was the same.' And it was not, he stressed, simply an Indian and Pakistani problem.

Certainly the picture is growing of a hydra-headed conspiracy threatening to subvert the game around the world. The reluctance of the authorities to admit to the existence of match-fixing, and their instinct to cover up embarrassing revelations, have clearly done cricket serious harm. And now, over a year since the lid was blown off the can of worms by the Cronje scandal, there is a further complication. The high-profile culprits exposed in the investigations in South Africa, India and Pakistan are fighting back. Cronje himself seems to have seen the light as far as the commercial possibilities of notoriety are concerned and put remorse behind him. He has appeared in a mini-series of velvet-gloved television interviews for the modest fee of £100,000, and the British PR guru Max Clifford has recently indicated that the sky is the limit for someone so drawn to lucre. Cronje is reputed to have got his golf handicap down to a creditable five, and seems to be coping with his enforced idleness better than might have been expected from his first media appearances as a tearful and guilt-racked penitent.

Not content simply to bask in lucrative infamy, Cronje has challenged the life ban imposed on him, and for good measure set his legal team to derail the King Commission, which has been prevented from reconvening on several occasions. Indeed, Cronje's lawyers have even challenged the Commission's legality, as well as questioning King's personal fitness to conduct the proceedings. Cronje was offered indemnity from prosecution in exchange for 'full disclosure', but there are still some important financial documents that have not been produced. It would be inconvenient to say the least if King were to decide that he had not fulfilled his part of the bargain, leaving the disgraced former captain exposed to possible charges of tax evasion and fraud.

Calling a halt to King would suit more people than just Cronje, and the view that the Commission has served its purpose has been widely and influentially disseminated. Ali Bacher, the managing director of the United Cricket Board, has said, 'We believe the Commission has done a good job. We have our doubts whether there's any more to come out. On that basis, the Commission's lifespan is short-lived, it's time to wrap it up.'

But as Owen Slot argued in the *Sunday Telegraph* in February 2001, the suggestion that the Commission has covered all the ground is 'preposterous'. He goes on, 'Bacher himself is not yet in the clear as King, in his interim report, questioned whether the South Africans' team management knew about an offer, to fix a match in Bombay in 1996, and kept quiet about it.' He also notes that the Commission were preparing subpoenas for 'a number of former international cricketers as new witnesses when the latest postponement stopped them'.

In the end, King succumbed to the mounting pressure and in February 2001 petitioned the government to wind up the hearings. In a statement he presented the decision as a pre-emptive strike to safeguard what the Commission had already achieved: 'This step I have taken has been precipitated by the threat of Mr Hansie Cronje's attorney to challenge the validity of my appointment.' King tried to put the best spin he could on the situation, but was clearly exasperated by the legal sniping and resigned to having to leave the job half done. He hinted that evidence against Cronje 'could be taken up by an appropriate agency', but declared that everyone else who had appeared before the Commission 'must be regarded as having been cleared'.

There have been similar developments in India, where Kapil Dev has challenged his punishment and threatened litigation on the grounds of defamation. Azharuddin is likewise contesting the legality of his life ban. Indeed, he has gone further, trying to deflect public opprobrium by spreading the blame. In January 2001, he pointed the finger at two other prominent former captains, Ravi Shastri and the legendary Sunil Gavaskar. Both are based in Bombay, the money capital of India, and both, according to Azharuddin, have suspiciously large assets. In a raid by the CBI on lockers in the Gymkhana Club, Bombay, an improbably large sum of money in US dollars was confiscated from Gavaskar's locker, while Shastri owns an unaccountably extensive portfolio of properties.

Charge and counter-charge, bare-faced denial, qualified admission and special pleading – it all replicates the 'dark chapter' in cricket's history when the boil of corruption in Regency England was finally lanced. The scale is, of course, vastly greater than when a match could be rigged by simply dropping in at the Green Man and Still with a seductively chinking purse, but the roots of the international match-fixing scandal remain the same. Perhaps the last word should be left with Sir Paul Condon, head of the ICC's Anti-Corruption Unit: 'Corruption is about opportunity and human weakness. Neither of these things will ever disappear.'

It's not cricket. But then, perhaps it never was.

NOTE

On 11 July 2001 it was announced that all corruption charges against Alec Stewart were dropped. Lord MacLaurin, Chairman of the England and Wales Cricket Board, said: 'Lord Condon's anti-corruption investigation has concluded there exists no substantive evidence justifying proceedings against Alec Stewart in relation to this matter. The matter is, therefore, closed.'

Bibliography

Akram, Wasim, with Patrick Murphy, *Wasim, The Autobiography of Wasim Akram* (Piatkus, 1998)

Bailey, Philip, Philip Thorn and Peter Wynne-Thomas (eds), *Who's Who of Cricketers* (1984, new edn Hamlyn, 1993)

Barker, Ralph and Irving Rosenwater, *England v Australia; A Compendium of Test Cricket between the Countries 1877–1968* (Batsford, 1969)

Barnes, Sidney, *It Isn't Cricket* (William Kimber, 1953)

Barrett, Norman (ed.), *The Daily Telegraph Chronicle of Cricket* (Guinness Publishing, 1994)

Barrington, Ken (as told to Phil Pillby), *Playing It Straight* (Stanley Paul, 1968)

Benaud, Richie, *The New Champions: Australia in the West Indies 1965* (Hodder & Stoughton, 1965)

Birley, Derek, *A Social History of English Cricket* (Aurum Press, 1999)

Blofeld, Henry, *It's Just Not Cricket* (Simon & Schuster, 1999)

Booth, Keith, *His Own Enemy; The Rise and Fall of Edward Pooley* (Belmont Books, 2000)

Botham, Ian and Peter Hayter, *The Botham Report* (CollinsWillow, 1997)

Brearley, Mike, *The Art of Captaincy* (Hodder & Stoughton, 1985)

Brodribb, Gerald, *Next Man in: A Survey of Cricket Laws and Customs* (1952; revised edn 1995, Souvenir Press)

Brookes, Christopher, *English Cricket; The Game and its Players Through the Ages* (Readers Union, Newton Abbot, 1978)

Cardus, Neville, *The Playfair Cardus* (The Dickens Press, 1963)

Cowdrey, Colin, *M.C.C. The Autobiography of a Cricketer* (Hodder & Stoughton, 1976)

Crace, John, *Wasim and Waqar: Imran's Inheritors* (Boxtree, 1992)

Docker, Edward Wybergh, *Bradman and the Bodyline Series* (Angus & Robertson, 1978)

Down, Michael, *Is It Cricket? Power, Money & Politics in Cricket Since 1945* (Queen Anne Press, 1985)

Edmonds, Frances, *Cricket XXXX Cricket* (Kingswood Press, 1987; reprinted Pan, 1988)

Fingleton, J. H., *Cricket Crisis: Bodyline and Other Lines* (first edn 1946; reprinted Pavilion Books, 1984)

Frindall, Bill (ed. and compiled), *The Wisden Book of Test Cricket 1876–77 to 1977–78* (Macdonald and Jane's, 1979)

Frith, David, *England versus Australia* (Lutterworth Press, revised edn 1981)

– *The Fast Men* (George Allen & Unwin, 1975; revised edn 1982)

– (with Jeff Thomson), *Thommo* (Angus & Robertson, 1980)

Gale, Frederick, *Echoes from Old Cricket Fields* (Simpkin, Marshall, 1871)

– *The Game of Cricket* (Sonnenschein, 1887)

Gatting, Mike, with Angela Patmore, *Leading from the Front: The Autobiography of Mike Gatting* (Macdonald/Queen Anne Press, 1988)

Geras, Norman and Ian Holliday, *Ashes '97: Two Views from the Boundary* (Baseline Books, Tisbury, 1997)

Girouard, Mark, *The Return to Camelot: Chivalry and the English Gentleman* (Yale, 1981)

Goodhart, Philip and Christopher Chataway, *War without Weapons* (W. H. Allen, 1968)

Goulstone, J., *Early Club & Village Cricket* (private publication, 1972)

Grace, W. G., *Cricket* (J. W. Arrowsmith, Bristol, 1891)

– *'W. G.' Cricketing Reminiscences & Personal Recollections* (James Bowden, 1899; reprinted with Introduction by E. W. Swanton, The Hambledon Press, 1980)

Green, Benny (ed.), *The Wisden Papers of Neville Cardus* (Guild Publishing/CenturyHutchinson, 1989)

Greig, Tony, *Test Match Cricket: A Personal View* (Hamlyn, 1977)

Harris, Lord (ed.), *The History of Kent County Cricket* (Eyre & Spottiswoode, 1907)

– *A Few Short Runs* (John Murray, 1921)

– and F. S. Ashley-Cooper (eds), *Kent Cricket Matches, 1719–1880* (Gibbs & Son, Canterbury, 1929)

Hill, Alan, *Peter May, A Biography* (Andre Deutsch, 1996)

Hopps, David, *A Century of Cricket Quotes* (Robson Books, 1998)

Hutton, Len, *Just My Story* (Hutchinson, 1956)

Igglesden, Charles, *66 Years' Memories of Kent Cricket* (*Kentish Express*, Ashford, 1947)

James, Alfred, *The 2nd Australian XI's Tour of Australia, Britain and New Zealand in 1880/81* (privately printed, Wahroonga, N. S. W., 1994)

Jardine, D. R., *In Quest of the Ashes* (Hutchinson, 1933)

Johnson, Ian, *Cricket at the Crossroads* (Cassell, 1957)

King, E. L., *Interim Report of Commission of Inquiry into Cricket Match Fixing* (Cape Town, August 2000)

Laker, Jim, *Over to Me* (Frederick Muller, 1960)

Lamb, Allan and Peter Smith, *Lamb's Tales* (Allen & Unwin, 1985)

– and Jack Bannister, *My Autobiography* (CollinsWillow, 1996)

Larwood, Harold, *Bodyline?* (Elkin Matthews & Marrot, 1933)

Lemmon, David, *The Crisis of Captaincy: Servant and Master in English Cricket* (Christopher Helm, 1988)

Lewis, Tony, *Double Century: The Story of MCC and Cricket* (Hodder & Stoughton, 1987)

McKinstry, Leo, *Boycs: The True Story* (Partridge, 2000)

McLean, Teresa, *The Men in White Coats: Cricket Umpires Past and Present* (Stanley Paul, 1987)

McLellan, Alastair (ed.), *Nothing Sacred: The New Cricket Culture* (Two Heads Publishing, 1996)

Magazine, Pradeep, *Not Quite Cricket: The Explosive Story of How Bookmakers Influence the Game Today* (Penguin Books India, New Delhi, 1999; revised edn, 2000)

Mailey, Arthur, *10 for 66 and All That* (Phoenix Sports Books, 1958)

Mangan, J. A., *Athleticism in the Victorian and Edwardian Public School* (Cambridge University Press, 1981; reprinted Falmer Press, 1986)

Marqusee, Mike, 'Tainted Love' (*Observer Sport Monthly*, October 2000)

Marshall, Michael, *Gentlemen and Players: Conversations with Cricketers* (Grafton Books, 1987)

Mason, Ronald, *Jack Hobbs* (Hollis & Carter, 1960)

Midwinter, Eric, *W. G. Grace: His Life and Times* (George Allen & Unwin, 1981)

Miller, Keith, *Cricket Crossfire* (Oldbourne Press, 1956)

– and R. S. Whitington, *Cricket Caravan* (Latimer House, 1950)

Mote, Ashley (ed.), *John Nyren's The Cricketers of My Time: The Original Version* (Robson Books, 1998)

Newbolt, Henry, *The Island Race* (Elkin Matthews, 1898)
– *Selected Poems of Henry Newbolt*, ed. Patric Dickinson (Hodder and Stoughton, 1981)

Oslear, Don, *Wisden: The Laws of Cricket (The 2000 Code and its Interpretation)* (Ebury Press, 2000)
– and Jack Bannister, *Tampering with Cricket* (CollinsWillow, 1996)

Parker, Eric, *The History of Cricket* (The Lonsdale Library, Seeley Service, n. d.)
Peebles, Ian, *Straight from the Shoulder: 'Throwing' – Its History and Cure* (*The Cricketer*/Hutchinson, 1968)
Polack, John and Duane Pettet, A *Definitive Overview of Cricket Match-fixing, Betting and Corruption Allegations* (CricInfo, May 2000)
Potter, Stephen, *Gamesmanship; or, The Art of Winning Games without actually Cheating* (Rupert Hart-Davis, 1947)
Pycroft, Revd J., *The Cricket Field* (Longman, 1851)

Rae, Simon, *W. G. Grace: A Life* (Faber & Faber, 1998)
Ramchand, Partab, *How the Match-fixing Drama Unfolded* (CricInfo, 1999–2000)
Rosenwater, Irving, *Sir Donald Bradman: A Biography* (Batsford, 1978)
Ross, Alan, *Through the Caribbean: The MCC Tour of the West Indies, 1959–1960* (Hamish Hamilton, 1960)

Smith, Rick, *ABC Guide to Australian Test Cricketers* (ABC Books, Sydney, 1993)
– and Ron Williams, *W. G. Down Under: Grace in Australia 1873–74 and 1891–92* (Apple Books, Tasmania, 1994)
Swanton, E. W. and John Woodcock (eds), *Barclays World of Cricket* (1966; revised edn Collins, 1980)

Tennant, Ivo, *Imran Khan* (H. F. & G. Witherby, 1994; paperback reprint, Gollancz/Witherby, 1995)
Thomson, A. A., *The Great Cricketer: A Biography of W. G. Grace* (Robert Hale, 1957; new edn, *The Cricketer*/Hutchinson, 1968)

Underdown, David, *Start of Play: Cricket and Culture in Eighteenth Century England* (Allen Lane, 2000)

Wakley, B. J., *Classic Centuries in the Test Matches between England and Australia* (Nicholas Kaye, 1964)
Walcott, Clyde, with Brian Scovell, *Sixty Years on the Back Foot* (Gollancz, 1999; paperback reprint, Orion Books, 2000)
Webber, J. R., *The Chronicle of W. G.* (The Association of Cricket Statisticians and Historians, 1998)

Welldon, J. E. C., *Youth and Duty: Sermons to Harrow Schoolboys* (Religious Tract Society, 1903)

West, G. Derek, *The Elevens of England* (Darf Publishers, 1988)

Wilde, Simon, *Letting Rip* (Orion, 1995)

Wisden Cricketers' Almanack (1864–2001)

Woolley, Frank, *The King of Games* (Stanley Paul, n. d.)

Worrell, Frank, *Cricket Punch* (Stanley Paul, 1959)

Wright, Graeme, *Betrayal: The Struggle for Cricket's Soul* (Witherby, 1993)

Wynne-Thomas, Peter, *England on Tour* (Hamlyn, 1982)

- *The History of Cricket* (The Stationery Office, 1997)

Newspapers, periodicals and specialist publications such as *The Cricketer* and *Wisden Cricketers' Almanack* are cited in the text.

Index